The Development of Institutions of Human Rights

Perspectives on Comparative Politics

Published by Palgrave Macmillan

The Struggle against Corruption: A Comparative Study
Edited by Roberta Ann Johnson

Women, Democracy, and Globalization in North America: A Comparative Study
By Jane Bayes, Patricia Begne, Laura Gonzalez, Lois Harder, Mary Hawkesworth, and Laura Macdonald

Politics and Ethnicity: A Comparative Study
By Joseph Rudolph

The Politics of Immigration in France, Britain, and the United States: A Comparative Study
By Martin Schain

Politics, Policy, and Health Care: A Comparative Study
By Paul Godt

Social Movements in Politics, Second Edition
By Cyrus Ernesto Zirakzadeh

The Development of Institutions of Human Rights: A Comparative Study
Edited by Lilian A. Barria and Steven D. Roper

The Development of Institutions of Human Rights

A Comparative Study

Edited by
Lilian A. Barria
and
Steven D. Roper

palgrave
macmillan

First published in 2010 by
PALGRAVE MACMILLAN®
in the United States—a division of St. Martin's Press LLC,
175 Fifth Avenue, New York, NY 10010.

Where this book is distributed in the UK, Europe and the rest of the world, this is by Palgrave Macmillan, a division of Macmillan Publishers Limited, registered in England, company number 785998, of Houndmills, Basingstoke, Hampshire RG21 6XS.

Palgrave Macmillan is the global academic imprint of the above companies and has companies and representatives throughout the world.

Palgrave® and Macmillan® are registered trademarks in the United States, the United Kingdom, Europe and other countries.

ISBN: 978–1–4039–7653–6 (paperback)
ISBN: 978–1–4039–7652–9 (lithocase)

Library of Congress Cataloging-in-Publication Data is available from the Library of Congress.

A catalogue record of the book is available from the British Library.

Design by Newgen Imaging Systems (P) Ltd., Chennai, India.

First edition: June 2010

10 9 8 7 6 5 4 3 2 1

Printed in the United States of America.

To Francesca Isabella, our joy

CONTENTS

Part IV Sierra Leone

Part V East Timor

Part VI Conclusion

SERIES EDITOR FOREWORD

The Development of Institutions of Human Rights: A Comparative Study by Lilian A. Barria and Steven D. Roper uses the comparative method to explore one of the most interesting and perhaps the most important development the continuing struggle to find ways to institutionalize protection of human rights. Here the emphasis is on how to create mechanisms of transitional justice in—or for—nations that have suffered the most egregious and long-lasting of human rights violations, imposed either by their own states or by forces those states were unwilling or unable to control. The goals are dual, and often in conflict: first, to achieve a measure of reconciliation between those who endured and those who inflicted the horrors of hatred run rampant, and second, to mete out sufficient punishment to the most guilty in order to deter the resumption of such behavior in the future. The task is complex and the pitfalls are many.

All books in this series, Perspectives in Comparative Politics, are designed to be scholarly, topic-oriented studies of a particular problem, accessible to upper-division students as well as to graduate students and professors. They begin with an introductory chapter, covering the relevant literature and laying out the problem, and end with a concluding chapter, summarizing what has been learned about the problems in the three or more nations covered, and elucidating the important comparative lessons learned. This book follows that format. It offers parallel consideration of its topic in four nations: Argentina, Bosnia-Herzegovina, Sierra Leone, and East Timor.

It is, however, a format that allows for considerable flexibility within the broader guidelines. Most of the books published thus far have been single author volumes, but of late the tendency has been toward edited volumes, with different authors covering the topic for different nations. The present book goes yet farther in the latter direction, as editors Barria and Roper have invited three different authors to address three topics for each of the four nations. Proceeding case by case , they present discussion of the three topics for each nation. Keeping the cases together, with parallel analyses, gives them readily apparent comparability, a feature enhanced by the very strong introductory and concluding chapters provided by the editors.

At the same time, the singularity and complexity of each aspect of each case receives the fully specialized treatment it deserves. Four experts have written on the historical backgrounds of the four cases, four have sought to explain and evaluate first stage efforts to establish suitable post-tragedy institutions in each nation, and yet another four have evaluated those first efforts, discussed second stage developments in the quest for justice, and offered their own evaluations of what has been accomplished and what remains to be done. The editors have not only provided the necessary scene-setting in the Introduction and Conclusion, but have carefully guided the contributors to make sure that within each case they build upon each other's work. Thus the twelve chapters work together to explain each case and to elucidate the differences and similarities among them, but at the same time remain separate and distinct, as indeed the developments they treat were in reality.

Comparative study is not the science of finding uniformity or homogeneity in vastly different contexts, treating variety as simply greater or lesser quantities of the same thing. Comparative politics is, rather, a science *and* an art together permitting us to recognize, organize and comprehend the infinite variety of political phenomena called by the same name. Here the phenomena we observe are the tragedy of mass violation of human rights and the subsequent quest for rectification. Can new institutions help nations so desperately tested find their way forward to truth, reconciliation and justice? What can the rest of us learn from the experiences of Argentina, Bosnia-Herzegovina, Sierra Leone, and East Timor?

I am very pleased to welcome *The Development of Human Rights: A Comparative Study* to the series Perspectives in Comparative Politics.

—Kay Lawson

PREFACE AND ACKNOWLEDGMENTS

This book began as many projects do as a casual conversation. We first met with the Series Editor, Kay Lawson, at an annual meeting of the American Political Science Association. At that time, we discussed a volume that would outline various forms of transitional justice and provide numerous country case studies ranging from Indonesia to Uganda. As faculty that have taught human rights and international law courses over the past few years, we felt that a comparative volume on transitional justice would make a contribution not only to scholarship but also to the classroom. Through further discussions, we began to re-conceptualize the volume—rather than focus on a number of countries and how a specific mechanism of transitional justice was implemented, we thought it more interesting to have fewer countries and compare within the same country the use of various forms of transitional justice. In so many cases since the 1970s, countries have attempted to deal with previous periods of human rights abuses using multiple methods rather than relying on any one. As we restructured the volume, we realized that an in-depth examination of a small number of countries and multiple mechanisms required country experts to provide a more nuanced understanding of the successes and limitations of transitional justice in each country. We have been very fortunate to work with contributors to this volume who have a detailed knowledge of the country, history, and attempt to deal with past abuses. Much of this volume has been written based on substantial fieldwork which is so important in good comparative research.

We have also been very fortunate to work with a wonderfully supportive editorial team at Palgrave Macmillan. Farideh Koohi-Kamali and Robyn Curtis have been very patient with us as we assembled the contributors and worked through the various stages of the project. Special thanks is due to Kay Lawson who has been encouraging and understanding throughout the process. She helped us to re-conceptualize the volume and her editorial suggestions were extremely helpful. Finally, we want to thank all the contributors to this volume for providing us such interesting, detailed, and thought-provoking chapters. Working with the contributors has been a real pleasure, and we have enjoyed reading and learning from all of them.

ABBREVIATIONS

Acronym	Translation
ACRM	Anti-Corruption Revolutionary Movement
AELM	Asia Pacific Economic Cooperation Economic Leaders' Meeting
AFRC	Armed Forces Revolutionary Council
APC	All People's Congress
APDH	Permanent Assembly for Human Rights
APEC	Asia Pacific Economic Cooperation
APODETI	Association for the Integration of Timor into Indonesia and Timorese Popular Democratic Association
ARBiH	Army of Bosnia-Herzegovina
ASDT	Timorese Social Democratic Association
BiH	Bosnia-Herzegovina
CAVR	Commission for Reception, Truth and Reconciliation
CDF	Civil Defense Forces
CELS	Center for Legal and Social Studies
CIA	Central Intelligence Agency
CNRM	National Council for Maubere Resistance
CNRT	National Council of Timorese Resistance
CONADEP	National Commission on the Disappearance of Persons
CPC	Criminal Procedure Code
CRA	Community Reconciliation Agreement
CRP	Community Reconciliation Process
CRRN	Revolutionary Council of National Resistance
CTF	Commission for Truth and Friendship
ECOMOG	Economic Community of West African States Monitoring Group
EU	European Union
Falintil	Armed Forces for the National Liberation of East Timor
Fretilin	Revolutionary Front for an Independent East Timor
GDP	Gross Domestic Product
HVO	Bosnian-Croat Army
IACHR	Inter-American Commission on Human Rights
ICTJ	International Center for Transitional Justice
ICTR	International Criminal Tribunal for Rwanda
ICTY	International Criminal Tribunal for the former Yugoslavia
ISU	Internal Security Unit

JNA	Yugoslavia National Army
NATO	North Atlantic Treaty Organization
NGO	Non-Governmental Organization
NPFL	National Patriotic Front of Liberia
NPRC	National Provisional Ruling Council
NRC	National Reformation Council
OCU	Ordinary Crimes Unit
OGP	Office of the General Prosecutor
OHR	Office of the High Representative
OSCE	Organization for Security and Co-operation in Europe
OTP	Office of the Prosecutor
PIC	Peace Implementation Council
RENETIL	National Resistance of East Timorese Students
RoR	Rules of the Road
RUF	Revolutionary United Front
SANU	Serbian Academy of Arts and Sciences
SCSL	Special Court for Sierra Leone
SCU	Serious Crimes Unit
SDA	Party of Democratic Action
SERPAJ	Service for Peace and Justice
SFOR	Stabilization Force
SLPP	Sierra Leone People's Party
SPSC	Special Panels for Serious Crimes
SRS	Serbian Radical Party
TNI	Indonesian Military
TRC	Truth and Reconciliation Commission
UDT	Timorese Democratic Union
UN	United Nations
UNAMET	United Nations Assistance Mission in East Timor
UNDP	United Nations Development Program
UNHCR	United Nations High Commissioner for Human Rights
UNICEF	United Nations Children's Fund
UNICIET	United Nations International Commission of Inquiry on East Timor
UNMISET	United Nations Mission in East Timor
UNMIT	United Nations Integrated Mission in Timor-Leste
UNPROFOR	United Nations Protection Force
UNTAET	United Nations Transitional Authority for East Timor
VRS	Army of Republika Srpska
WCC	War Crimes Chamber
WCU	War Crimes Unit

ABOUT THE AUTHORS

Lilian A. Barria is an Associate Professor of Political Science at Eastern Illinois University. Her research focuses on international law and human rights. She is co-author of *Designing Criminal Tribunals: Sovereignty and International Concerns in the Protection of Human Rights* (2006). Her articles have appeared in several journals including the *Journal of Conflict Resolution, International Journal of Human Rights,* and *Human Rights Review*. She is a past President of the Human Rights Section of the American Political Science Association. She can be reached at: labarria@eiu.edu.

Janine Natalya Clark is a Lecturer in the Politics Department and the Post-War Reconstruction and Development Unit at the University of York. Clark's research interests include post-conflict societies (particularly in the Balkans and Africa), reconciliation and trust-building processes, war crimes, and restorative justice mechanisms. Her first book, *Serbia in the Shadow of Milosevic: The Legacy of Conflict in the Balkans*, was published in 2008. Her recent publications include articles in journals such as *Journal of International Criminal Justice, European Journal of International Law,* and *International Criminal Law Review*. She can be reached at: jc817@york.ac.uk.

Emilio Crenzel holds a PhD in social science and is a Researcher at the National Council of Scientific Research and Professor of Sociology at the Faculty of Social Science at the University of Buenos Aires. His books include *La historia política del Nunca Mas: La memoria de las desapariciones en la Argentina* (2008). He is an author of various articles on transitional justice, human rights, and social memories of political violence and state terrorism in the Southern Cone of Latin America and has published in European, Canadian, Israeli, Brazilian, and Mexican journals. He can be reached at: ecrenzel@retina.ar.

Mario Di Paolantonio is a Professor of Philosophy of Education at York University (Toronto, Canada). His research currently explores the pedagogical implications of artistic memorial practices that arise due to state sanctioned initiatives to come to terms with historical wrongs. His work has appeared in journals such as the *Journal for Cultural Research, Social & Legal Studies, Political Culture,* and *Pedagogy & Cultural Studies*. He is an Adjunct Professor at the University of Toronto and an International Research Associate with the Unit for Global Justice at Goldsmiths College, University of London and at the Centro de Estudios en Pedagogias Contemporaneas at the Universidad Nacional de San Martin. He can be reached at: mdipaolantonio@edu.yorku.ca.

Zoe Dugal holds a MA degree in political science from McGill University. She started her career working as a Research Officer for the Truth and Reconciliation Commission for Sierra Leone and has been involved in all the activities of the commission. She also worked on a community disarmament program for UNDP Sierra Leone. She has been a short-term consultant for the International Center for Transitional Justice. She is currently the Project Manager for West Africa for the Pearson Peacekeeping Center, a Canadian nonprofit organization building capacity for police services in Africa. She can be reached at: zoedugal@hotmail.com.

Clinton Fernandes is a Senior Lecturer in Strategic Studies at the Australian Defense Force Academy campus of the University of New South Wales. His principal area of research is in international relations and strategy. He focuses on the national interest in Australia's external relations. He is a historian of the twenty-four-year occupation of East Timor by Indonesia in its multiple dimensions. He teaches courses on the role of modern intelligence, modern political ideologies, strategic studies, and the comparative politics of Southeast Asia. He can be reached at: c.fernandes@adfa.edu.au.

Wendy Lambourne holds a PhD and is Senior Lecturer and Academic Coordinator at the Center for Peace and Conflict Studies, University of Sydney. Her research is concerned with analyzing and evaluating transitional justice, reconciliation, and peace-building after mass violence, with a regional focus on Africa and Asia/Pacific. Her publications include chapters in *Reconciliation, Justice, and Coexistence: Theory and Practice*, ed. Mohammed Abu-Nimer (2001) and *The Challenge of Conflict: International Law Responds*, ed. Ustinia Dolgopol, and Judith Gardam (2006). Her recent articles have been published in the *Journal of Peacebuilding and Development*, *International Journal of Transitional Justice,* and *Global Change, Peace and Security.* She can be reached at: wendy.lambourne@usyd.edu.au.

Ryan Lowry is a MA student at the University of Nebraska. His research interests are ethnic conflict and transitional justice. He can be reached at: ryan.lowry@huskers.unl.edu.

Abu Karimu Mboka holds a BSc and BA (Hons), MA in communication studies and a PhD in justice studies. He is the author of *The Politics of Chapter VII Interventions in Violent Conflict: A Comparative Analysis of Bosnia, Iraq, Rwanda, and Sierra Leone.* He has taught classes in Human Rights, Global Human Rights Communication, and Conflict Negotiation at Arizona State University. He is an Assistant Professor of Criminal Justice at California State University-Stanislaus where he teaches Constitutional Rights of Prisoners, Violence against Children, Judicial Process, and Youth Violence. Current research activities focus on state responses to criminal tendencies and behaviors. He can be reached at: amboka@csustan.edu.

Patrice C. McMahon is an Associate Professor at the University of Nebraska. She is author of *Taming Ethnic Hatred: Ethnic Cooperation and Transnational Networks in Eastern Europe*. Her research has appeared in *Foreign Affairs*, *Journal of Conflict Studies, Human Rights Quarterly, Political Science Quarterly,*

Democratization, and *Ethnopolitics*. She can be reached at: pmcmahon2@unl-notes.unl.edu.

Christina M. Morus holds a PhD and is an Assistant Professor of Comparative Genocide and Rhetorical Studies at The Richard Stockton College of New Jersey. She is currently a Fulbright Scholar at the University of Belgrade and is a volunteer and activist with Belgrade's *Women in Black*. Her past research analyzed the affects of historical narratives on the normalization of violence in the former Yugoslavia (as well as in Rwanda, Cambodia, and South Africa). She is presently working on a book analyzing the ways locally grown grassroots NGOs use historical narratives to affect sustainable stability in postconflict transition. She can be reached at: christina.morus@stockton.edu.

James DeShaw Rae is an Assistant Professor of Government at California State University, Sacramento. His most recent publication is *Peacebuilding and Transitional Justice in East Timor*. He can be reached at: rae@saclink.csus.edu.

Steven D. Roper is a Professor of Political Science at Eastern Illinois University and Associate Editor of *Human Rights Review*. His research focuses on constitutional development, conflict resolution, and human rights. He is the author of *Romania: The Unfinished Revolution* (2000) and co-author of *Designing Criminal Tribunals: Sovereignty and International Concerns in the Protection of Human Rights* (2006), and co-editor of *Public Finance and Post-Communist Party Development* (2008). He can be reached at: sdr@steven-droper.com.

Ellen Emilie Stensrud is a PhD candidate and Research Fellow in the Department of Political Science at the University of Oslo. Her current research interests include transitional justice and genocide studies. She has published in the *Journal of Peace Research* as well as has contributed a chapter to *The Black Book of Genocide*. She can be reached at: ellen.stensrud@stv.uio.no.

Timothy D. Wilson is an Assistant Professor of Spanish at the University of Alaska Fairbanks. He has spent several years in Argentina and holds a PhD in Argentine literature from the University of Illinois at Urbana-Champaign. His research interests include Argentine rock music and dictatorship and government-sponsored terror and cultures of resistance. He can be reached at: tim.wilson@alaska.edu.

PART I

Introduction

CHAPTER 1

Mechanisms of Transitional Justice

LILIAN A. BARRIA AND STEVEN D. ROPER

Introduction

How should countries emerging from authoritarian rule or protracted civil war deal with the human rights abuses committed by the previous regime and members of society? This is an important question because how governments address the past human rights abuses affects the present and future relationship between perpetuators and victims, as well as a country's transition to democracy and the legitimacy of the new political system. Over the last three decades, various mechanisms of transitional justice have been developed with the objectives of uncovering the truth of events, providing accountability for crimes, and promoting individual and societal reconciliation. The study of transitional justice has produced a broad literature that explores under what conditions different accountability mechanisms, whether domestically driven or internationally inspired, are capable of addressing the human rights violations and assisting in the consolidation of democracy.

This volume draws on that literature and uses the comparative method to carry the inquiry forward. It examines the use of diverse transitional justice mechanisms in four of the most war-torn countries since World War II: Argentina in South America, Bosnia-Herzegovina (BiH) in Europe, Sierra Leone in Africa, and East Timor in Southeast Asia. For each of the four country case studies, one chapter discusses in-depth the human rights violations that were perpetuated by either government forces under authoritarian rule or members of society during a civil war. These countries faced extreme periods of violence that included abductions, torture, rape, disappearances, and murder. The introductory chapter for each section provides the context in which the violence occurred and a discussion of the various actors in each country. The type of violence and the political transition in each country sets the stage for the type of transitional justice mechanism that was adopted.

As authoritarian rule or civil war ended in Argentina, BiH, Sierra Leone, and East Timor, the newly elected democratic governments were confronted with the question of how to address the human rights violations that occurred under the previous regime and what type of transitional justice mechanism should be adopted. For each of the country case studies, two transitional justice mechanisms were employed and each of the mechanisms will be discussed to determine whether they accomplished the goals of providing justice and reconciliation. In the four countries, different mechanisms were implemented (some simultaneously). In some cases, these efforts included domestic trials, amnesties, and truth and reconciliation commission (TRCs). In other cases, mechanisms that involved only domestic actors were not feasible, and thus the international community worked through the United Nations (UN) to craft institutions to deal with the human rights abuses. Ultimately, through the selection of different transitional justice mechanisms, all four governments attempted to hold individual perpetuators accountable (especially public officials), provide justice to victims, and help heal society.

Transitional justice mechanisms aim at assisting societies to move forward, psychologically and even physically (for example, re-building the judiciary). Seeking reconciliation between perpetuators and victims is important in order for society to acknowledge the past but also look into the future in order to consolidate democracy and assure lasting peace. The relationship between former enemies has to be transformed in order to re-integrate perpetuators into society and provide justice to the victims.

However, as the chapters in this volume demonstrate, no transitional justice mechanism, individually or in combination with others, necessarily fulfills all the goals of justice and reconciliation. The limitations associated with transitional justice mechanisms have less to do with any specific method than with more general problems of implementing policy and involving the whole society in the process of ending impunity and fostering reconciliation. This chapter provides a general overview of each mechanism that is available to any government after a transition to democracy, presents the logic of the volume, and concludes with a summary of the various country case chapters.

Human Rights and Wrongs

Human rights are the rights that individuals are entitled to as humans. Natural law theorists from the early Greeks through Grotius and John Locke argued that basic human rights can be discerned either through reason or in some cases through an understanding of God's law (Shestack 1998). These universal human rights can be expressed in national constitutions and through international instruments such as the Universal Declaration of Human Rights, the International Covenants for Civil and Political Rights, and the International Covenant for Social, Economic and Cultural Rights. While legal positivists argue that human rights exist on the basis of the consent of the state, international human rights law since the 1970s has developed based on notions of the universality of rights. Thus, no state can legalize crimes such as genocide, war crimes, and crimes against humanity, and states have an absolute obligation to prosecute individuals charged with these crimes. Whereas states are expected to uphold these universal rights for their citizens, abuses have taken place across the world during periods of authoritarian rule, civil war, or a struggle for independence. It is during these periods that governments are pitted against society and target those who are perceived to be enemies of the regime. To deal with the abuses committed by the previous regime, democratizing states (with the support of the international community) can decide to adopt one or more method of transitional justice to address past violence.

One issue that must be considered when selecting a mechanism of transitional justice involves the relative strength of the outgoing authoritarian regime, colonial power, or civil war leadership. When the previous regime has been thoroughly defeated, then a domestic trial is possible as the vanquished leaders have no choice but to abide by the court's decision. In democratic countries in which individuals are charged with violating human rights, it is natural to leave the matter to the judiciary in order to ensure the rights of the accused as well as fairness to the victim. However, in countries transitioning to democracy, the rule of law and impartiality of the judiciary may not be fully developed. Therefore, trials may become a form of "victor's justice" for the new regime in which the accused may not receive a fair trial. To ensure fairness to both the accused and victims, trials can involve international judges and prosecutors in collaboration with the local judiciary to promote the rule of law. In some cases however, the domestic judiciary is either so discredited or weak that any domestic legal process is impossible. In these situations, a purely international judicial process may be necessary to protect the accused while providing justice to victims.

Another possible scenario after a transition to democracy involves high-ranking government officials and military leaders continuing to wield considerable power, which can be used against the new, fragile political system if they are charged with crimes. In these cases, amnesties can provide officials protection from prosecution that removes the threat of violence toward the new government; however, this is done at the cost of justice for victims. Finally, TRCs are a more likely outcome "when the relative strength of the demands [between the outgoing and current regime] is roughly equal" (Skaar 1999, 1110). TRCs are seen a "compromise solution" in which trials or doing nothing (*i.e.*, amnesties) is rejected by either side in a post-conflict, democratic transition. In the following section, we discuss more thoroughly the options available to democratizing states for addressing the human rights violations of the previous regime.

Transitional Justice Mechanisms

Domestic Trials

The Treaty of Westphalia of 1648 established that states and their governments have the ultimate political authority over the territory they control. States are sovereign and thus are entrusted with creating, upholding, and penalizing any violations of the law. Judiciaries play a critical role in applying laws and penalizing those who break them. Domestic courts are established to address breaches of the law so when governments and citizens violate the law, the first recourse for remedy is assumed to be the domestic judicial system, particularly in societies where a legal culture of accountability exists, and the rule of law is well ingrained. Domestic trials are a good option when the judiciary is well-established and impartial, and most importantly not perceived to have been an accomplice to the outgoing regime (Dakolias and Thachuk 2000).

What happens when the domestic judiciary is weak or is perceived to have been a collaborator in the human rights violations during authoritarian rule or colonialism? In the case of consistent and pervasive abuses, the traditional mechanisms for enforcing human rights norms, such as the judiciary and law enforcement, are undermined (Snyder and Vinjamuri 2003/2004). Sometimes, judiciaries are silent during authoritarian or colonial rule, or the judicial system might have collapsed during the authoritarian period. If society places pressure on the state to address widespread and systematic abuses and if the judicial system has ceased to function independently or effectively, domestic trials might not be the best option (Kaye 1997). This might necessitate the use of alternative judicial mechanisms.

International Criminal Tribunals

The struggle to provide justice for individuals who have been the victims of violations of human rights has often been a struggle against nation-state sovereignty (Chopra and Weiss 1992). Historically, international law regulated the conduct and relationship among states and ignored the individual as a subject of the law. The only area of international law that addressed violations of individual rights by states concerned actions by governments against citizens of other states. During the cold war, heads of state could act with impunity against their own citizens because of the lack of consensus among UN Security Council members (Mingst and Karns 2000). During this period, heads of state could use state sovereignty to justify their actions and to protect them against criminal charges. However, with the end of the cold war, the international community has become more active in ensuring that individuals who have committed gross human rights violations are prosecuted.

There are a number of reasons why under international law, individuals should be held accountable when the domestic judiciary is either unable or unwilling to prosecute the perpetrators of a crime. First, the pursuit of accountability serves to provide victims with a sense of justice and closure. Second, in transitional regimes, accountability can help promote national reconciliation and help society come to terms with the reasons why the law was violated. Third, accountability may deter future violations either by demonstrating to those contemplating such violations the prospect of punishment or more generally by promoting justice, government reform, and the rule of law. Finally, the rehabilitation of the offender is regarded as an essential result of accountability and reconciliation.

The International Criminal Tribunal for the former Yugoslavia (ICTY) and the International Criminal Tribunal for Rwanda (ICTR) were established as auxiliary organs of the UN in 1993 and 1994, respectively, to deal with a range of crimes committed under international law. These two tribunals were guaranteed financing as part of the UN budget under Chapter VII authority. In addition, states were required to cooperate with these tribunals, especially in the apprehension of suspects. Both tribunals were staffed by purely international judges and seated in international venues (The Hague, Netherlands and Arusha, Tanzania, respectively). The international community, acting through the UN, determined that the conditions in the former Yugoslavia and Rwanda did not allow for domestic trials that would ensure fairness and impartiality and conform to international standards of justice. In the case of Yugoslavia, domestic legal institutions were in shambles after the country disintegrated into several newly independent states while in the case of Rwanda, the ICTR was created soon after one of the most shocking genocides since World War II.

Hybrid Criminal Tribunals

The year 2000 marked a turning point in the development of international tribunals. The international community had become reluctant to finance additional criminal tribunals through the UN budget (Roper and Barria 2006). This concern, coupled with the resistance of some states to relinquish sovereignty over individuals to an international process, led to the innovation of hybrid or mixed criminal tribunals. Within the span of eights months in 2000, three hybrid criminal tribunals were established including the Serious Crimes Unit (SCU) for East Timor in March, the Extraordinary Chambers in the Courts of Cambodia (ECCC) in July, and the Special Court for Sierra Leone (SCSL) in August.

These hybrid courts are a movement away from an ICTY and ICTR international criminal tribunal model to a mixed model involving both international and domestic actors. While these criminal tribunals vary considerably in their jurisdiction, composition, and financing, the SCSL, the ECCC, and the SCU include a combination of domestic and international judges, utilize domestic and international laws, and are administered by a prosecutorial team composed of domestic and international lawyers. In many respects, the institutional changes have been brought about because of criticisms of the ICTY and the ICTR model. These new hybrid criminal tribunals also represent an attempt by states to re-insert themselves into the post-conflict legal process by incorporating, to the fullest extent possible, domestic legal institutions and laws.

One of the main arguments in support of hybrid criminal tribunals is that they can provide the basis for re-building the judicial system in post-conflict societies, provide training for local judicial officials, and at the same time serve the essential functions of a judiciary. Fritz and Smith argue that "[k]nowledge gained, skills acquired, and personnel empowered may act as catalysts for the establishment of new institutions, structures, and cultures that will better safeguard the rule of law and outlive the existence of [hybrid courts]" (2001, 406). Hybrid criminal tribunals can provide greater educational and training benefits than international tribunals, and also offer local ownership of the judicial process while at the same time ensuring international standards of justice. Moreover, because the tribunal is located in the country and the prosecutorial team includes individuals selected by the government, there is a greater likelihood that this type of legal institution will bring a greater sense of justice than purely international tribunals, which are often viewed as too distant from the citizenry.

Amnesties

Amnesties are pardons granted by a government to an individual or group of individuals that gives them immunity from criminal prosecution. Amnesties can be granted by the outgoing regime to itself in order to avoid future prosecutions, or they can be granted by the new democratic regime that is fearful that criminal prosecutions could undermine its legitimacy and bring back to power the officials who were responsible for the previous human rights violations. While amnesties have been used by various successor governments for a wide range of crimes, there remains the question whether any government can provide an amnesty from prosecution for crimes including genocide, war crimes, and crimes against humanity. Since these crimes involve the violation of universal human rights, no government has the power to waive prosecution, and under customary international law, states actually have an obligation to prosecute individuals, including previous government officials, for these crimes.

Truth and Reconciliation Commissions

A TRC is a body that is created to uncover past wrongdoings committed by the government and society. However, a TRC is not a judicial body that can punish perpetrators. According to Hayner (1994), a TRC is defined by the following characteristics: First, a TRC focuses on the past (a specific period of time). Second, a TRC is not focused on a single event but attempts to paint an overall picture of human rights abuses. Third, a TRC is established for a predefined period of time and ceases to exist with the submission of a final report of its findings. Fourth, while not a judicial body, a TRC is vested with some sort of government authority, which allows it greater access to information and to individuals.

Based on the composition of the TRC, national, mixed, and purely international TRCs have been formed. One of the most prominent examples of a national TRC is the one adopted by South Africa, in which all of the commissioners were South African. The Guatemalan Historical Clarification Commission was composed of both national and international commissioners while the UN Truth Commission for El Salvador was composed of only international commissioners. Individuals of high social standing are selected to be members of a TRC either by the government, the UN, or both. The role of commissioners is to meet with individuals and groups to gain testimony that establishes a historical record of events and produce a report that optimally would be available for citizens.

Government officials and victims are asked to testify in order to create a social narrative about the events that took place in order to assist members of society to move forward and reconcile with perpetrators. TRCs can also provide amnesties to encourage perpetrators to come forward and testify and can help put specific incidents into a broader social and political context in order to understand the factors that created the conditions for the crimes to occur and to suggest ways to prevent their recurrence (Buergenthal 2006/2007). TRCs are viewed as being victim-centered in that revelations by perpetuators can restore dignity to victims and provide healing. Based on the mandate of the TRC, the final report can provide specific recommendations, including the prosecution of individuals, judicial reform, and changes within the military and law enforcement in order to enhance the effectiveness of the rule of law.

The International Criminal Court

While none of the countries covered in this volume has a case before the International Criminal Court (ICC), it is important to briefly mention this new international mechanism of accountability. All courts, whether domestic, international, or hybrid, must ensure fairness and impartiality for the accused and the victim. Since the end of the cold war, in cases in which domestic trials are not possible, the international community has selectively used international and hybrid criminal tribunals to prosecute those responsible for human rights violations. However, because these criminal tribunals are temporary, selective (established only for certain countries), and require significant startup time, many states argued in favor of a permanent criminal court. Indeed, discussions concerning the need for a permanent international criminal court have been ongoing since the end of World War I (Hudson 1938). In addition, the creation of the Nuremberg and the Tokyo military tribunals after World War II focused attention on the need for an international criminal court to end impunity for human rights violations (Pella 1950).

With the end of the cold war, states were more willing to consider a permanent international body to prosecute violations of human rights. During the diplomatic conference in Rome in 1998 to finalize the statute of the ICC, one of the key concerns was the relationship of the ICC to states and the obligations that states would have to the ICC *vis-a-vis* their own citizens and citizens of other states (Scheffer 2000). One of the lessons learned from the experiences of international criminal tribunals such as the ICTY and the ICTR, as well as hybrid criminal courts like the SCSL and the SCU, was that the noncompliance of states greatly undermines the effectiveness of these courts. Although the ICC has been overwhelmingly supported by the international community, states such as the United States, China, and India still remain outside of the ICC system (Mayerfeld 2003).

The Logic of This Volume

During the transition to democracy from a period of authoritarian rule or civil war, states have used various methods to address the human rights abuses of the previous regime in power. This volume examines the choices made by four countries, often with substantial international involvement, to confront human rights violations. We chose Argentina, BiH, East Timor, and Sierra Leone for many reasons. First, these four countries cover different regions, which demonstrates that transitional justice is truly a global concern and that transitional justice mechanisms can be used in different regional and cultural settings. Second, the four countries in this volume provide a broad sample of the different accountability mechanisms available to states and the international community (*e.g.*, domestic trials, amnesties, international and hybrid criminal tribunals, and TRCs). These different methods of transitional justice are not mutually exclusive, and each country chose to use more than one mechanism to address the same violations. Third, the cases highlight the particular concerns of countries that are either transitioning to democracy after a period of authoritarian rule or civil war (*e.g.*, Argentina and Sierra Leone) or are transitioning to democracy as part of the building of a new state (*e.g.*, BiH and East Timor). The violations covered in this book span a period of over twenty-five years. The "Dirty War" in Argentina took place between 1976 and 1983 while the international war in BiH and the civil war Sierra Leone occurred in the 1990s. In the case of East Timor, violations span the period 1975–1999 during the struggle for independence as Indonesia governed the territory.

For each of the country cases, one chapter provides a historical overview concerning the causes of the conflict and the forms of violence that occurred. Afterward, two subsequent chapters highlight a different method of transitional justice implemented by the country. In the case of Argentina, the first transitional justice mechanism was a TRC followed by domestic trials and amnesties. In BiH, the ICTY was created to prosecute individuals and only a decade later were some of the ICTY cases devolved back to the BiH judiciary for domestic trials. In Sierra Leone and East Timor, a TRC and hybrid court existed concomitantly to address human rights abuses. We have been fortunate to draw on the expertise of scholars who have spent significant time in the field conducting interviews that provide an in-depth understanding not only about the mechanism but also the larger social questions and problems involved in transitional justice.

In Part I, devoted to Argentina, Chapter 2 by Timothy Wilson focuses on the military regime and the Dirty War from 1976 to 1983. As part of a policy to eliminate the enemies of the regime, tens of thousands of individuals disappeared, never to be found alive. While some of these individuals opposed the regime, others were innocent victims. As Argentina transitioned to democracy at the end of 1983, civil society groups demanded accountability for those who disappeared during the previous regime. In order to address these demands, the newly elected government of President Raul Alfonsin took a two-track approach: Establishing a TRC while also supporting the trial of top military leaders. However, in order to avoid the possibility of a military coup, Alfonsin had to ultimately grant amnesties to military officials in order to maintain the country's fragile democracy.

The next two chapters consider the transitional justice mechanisms implemented in Argentina to address the violence known as the "Dirty War." In Chapter 3, Emilio Crenzel examines the successes and the limitations of the investigation by Argentina's National Commission on the Disappearance of Persons (CONADEP). This TRC was established in December 1983, and over the course of nine months, it heard testimony from relatives of the disappeared, survivors, and other witnesses and gathered evidence about the clandestine detention centers where the victims were held. The commission's final report, entitled *Nunca Mas* (*Never Again*), was published in November 1984 and was groundbreaking in terms of its discussion about the violence during the military regime. *Nunca Mas* was used as a basis for the subsequent prosecution of officials involved in the Dirty War.

Mario Di Paolantonio in Chapter 4 discusses the "Trial of the Military," which occurred in 1985. This trial involved nine junta leaders deemed responsible for the violations committed during the military regime. Di Paolantonio discusses the selective strategy of prosecution as well as the passage of amnesty laws enacted to prevent further trials. He notes that the government, amid the instability of the transition to democracy, chose to use amnesties in order to avert a return of the military to power.

In Part III, we turn to Bosnia-Herzegovina. Christina Morus discusses in Chapter 5 the historical antecedents and role of ethnicity in the former Yugoslavia. As the country disintegrated in the early 1990s, cynical politicians used nationalism to carve up territory and populations. The "New World Order" of the 1990s unleashed decades-old, if not centuries-old, animosities with a fury not seen since World War II. The creation of concentration camps such as Keraterm brought back ghastly images of the Holocaust. The genocide in Srebrenica is not only the most horrific event of the war in BiH, but is a painful symbol of the failure of the international community to take action in the face of a humanitarian and human rights catastrophe.

Chapters 6 and 7 examine different forms of transitional justice in the aftermath of the wars in the former Yugoslavia. Chapter 6 focuses on the role of the international community to bring to justice those most responsible for the conduct of the war while Chapter 7 examines international attempts to assist local officials in developing the domestic judiciary to try perpetrators. As the ICTY's mandate nears its end (it is scheduled to cease operations in 2013) and cases are returned to BiH, an analysis of the successes and failures of the tribunal is timely. The chapter by Janine Clark examines the ICTY's communication with the Bosnian, Serbian, and Croatian population to assess its overall effectiveness. Given that the trial chambers of the ICTY are located in The Hague, Clark argues that outreach was imperative to explain the decisions of the tribunal in order to promote a sense of justice and reconciliation. The chapter by Ryan Lowry and Patrice McMahon is a cautionary tale about the obstacles and the challenges to domestic judiciaries prosecuting human rights violations. While chapters in this volume highlight some of the weaknesses of the international community in prosecuting human rights violations, the Lowry and McMahon chapter addresses the significant difficulties facing domestic courts as transitional justice mechanisms in prosecuting complex human rights cases.

Sierra Leone is the focus of Part IV. To begin, Abu Mboka addresses the fundamental question of the underlying causes for the conflict and human rights violations in Chapter 8. Throughout the 1990s, Sierra Leone was engulfed in civil wars, which led to some of the worst human rights atrocities committed in West Africa. The presence of child soldiers as both victim and perpetrator is one of the defining legacies of the human rights abuses in Sierra Leone. Mboka explores the complex pre- and post-colonial history, which undermined attempts at establishing democracy and the rule of law. He explains how the civil war in the country was at the same time part of the larger West African wars of the 1990s. The complex historical narrative that he provides sheds light on why finding the "truth" about events in Sierra Leone was so difficult.

Zoe Dugal discusses the Sierra Leone TRC in Chapter 9 as a means of dealing with the past in order to move forward. This TRC was part of the Lome Peace Agreement in 1999 but took three more years to actually implement. At the beginning of the commission's work, the general perception of the international community was that conflict in Sierra Leone was resource-driven (*i.e.*, diamonds) and part of the larger West African conflict. The commission concluded that this view of the conflict was too simplistic and tended to negate Sierra Leone's own troubled past. As Dugal notes, the creation of a historical narrative of human rights abuses is one of the central missions of a TRC. Chapter 10 by Ellen Stensrud addresses the strengths and the weaknesses of the SCSL as a hybrid model of transitional justice. As one of the three hybrid courts established in 2000, the SCSL was to try those most responsible for the human rights abuses of the 1990s as well as to ensure that the different warring parties were held equally liable for violations. The current trial of Charles Taylor at The Hague is the last prosecution of the SCSL and involves the first former African head of state being tried for international human rights violations.

In Part V, we turn to East Timor. In Chapter 11, Clinton Fernandes details the struggle for independence in East Timor beginning in 1975 when it was annexed by Indonesia. During the period from 1975 to 1999, the Indonesian government waged a war against the various groups that were fighting for independence. It is estimated that over 100,000 Timorese perished, and it was not until 1999 that a UN-sponsored referendum resulted in the creation of the newly independent state of East Timor. However, as Indonesian forces departed, they engaged in horrific violence and the destruction of much of the infrastructure of East Timor. With the assistance of the UN, a new government took power in 2002 and both a TRC and a hybrid tribunal were established.

In Chapter 12, James Rae discusses the bargaining among Indonesia, East Timor, and the UN concerning the creation of the SCU hybrid court. While most of the human rights violations were committed by personnel in the Indonesian military, the Indonesian government refused to participate in the SCU and instead created their own separate judicial process to try individuals (Roper and Barria 2005). The inability of East Timor to arrest Indonesian military officials severely hampered the efforts of the SCU. Like Sierra Leone, East Timor established a TRC at the same time as the hybrid court. Wendy Lambourne in Chapter 13 discusses the East Timorese Commission for Reception, Truth, and Reconciliation (CAVR). This TRC focused on three major activities: Facilitating the reintegration of East Timorese refugees, establishing a historical record about human rights abuses, and recommending legal reforms to protect human rights in the future. As Rae discusses in terms of the SCU, the CAVR's work and activities were undermined by the lack of involvement of Indonesian officials.

Conclusions

The chapters in this book provide details of the atrocities committed in each country and the efforts by both domestic actors and the international community to end impunity and provide justice to victims and reconciliation for society. Part of the debate surrounding the appropriateness of each transitional justice mechanism centers on the relationship between justice and peace. There is always a balance between achieving accountability and nurturing a stable democratic transition. Many argue that peace and stability should take center stage after a transition to democracy, and this can be better achieved by adopting a TRC and granting amnesties. By contrast, others argue that peace is not possible without justice for victims. Therefore, trials, whether domestic, international or mixed, are absolutely necessary for the long-term prospects of democracy and peace. While the country cases in this volume involved human rights violations in the 1970s, 1980s, and 1990s, the current genocide in Darfur, ICC indictment against President Omar Bashir, and possible intervention by the UN Security Council to prevent his arrest, all demonstrate that the debate over peace and justice is far from over.

References

Buergenthal, Thomas. 2006/2007. "Turth Commissions: Between Impunity and Prosecution." *Case Western Reserve Journal of International Law* 38:217–223.

Chopra, Jarat, and Thomas G. Weiss. 1998. "Sovereignty is No Longer Sacrosanct: Codifying Humanitarian Intervention." In *International Law: Classic and Contemporary Readings*, ed. Charlotte Ku, and Paul F. Fiehl. Boulder, CO: Lynne Rienner Publishers.

Dakolias, Maria, and Kim Thachuk. 2000. "Attacking Corruption in the Judiciary: A Critical Process in Judicial Reform." *Wisconsin International Law Journal* 18:353–406.

Hayner, Priscilla. 1994. "Fifteen Truth Commissions—1974 to 1994: A Comparative Study." *Human Rights Quarterly* 16:597–655.

Hudson, Manley O. 1938. "The Proposed International Criminal Court." *The American Journal of International Law* 32:549–554.

Kaye, Mike. 1997. "The Role of Truth Commissions in the Search for Justice, Reconciliation and Democratisation: The Salvadoran and Honduran Case." *Journal of Latin American Studies* 29:693–716.

Mayerfeld, Jamie. 2003. "Who Shall Be Judge?: The United States, the International Criminal Court, and the Global Enforcement of Human Rights." *Human Rights Quarterly* 25:93–129.

Mingst, Karen A., and Margaret P. Karns. 2000. *The United Nations in the Post-Cold Wart Era*. Boulder, CO: Westview Press.

Pella, Vespasian V. 1950. "Towards an International Criminal Court." *The American Journal of International Law* 44:37–68.

Roper, Steven D., and Lilian A. Barria. 2006. *Designing Criminal Tribunals: Sovereignty and International Concerns in the Protection of Human Rights*. Aldershot: Ashgate Publishing.

Roper, Steven D., and Lilian A. Barria. 2005. "Assessing the Record of Justice: A Comparison of Mixed International Tribunals versus Domestic Mechanisms for Human Rights Enforcement." *Journal of Human Rights* 4:521–536.

Scheffer, David J. 2000. "The U.S. Perspective on the ICC." In *The United States and the International Criminal Court*, ed. Sarah B. Sewall, and Carl Kaysen. Lanham, MD: Rowman & Littlefield Publishers.

Shestack, Jerome J. 1998. "The Philosophic Foundations of Human Rights." *Human Rights Quarterly* 20:201–234.

Skaar, Elin. 1999. "Truth Commissions, Trials—or Nothing? Policy Options in Democratic Transition." *Third World Quarterly* 20:1109–1128.

Snyder, Jack, and Leslie Vinjamuri. 2003/2004. "Trials and Errors: Principle and Pragmatism in Strategies of International Justice." *International Security* 28:5–44.

PART II

Argentina

Map from the United States Central Intelligence Agency's World Factbook.

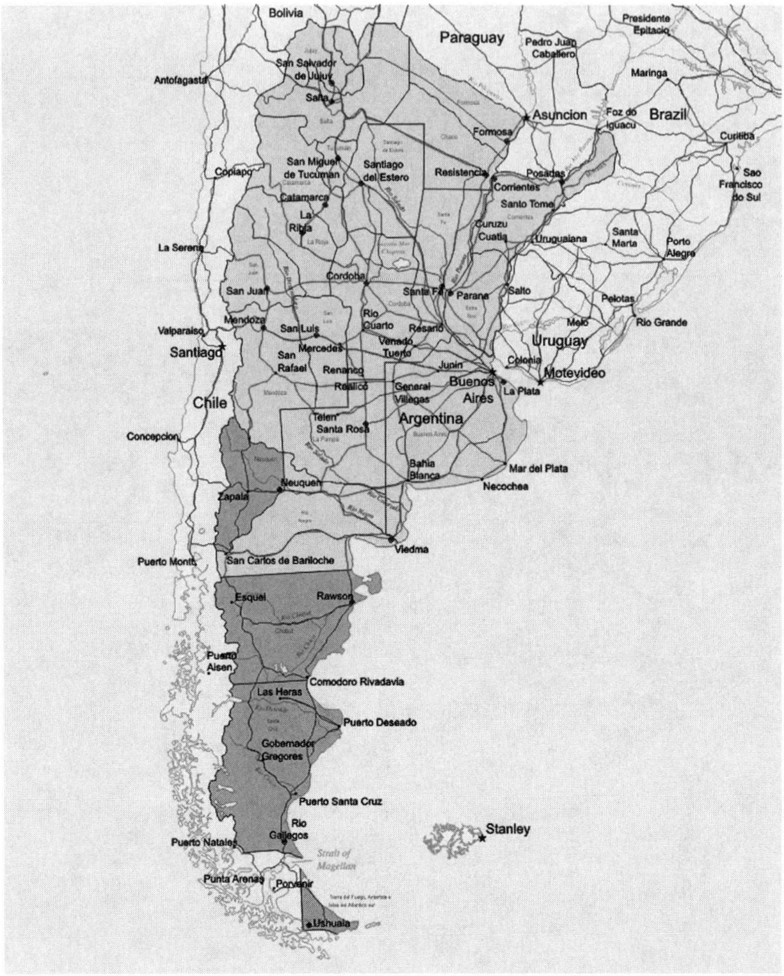

Map created by TownDown and accessed via Wikimedia Commons.

CHAPTER 2

Argentina's Proceso: *Societal "Reform" through Premeditated Terror*

TIMOTHY WILSON

Introduction

The "Dirty War," officially called "The War against Subversion" by the Argentine military, was a campaign in the 1970s and early 1980s to eradicate extremist leftism and terrorism in that country. It mostly—though not fully—coincides with the period of military dictatorship that ruled Argentina from 1976 to 1983. The violence is often defended as the unfortunate and necessary steps taken by a regime beset by leftist attacks; it is said that the country was spiraling out of control, and a firm hand was necessary to stop leftist extremists from causing damage. However, by all accounts, the degree of state repression during that time was extreme, far outstripping the ostensible danger from terrorists. The best estimates, by newly discovered documents from within the regime itself, put the number of tortured and killed ("disappeared") in Argentina's Dirty War at 30,000 (Dinges 2004). In 1977, Amnesty International won the Nobel Prize for Peace for their exhaustive investigation of the abuses of the Argentine military regime. Their report concluded that the extreme measures taken by the state were in no way commensurate with the relatively limited threat posed by leftist terrorists (Amnesty International 1977). The question, then, is why were so many treated so harshly?

If one takes the traditional view of the Dirty War in Argentina as a conflict between leftist extremists and the military government in which the situation "got out of hand," then the terrible acts of sadism that have been documented make no sense. If one accepts the military junta's official rationale that force was necessary to "establish security," and that their goal was to establish peace and stability the good of the country, then the crimes they committed are simply bewildering; they are, as Naomi Klein puts it, "just random, free-floating bad event... to be condemned by all people of conscience but impossible to understand" (2007, 120). Without an understanding of the larger plan of the

Dirty War, of the true purpose of the violence, and of the powerful interests behind that project, then the Dirty War is simply incomprehensible.

In fact, the perpetrated violence was in no way random, but rather very carefully planned as part of a long-term ideological project. The regime used the pretense of "establishing security" as a justification for what was actually a premeditated plan to reshape the country ideologically and economically. The military and the leftist extremists were far from the only players in this gruesome game. Many others had a role: On one side, the Argentine elite, the U.S. Department of State, the Central Intelligence Agency (CIA), and multinational corporations such as Ford, certainly took part in some measure. On the other side, not just extremists, but all the Argentine people, the famous and the faceless, suffered to some extent. The military regime that called itself the "process of national reorganization" used terror as a tool to impose its ideological project of re-aligning the country farther to the right. It planned to revamp the economy, the media, and even the very minds of Argentines. Many of the actors in these events, as well as their strategies, were surprising and many of the outcomes were unexpected. In a very real way, the secrets and the legacies of the Dirty War are still being unearthed today.

Historical Background of Argentina Leading Up to the Violence

Since the nineteenth century, most of the wealth in Argentina had been in the hands of merely 300 rural landowning families, and political power was passed from hand to hand among a tight oligarchy drawn from the Argentine Rural Society. In the twentieth century, a new dynamic was formed. As immigration swelled the population of cities, the center-left Radical Party, and to a lesser extent, the Socialists, won wide popular support among the new urban and industrial classes. In the elections of 1916, the oligarchy was finally removed from power, and President Hipolito Irigoyen and the Radicals enjoyed fourteen years of democratic rule.

Their loss of power was cause for alarm to Argentina's traditional ruling class, and their fears were shared by the military. Irigoyen was removed in a military coup in 1930, without finishing his second term. This use of military force set a precedent for very confrontational politics, which dictated the remainder of the twentieth century. Since 1930, the tension between populists and the military has been a constant thread in the fabric of Argentine society.

This gap was bridged in the twentieth century briefly by Colonel Juan Domingo Peron, who cultivated the support of the masses through an uncommon blend of military power and left-wing social programs, and was elected to the presidency in 1946. But he too was ousted by rival factions of the military in 1955 and went into exile in Spain. The tensions between military and populists that Peron had temporarily assuaged were not gone, and while Peron was in exile, left- and right-wing factions of Peronism emerged. Increasingly, far-left-wing Peronist revolutionary organizations such as the *Montoneros* carried out campaigns of kidnappings and bombings. Upon his long-awaited return from exile, Peron was again elected to the presidency in

1973, but the now-elderly leader soon died in July 1974 and was succeeded in the presidency by his third wife and vice-president, the former dancer Isabel Martinez de Peron. She proved to be a weak, ineffectual leader, and soon after Juan Peron's death, the *Montoneros*, claiming to be the bearers of authentic Peronism, implemented terrorist tactics against her government.

Perhaps under the influence of her aide Jose "Witchdoctor" Lopez Rega, Isabel Peron signed decrees authorizing the military and the police to "annihilate" left-wing subversion throughout the country (McDonnell 2007). Lopez Rega is also credited with the founding of the right-wing paramilitary group, the Argentine Anti-communist Alliance, or Triple A, whose death squad operations were soon claiming hundreds of victims. On the other side, the leftist People's Revolutionary Army (ERP) and the *Montoneros* targeted military installations, private companies, and business executives. The situation escalated: In 1975 alone, 137 military and police were killed as a result of terrorist activity (Wright 2007) while 359 assassinations were carried out by paramilitary groups, principally Lopez Rega's Triple A death squad (*Nunca Mas* 1986).

Finally, a coup d'etat overthrew Isabel Peron on March 24, 1976. In her place, a military junta was installed, with a representative from each of the three branches of the military: General Jorge Videla (commander-in-chief of the Army), Admiral Emilio Massera (head of the Argentine Navy), and Brigadier Orlando Agosti (head of the Air Force) with Videla acting as president. The junta took the official name of "Process of National Reorganization" (*Proceso de Reorganizacion Nacional*, often simply referred to as *El Proceso*) in order to reflect its desire to completely reverse the situation of the country. As General Videla had declared months before leading the coup, "in Argentina as many people will die as is necessary to make the country secure" (H.I.J.O.S. 2006). And they did die. General Iberico Saint Jean, governor of the Province of Buenos Aires, gleefully prognosticated that "[f]irst we will kill all the subversives, then their collaborators, then the sympathizers, after that we'll kill the indifferent, and finally we'll kill the timid" (Presman 2007). And indeed, those who perished during these years were by no account all armed terrorists. But neither were they just random victims of bloodthirsty dictators who were drunk on sadism and personal power. What happened was more scientific, more "terrifyingly rational" (Klein 2007). As has been suggested above, the killings were part of a premeditated plan of strategic extermination, designed to reinforce a certain ideology and support a certain economic policy. To completely address this point, however, it will be necessary to understand the wider international scene in the years preceding the Dirty War. For although the historical tensions between the left and right within Argentina set the stage for the *Proceso*, it could not have taken place without actors of many nationalities who facilitated, advised, and even helped plan the bloody events.

The Influence of International Actors

The Argentine Dirty War was not a result of ideas held or actions taken by the Argentine military alone; a number of international factors and interests heavily influenced the events that unfolded. In fact, it could be said that the Argentine *Proceso* was born not in 1976 in Buenos Aires, but three years earlier in Santiago de Chile, or perhaps ten years before that, in Cuba or in Washington. In Washington, there was a palpable fear that other Latin American countries would follow Cuba's example of socialism. The fear was so palpable that when it became apparent that socialist Salvador Allende would win the 1970 presidential elections in Chile, great pains were taken to prevent Allende's victory. Secretary of State Henry Kissinger said that "I don't see why we need to stand by and watch a country go communist due to the irresponsibility of its own people. The issues are much too important for the Chilean voters to be left to decide for themselves" (Jones 1973, 93). It was determined that Allende's election should be prevented if possible and, if not, that he should be overthrown. President Nixon ordered the CIA to "[m]ake the economy scream [in Chile to] prevent Allende from coming to power or to unseat him" (CIA 2002).

After three years of sabotage of the Chilean economy and millions of dollars of funding for covert CIA operations, trainers, and materials, the previously staunchly democratic country was coaxed into overthrowing its government in a military coup (Klein 2007, 76). The new government lost no time in dismantling the social programs of Allende's government and implementing neoliberal economic policies. Earlier that year, Uruguay had turned to a military government, as had Brazil a number of years earlier. This meant that with the exception of Argentina, the entire Southern Cone region—the countries that had previously been the most socially progressive in Latin America—were now all run by U.S.-backed military governments, which imposed extreme free-market policies (Klein 2007).

It was clearly not by chance that military government was brought about in Argentina as well. The coup has normally been painted by the regime and its apologists as a last resort to finally put a stop to leftist violence, but it has become clear in recent years that the opposite is true: That the War against Subversion was merely a pretense to seize power. As early as six months before the coup, in September 1975, General Videla had begun planning the takeover (Wright 2007). The Argentine military worked with its more experienced neighbors to create a plan of attack; newly declassified documents reveal that Argentine generals contacted Pinochet and the Brazilian junta before the coup to "outline the main steps to be taken by the future regime" (Klein 2007, 88). Preparations were made long in advance to pave the way for the planned repression: Long before the coup, military and police intelligence services made lists of suspected leftists and targeted them for disappearance (Wright 2007).

The Argentine coup plotters had learned lessons from watching the Chilean experiment three years before and knew they would have to take a different tack in order to be successful. In Chile, Pinochet tried to make the coup as dramatic and traumatic as possible. The violence was purposely very open, as a strategy to terrify Chileans into docility. In the days following the coup, 13,500 civilians were rounded up in trucks and imprisoned, according to a declassified CIA report (Berryman 1993). Many were taken to one of the two main soccer stadiums in Santiago, the Chile Stadium, and the huge National Stadium, where they were held for days without food and water, and many were tortured and killed. Famous persons were treated no better, to the contrary: High-profile detainees, such as singers and politicians, served all the better as warning examples to Chileans. On September 15, 1973, four days after the coup, the internationally famous folk singer and activist Victor Jara was arrested and taken to the national stadium with 5,000 others. There, he was tortured—perhaps in one of the same basement rooms where so many times before he had prepared to perform. Finally he was machine-gunned to death—his body thrown into the street (Jara 1983). It soon became clear to Chileans that resistance would be fatal.

However, not only Chileans got the message: Pinochet's cruel campaign soon sparked an outcry around the world, resulting in calls for trade sanctions in Europe and North America, not the most favorable outcome for a regime that had dedicated itself to free trade (Klein 2007). Videla and the other Argentine military leaders were keenly aware of the dangers of bad publicity. When they were preparing for their 1976 coup, they were determined "to avoid suffering an international campaign like the one that has been unleashed against Chile" (Reuters 2007). They chose a lower-profile method: Less sensational repression tactics that would be capable of spreading terror and yet allow them to avoid pressure by the international press (Klein 2007). As one officer stated: "We are not going to use the firing squad like [Spanish dictator] Franco and [Chilean dictator] Pinochet, because then everyone up to the Pope will ask us not to do it" (Mignone 1991, 60).

One of the powerful entities that hoped the Argentine junta would be discreet was the U.S. government. The U.S. Department of State has publicly long clung to the illusion of the Dirty War as a struggle against dangerous leftists, a struggle that sometimes resulted in unfortunate excesses but one worthy of U.S. support. However, recently de-classified documents show that Washington knew even at the time that this was not the case. Two days after the military coup, Kissinger was advised by former Secretary of State William Rogers that he could "expect a fair amount of repression, probably a good deal of blood, in Argentina before too long" and that the Argentine military would have to "come down very hard not only on the terrorists but on the dissidents of trade unions and their parties." Yet Kissinger ordered immediate support for the new regime in spite of his staff's warnings. "Whatever chance they have, they will need a little encouragement... because I do want to encourage them" (U.S. Department of State 2006b). Later that year, it became clear in Washington how excessive the tactics were becoming. Kissinger's own note taker took testimony from the recently freed U.S. citizen Gwenda Loken Lopez, who had been detained and tortured in Argentina for handing out leaflets. She said that "they started using [an electric prod]. Then they tied me down and threw water on me... They questioned me but it was more 'just give it to her. There. There. There.' In the genital area... They said they'd fix me so I couldn't have children" (U.S. Department of State 2002). Only three days later, Kissinger met with Argentine foreign minister Cesar Augusto Guzzetti, to whom he gave his full support. He asked only that Guzzetti hurry before the U.S. Congress cut military aid because they were about to approve sanctions against the Argentine regime due to reports of human rights abuses. Kissinger stated that "[l]ook, our basic attitude is that we would like you to succeed. I have an old-fashioned view that friends ought to be supported... The quicker you succeed the better... If you can finish before Congress gets back, the better" (U.S. Department of State 2006a).

Thus, the U.S. State Department gave its tacit approval while the Argentine regime was waging a Dirty War of abduction and torture, and the U.S. government also clearly had a role in supporting the generals with military aid. What is not clear is how directly involved U.S. personnel may have been in the tactics of the Dirty War; that is, to what extent the United States shared "expertise" with the Argentine regime, or exactly what the role of the CIA might have been in providing training in interrogation techniques. However, it may be surmised from the evidence of surrounding countries: The U.S. training of Brazilian and Uruguayan police in torture methods has been heavily documented (Klein 2007). Furthermore, a 1975 U.S. Senate investigation ascertained that the CIA also provided the Chilean military with training in methods for "controlling subversion" (U.S. Senate 1975). Additionally, just before his death at the hands of the regime, the legendary Argentine investigative journalist Rodolfo Walsh described in an open letter the involvement of the CIA in training the Argentine police (McCaughan 2002).

Argentina could not have carried out its Dirty War mission without the collaboration of other countries in the region as well. "Operation Condor" was the code name for an international pact between cooperating intelligence services such as Argentina's *Secretaria de Inteligencia del Estado,* the Chilean *Direccion Nacional de Inteligencia,* and Uruguay's *Servicio de Inteligencia de Defensa.* It was established to share intelligence collected on leftists, communists, and Marxists in South America. Reportedly, the members showing the most enthusiasm were Argentina, Uruguay, and Chile (U.S. Department of Defense 1999). Since "subversives" sought by a particular regime frequently went into exile in neighboring countries, the Condor member states worked together to deliver them back to their country of origin (Documentation Center 2003). Another grisly collaboration was the trading of tips about the most effective means to extract information from prisoners. Torture survivors recount "the unexpected detail that there were Brazilian soldiers in the room offering advice on the most scientific uses of pain" (Klein 2007, 92).

Measures Taken by the Military Government and Domestic Supporters

All the expertise and foreign aid from abroad were put to use within Argentina in an attempt to force an "extreme makeover." It is important to remember that the violence was not random, but a tool, and part of a "Process of National Reorganization." The regime would control the economy, the media, and even attempt to control the minds of Argentines in order to recreate in its own image the "*Ser nacional*" (the "National Being")—an idealized nationalistic concept of Argentine-ness projected by the junta.

Control of the Economy

Too often the carnage that resulted from the Dirty War is characterized as a murder scene, the result of a wanton killing spree. In reality, says Naomi Klein, it should be thought of as the scene of an armed robbery—grisly and premeditated (2007). What many fail to take into account is that the tortured and disappeared were not the only victims of the junta's policies. Most statistics on the abuses of the *Proceso* make no mention of the dramatic reversal of programs to redistribute wealth, and the resultant deepening and widespread poverty in this once very prosperous and middle-class country. Many Argentine economists who were trained in the "Chicago school" (a form of economic libertarianism) landed in key posts in the new regime—the secretary of finance, the president of the Central Bank, the director of the Treasury Department, as well as numerous lower-level consulting and advising positions—and they soon put in place extreme free market policies. To attract investment, the Argentine government issued a thirty-one-page advertising supplement in *Business Week*, produced by the PR giant Burson-Marsteller, declaring that "few governments in history have been as encouraging to private investment... we are in a true social revolution, and we seek partners. We are unburdening ourselves of statism, and believe firmly in the all-important role of the private sector" (Klein 2007, 89).

The regime itself made clear its revolutionary ambitions to remake society, but played down the financial agenda and its implementation of neoliberal economic policies. In reality, however, what was supposed to be a war against dangerous Marxist terrorists was in many ways a war against workers. One example is the focused attack on trade unionism; the military carried out surgical strikes against members of the trade unions on either the day of the coup or the following day. These attacks were clearly planned well in advance, as they were timed to coincide with—and be concealed by—the initial chaos of the coup (*Nunca Mas* 1986). Thus, the excuse of fighting terrorism was used as a smokescreen to target nonviolent labor activists. Factory owners who could benefit from a dismantling of trade unionism also became collaborators with the regime. The repression of organized labor was a concerted effort: There is abundant evidence that not only the military, but even multinational corporations such as Ford took part in the regime's attack on unionists. The Ford factory in suburban Buenos Aires allowed 100 soldiers to be quartered on the grounds, and management singled out union organizers for arrest. There was even a torture center set up within the factory itself.

Another group that stood to gain from cooperation with the new regime was the Argentine elite, as reversal of previous labor laws would help to protect their traditional privilege. One of the new regime economists was Minister of the Economy Jose Alfredo Martinez de Hoz, a representative of the landed aristocracy. He worked quickly to implement the new policies: Strikes were banned, companies were allowed to fire workers at will, price controls were lifted, and restrictions on foreign ownership were also removed. It can truly be said that in large part the coup represented a "revolt of the elites, a counterrevolution against forty years of gains by Argentina's workers" (Klein 2007, 88).

Control of the Media

Another important element in the junta's carefully coordinated plan beginning the day of the coup was a cultural "blackout." It consisted of an immediate seizure of the media—all print, and visual and audio media were strictly controlled—and the prohibition of public meetings: labor unions were banned and not even professional guilds or student groups were allowed to meet. In effect, all meetings or exchange of ideas was forbidden in public spaces. One indicator of the tight control on media is the alarming decline in the number of books published: From 21.4 million per year before the *Proceso*, down to only 2.7 million just five years later (National Institute of Statistics 1979). For Argentina, an educated country with a literacy rate of 97 percent, this decline constituted a rapid cultural impoverishment. This same decline was also felt in the education system, since the clampdown especially targeted schools: Eight thousand "ideologically suspect" leftist educators were quickly purged as part of Operation Clarity (Feitlowitz 1998). In high schools, they even prohibited group projects (Taylor 1997). Any intellectual undertaking was suspicious, and many intellectuals and artists fled the country during this time. According to Feitlowitz, "the Dirty War regime eviscerated the best-educated generation in the history of Argentina" (1998, 10).

Control of the Mind

The policies of the regime aimed to eliminate collectivism—not only from the culture, but from the mind itself. As an early junta editorial noted in 1976 that "minds too must be cleansed, for that is where the error was born" (Feitlowitz 1998, 153). The way this was to be achieved was through a complete control over public language. The regime's policies amounted to a systematic redefinition of words akin to Orwellian Newspeak: "The purpose of Newspeak was not only to provide a medium of expression for the World-view and mental habits proper to the devotees of Ingsoc, but to *make all other modes of thought impossible*" (Orwell 1949, 312, emphasis mine). Almost stranger than fiction, the junta in Argentina set out to manipulate language so as to control what could be thought: "We know that in order to repair so much damage we must recover the meanings of many embezzled words," said junta member Admiral Emilio Massera in a speech in 1976 (Massera 1979, 146). As Taylor puts it, "[d]uring the Dirty War, nation-ness was resemanticized. The ideal citizens were those who self-consciously controlled their... every word" (1997, 95).

Survivors of the *Proceso* explain that the terribly maddening aspect about the regime's discourse was that it constructed a national language that was almost believable, and that one was required to believe—or at least to use—yet in so many ways conflicted with what was seen with one's own eyes.

The national language constantly emphasized rationality and life, whereas the regime's own tactics consisted of the senseless destruction of life. The junta railed against subversion while its own subversion of words bankrupted language. Even as victims were tortured or disposed of in death camps, language itself was tortured—with words given new, horrible meanings. In the clandestine camps, "there developed an extensive argot in which benign domestic nouns, medical terms, saints, and fairy-tale characters were appropriated as terms pertaining to physical torture. Comforting past associations were translated into pain, degradation, and sometimes death" (Feitlowitz 1998, 49–50).

The junta characterized language as either "rational" or irrational and hysterical. In another speech (of which there were many), Massera warns his audience to beware of words. They are "unfaithful," he said. "The only safe words are our words" (1979, 19). Essentially, the regime dichotomized language and literally appropriated one segment ("our words"), which it considered the official, logical, and rational, and which it claimed for the national cause. As a result, a severe discrepancy arose between what people were told in the media and what they themselves had witnessed. Even as bodies washed up on the shore in Buenos Aires, news reports made no mention of the growing number of disappearances that happened daily throughout the country. The official version of reality, the rhetoric of the regime that was transmitted through the media, seemed more like fiction.

Obfuscation of misdeeds by politicians is clearly nothing new; what sets the *Proceso* apart is its scope: Massera's illogic represents a complete re-writing of reality. Not only junta members themselves, but also spokespersons and supporters of the junta, seemed to revel in the reversal of meaning. "Peace," said General Osiris G. Villegas, "is the continuation of war by other means" (Feitlowitz 1998, 32). Women's magazines (such as *Para ti*, whose language mirrored that of the regime) had recurrent themes that included "the benefits of limits" and "authority is not dictatorship" (Feitlowitz 1998, 39). Finally, the most tragic example is from an "open letter to the nation" that appeared in *Para ti* that redefined innocence as guilt:

> We are prepared to demand a great deal of ourselves, but we are going to demand a lot of others as well. Of those who govern us, that they keep their word, fulfill their promises to the ultimate consequences. To those who *disappeared themselves* [we say] return, show your face if your conscience permits. (Feitlowitz 1998, 39–40, emphasis in original)

This quote is exemplary of the maddening rhetoric of the regime and its supporters. The injustice of the accusation, which blames the *desaparecidos* themselves for crimes committed against them, is simply perverse. Yet the government's relentless discourse of double-talk made such blatant untruths begin to seem plausible. The so-called rational discourse of the regime had a logic so twisted, and undermined expression to such an extent that language became unreliable. In this way, and reinforced by terror and torture, the regime sought to re-fashion the "national being" and achieve a level of control that included the mind itself.

Enemies and Victims of the Regime

Leftist Extremists

It was asserted earlier in the discussion that the *Proceso* regime used the pretense of establishing security as a justification for a project the generals wanted to carry out from the start: A Dirty War against the Argentine people to reform society ideologically and economically. The generals claimed that the *Montoneros* left-wing guerrilla group specifically was such a threat that they had no choice but to impose martial law and use whatever force necessary to defeat them. We now know that this was absolutely false, as shown by abundant evidence to the contrary. The truth is that by the time of the coup, the battle against the revolutionary groups was actually winding down. Months before the coup, in January 1976, General Videla himself had already commented that the "terrorist organizations" were "absolutely impotent," that they had "little fighting capability," and were unable to "reach a military level" (Wright 2007, 102). It is true that Argentina's *Montoneros* had been an armed group whose daredevil attacks posed a real threat to military and corporate targets, but they were finished off in the first months after the coup (Klein 2007).

Foreign Minister Guzzetti told Kissinger in a meeting on October 7, 1976 that the "terrorist organizations have been dismantled. If this direction continues, by the end of the year the danger will have been set aside" (U.S. Department of State 2006a). So although the terrorist danger had been neutralized already, for the next seven years, the regime continued to make "disappear" tens of thousands of citizens. Not only were the organizations broken up, but the leftists themselves had been virtually wiped out during the earliest years of the regime. An official communique from Videla in early 1978 made clear that they had already achieved "the virtual annihilation of subversive organizations, with the elimination of approximately 90 percent of personnel" (Directive 504/77). The real goal of the regime was, of course, much broader: The elimination of anything they considered leftist. In another directive, the commander-in-chief describes his objective as "normalization in all areas, meaning the affirmation of the values which comprise our 'National Being,' and the elimination of any Marxist elements (ideologies, activists, written material, etc.)" (Directive 604/79). Though the cover story was that the enemy was any armed leftist, in the bewildering double-talk typical of the *Proceso*, Videla also once told the press that "[a] terrorist is not just someone who carries a bomb or a pistol, but also anyone who spreads ideas that are contrary to our Western Christian civilization" (Presman 2007).

The Disappeared

The exact number of actual guerrilla fighters who took up arms against the state is unknown—it partially depends upon whether one uses General Videla's broad definition or not—but some estimates put it as low as 2,500 (Lewis 2001, 46). To the military government, it did not really matter that unarmed leftists would be killed: As Videla stated, their ideas were also weapons. General Luciano Menendez, commander of the Third Army Corps, had an expansive view of the "work" that would have to be done to cleanse the country. "We are going to have to kill 50,000 people: 25,000 subversives, 20,000 sympathizers, and we will make 5,000 mistakes" (Lewis 2001, 147). In the view of the junta, it did not really matter whether the person was "guilty" or not; if they were, their death would remove them as a threat, and if they were not, they at least served as a warning to others who might be thinking of resisting.

In reality, there were no unintended victims. The disappeared who were not armed insurgents—perhaps as many as 27,000—were also intended targets. The killings were too uniform, too organized to be an accident. Argentine federal judge Carlos Rozanski, in handing down a sentence against one high-ranking official, stated that there had been a "plan of extermination carried out by those who ruled the country" (Walsh 2006). The killings were "part of a system, planned far in advance, duplicated in identical fashion across the country, and committed with clear intent not of attacking individual persons but of destroying the parts of society that those people represented" (Klein 2007, 101). It was a premeditated plan to annihilate a group. The target group consisted quite simply of anyone who might be opposed to the regime's ultra-conservative view. Certainly, this included particular suspicious occupations such as union workers, students, teachers, journalists, entertainers, and, of course, social workers, community activists, and labor leaders of any kind. Given what is known about the junta's economic project, it is no surprise that so many of the victims were trade unionists and social workers. Yet more than any other demographic group, it was the youth who best fit the junta's distorted definition of "subversive."

Youth

It has been shown that of all the people swept up in Dirty War raids, a huge percentage were not leftist terrorists or even necessarily politically active, but ordinary people who were simply seen as representing values contrary to those of the military rulers. Most *desaparecidos*, the great majority in fact, had something else in common as well, their youth. Eighty-one percent of the disappeared were in their teens or twenties (Marchak 1999). This targeting of youth was a deliberate tactic on the part of the regime, part of a plan to re-educate the young—or to exterminate them, if necessary. It was a macabre investment in the future of Argentine society. Among the youngest were a group of high-school students who, in September 1976, banded together to ask for lower bus fare. For the junta, the collective action showed that the teenagers had been infected with the virus of Marxism, and it responded with genocidal fury, torturing and killing six of the high-schoolers who had dared to make this subversive request (Marchak 1999).

As junta leader Videla said in his first of many addresses to the nation that "the goal of the *Proceso* is the profound transformation of consciousness" (Troncoso 1984, 29). One of the first steps in this process was a reimagining and public reshaping of youth identity. In the bombardment of public communiques from the junta, the image of the "suspect youth" was carefully cultivated. These pronouncements described how young people were initiated into rock music—portrayed as a secret society celebrating drugs and free love with ritual clothing and music—and then inevitably end up in the guerrilla forces (Vila 1987). This association of youth with subversion assured that the so-called "war against subversion" would essentially be a war on youth. In this war, young people disappeared—literally and figuratively—from the national scene. In many different areas of public discourse, it was as if they had been proclaimed to not exist. "Even in ads you saw absolutely no young people. Only older people and very young children who were smiling, well groomed, and of course completely obedient" (O'Donnell 1984). In addition to this figurative disappearance, of course, was the literal physical disappearance of teenagers and twenty-somethings into a network of more than 300 concentration camps and secret torture centers.

Concerts: An Alternative Form of Gathering and Expression

During these years, young people were singled out and isolated, since all public gatherings—even school clubs—were expressly prohibited. But young people found ways to continue their meeting. Many young Argentines discovered that the extremely public nature of huge concerts made it difficult for police to carry out secret abductions. Thus, concert halls developed a new function as countercultural meeting places; during these years, attendance at concerts reached new heights. For their part, *Proceso* junta leaders, still wary of the bad press the Chilean dictatorship had received, never dared to do more than just threaten Argentine singing stars, though musicians' work was often heavily censored (Wilson 2008). This combination of factors made possible a level of public expression in concerts that was unthinkable in any other venue. The new-found freedom made these concerts hugely popular and they drew mega-crowds. Toward the end of the regime in the early 1980s, shows regularly had up to 60,000 fans in attendance. Fans reveled in the savvy lyrics that singers such as Charly Garcia devised, which were clever enough to outwit the censors. One well-known song, "*cancion de Alicia en el pais*," played on Lewis Carrol's "Alice" to describe a country (clearly Argentina) where everything is backwards. It describes a turtle and a walrus—caricatures of former presidents Illia and Ongania—and a cruel *brujo* (witchdoctor) who could be none other than former minister Lopez Rega.

But singers were not the only ones to perform: In these mass concerts, the audience members were literally as much participants as the musicians themselves. One very active form of expression on the part of listeners was the soccer chants that sometimes overtook an entire stadium. Often these would be directed against the government, innocently at first, such as "*el que no salta es un military*" ("anyone who does not jump is a military man"). This provoked the curious spectacle of the whole stadium jumping in unison upon their seats (Vila 1987). However, as time went on, another chant became more common "*se va a acabar, se va a acabar la dictadura military*" ("it is going to end, it is going to end, the dictatorship is going to end"). Such a phenomenon actually converted bemused musicians into a sort of audience that could only watch and interpret. At times, the public anonymity of being part of a crowd of over 50,000 freed audience members to make truly audacious statements for the time, such as "*paredon, paredon, a todos los milicos que vendieron la nacion*" ("firing squad to all those military men who sold out our nation"). This expression reached its culmination in a mass concert by Charly Garcia toward the end of the regime. At one point, fans begin chanting "*los desaparecidos, ¡que digan donde estan!*" ("the disappeared—tell us where they are!"). The singer actually responded to the audience, though he was careful to use no specifics or mention any names. He said that "I don't think anyone's going to answer you, so let us go on with the music. But, those who are disappearing now soon will not disappear anymore. And let me tell you, what we have got now will soon have to disappear. You can count on that" (Rebelde 2003). The fact that any musician would feel emboldened to make even such a circumspect statement shows that youth and artists had found a chink in the armor of the regime, a way to express themselves, despite the tight controls of the regime.

The Madres of Plaza de Mayo

Another group that found a way to exploit the regime's fear of international criticism was the now famous *Madres de Plaza de Mayo*. They are a very courageous group of human rights activists, mothers who wanted to protest the loss of their disappeared children, and discovered that there was relative safety in numbers. During the height of the repression, they began to meet every Thursday to march in Buenos Aires' Plaza de Mayo, in front of the presidential palace. Instead of protest signs, they held only photos of their lost children with the caption "Where are they?" They circled silently wearing the white head scarves that have become their symbol. Some of the mothers were also themselves disappeared, but the group did not desist, and they outlasted the regime. They continue to march today, to raise awareness of Dirty War crimes.

Conclusions: The Aftermath

The eight-year Dirty War waged against the Argentine people by its military leaders lasted until the end of 1983. Videla served as president for the first five years until he handed over power to General Roberto Viola in March 1981. Yet after Videla relinquished power, the political situation deteriorated relatively quickly. Viola held power for only eight months before he was ousted by a military coup in December 1981 and was replaced by commander-in-chief of the Army, Lieutenant General Leopoldo Galtieri. He, in turn, lasted only six months before his disastrous military incursion in the Falkland/Malvinas Islands resulted in a humiliating defeat by Britain and prompted protests in Argentina against the military government, thus hastening the downfall of the regime. Finally, retired General Reynaldo Bignone served as interim president for the last eighteen months of the dictatorship and oversaw the transition to democracy. On December 10, 1983, democratically elected President Raul Alfonsin took office, thus bringing an end to the years of institutionalized societal reform through premeditated state-sponsored terror.

Though some found solace at certain moments in song, and others found refuge in exile to Europe or North America, the fact is that many, many people were killed in the purges of the Dirty War. Although initially only a portion of the disappearances could be officially corroborated (9,089 disappeared were listed by the National Commission on the Disappearance of Persons report in the 1980s), human rights organizations have long calculated the number to be about 30,000. This number can now be confirmed: According to a newly unearthed Argentine secret intelligence report, by 1978 already 22,000 people had been murdered or disappeared by the Argentine military (Dinges 2004). This is significant for a number of reasons. For one thing, it is the only known report of a calculation by the Argentine military itself of the number of people they had killed in the repression. Secondly, since we know that the disappearances continued for several more years, the full number can be extrapolated far beyond the original 22,000 who were counted in 1978.

Besides the damage counted in human lives, another terrible legacy of the Dirty War is the less spectacular but nevertheless heavy toll of misery due to economic hardship that Argentines have had to endure as a result of the junta's experimentation with the free market. Indeed, according to Argentine investigative journalist Rodolfo Walsh, the economic policy was worse than the torture. Walsh, in a courageous "Open Letter from a Writer to the Military Junta," decries the torture techniques used against the Argentine people. He asserts, however, that an even greater evil was the economic model adopted by the regime, the Chicago school neoliberalism. He writes to the generals that the torture is "not, however the greatest suffering inflicted on the Argentinean people nor the worst violation of human rights which you have committed. It is in the economic policy of this government where one discovers not only the explanation for the crimes, but a greater atrocity which punishes millions of human beings through planned misery" (McCaughan 2002). In the 1960s, Argentina was a model of development for other countries in Latin America. It had a healthy industrial sector with a strong tradition of labor unions, a well-developed and growing middle class, and a social system that provided good public education and health care. Argentina had a very low poverty rate—at 9 percent, it was lower than that in France or the United States—and a very low unemployment rate at 4 percent (Klein 2007). But within a year of the coup, wages declined drastically and the number of poor soared.

One final outcome that cannot yet be measured is the psychological effect of the *Proceso* years—not only the effect on individuals who suffered brainwashing and torture but also the effect on the entire society. It remains to be seen in this generation whether the lessons of terror sown by the Dirty War generals on the fields of Argentine youth took root and changed them forever, or whether the timidity born of terror can be overcome. It was hoped that the truth and reconciliation commission and the military trials discussed in the next two chapters would provide individual and social healing; however, Argentina still suffers from the events of the Dirty War.

References

Amnesty International. 1977. *Report of an Amnesty International mission to Argentina, 6–15 November 1976*. London: Amnesty International Publications.

Berryman, Phillip E. 1993. *Report of the Chilean National Commission on Truth and Reconciliation*. Notre Dame, IN: University of Notre Dame Press.

CIA. 2002. "Notes on Meeting with the President on Chile, September 15, 1970." Available at: www.gwu.edu/~nsarchiv/NSAEBB/NSAEBB8/ch26-01.htm.

Dinges, John. 2004. *The Condor Years: How Pinochet and His Allies Brought Terrorism to Three Continents*. New York: New Press.

Directive No. 504/77. 1978. Available at: www.nuncamas.org/document/militar/50477.htm.

Directive No. 604/79. 1979. Available at: www.nuncamas.org/document/militar/60479.htm.

Documentation Center. 2003. "Relacion de requeridos del OPR-33." Available at: www.gwu.edu/~nsarchiv/NSAEBB/NSAEBB185/Front of Relacion de requeridos19760500 FAU ROE OPR 33 R008F1761.pdf.

Feitlowitz, Marguerite. 1998. *A Lexicon of Terror: Argentina and the Legacies of Torture*. New York: Oxford University Press.

H.I.J.O.S. 2006. "Discurso escrache a Videla." Available at: www.hijoscapital.org.ar/index.php?option=com_content&task=view&id=4&Itemid=47.

National Institute of Statistics and Census. 1979. *Statistical Annual 1979–80*.

Jara, Joan. 1983. *Victor: An Unfinished Song*. London: Jonathan Cape.

Klein, Naomi. 2007. *The Shock Doctrine: The Rise of Disaster Capitalism*. New York: Metropolitan Books.

Lewis, Paul. 2001. *Guerrillas and Generals: The Dirty War in Argentina*. Westport: Praeger.

Marchak, Patricia. 1999. *God's Assassins: State Terrorism in Argentina in the 1970s*. Montreal: McGill-Queen's University Press.

Massera, Emilio. 1979. "La Postergacion de un destino." *El Camino a la democracia*. Buenos Aires: El Cid Editor.

McCaughan, Michael. 2002. *True Crimes: Rodolfo Walsh*. London: Latin America Bureau.

McDonnell, Patrick J. 2007. "Isabel Peron's Arrest Signals Shift in Argentina." *Los Angeles Times*. (13 January). Available at: www.latimes.com/news/nationworld/world/la-fg-isabel13jan13,1,437158.story?coll=la-headlines-world.

Mignone, Emilio. 1991. *Derechos humanos y sociedad: El caso Argentino*. Buenos Aires: Colihue.

Nunca Mas: The Report of the Argentine National Commission of the Disappeared. 1986. New York: Farrar Straus Giroux.

O'Donnell, Guillermo. 1984. "Democracia en la Argentina: Micro y macro." In *Proceso: crisis y transicion democratica*, ed. Oscar Oszlak. Buenos Aires: Centro Editor de America Latina.

Orwell, George. 1949. "The Principles of Newspeak." *Nineteen Eighty Four*. London: Secker & Warburg.

Presman, Hugo. 2007. "24 de Marzo—A 31 anos del Golpe oligarquico militar: La derrota y sus lecciones." Available at: www.rodolfowalsh.org/spip.php?article2917.

"Rebelde: El rock Argentino en los anos '70." 2003. Available at: www.dospotencias.com.ar/rebelde/aldia/18.htm.

Reuters. 2007. "Argentine Military Warned Brazil, Chile of '76 Coup."

Taylor, Diana. 1997. *Disappearing Acts: Spectacles of Gender and Nationalism in Argentina's "Dirty War."* Durham: Duke University Press.

Troncoso, Oscar. 1984. *El Proceso de Reorganizacion Nacional*. Buenos Aires: Centro Editor de America Latina.

U.S. Department of Defense. 1999. "Chile Declassification Project." Available at: www.gwu.edu/~nsarchiv/NSAEBB/NSAEBB185/19761001 Special Operations Forces small.pdf.

U.S. Department of State. 2002. "Document 4: October 4, 1976." Argentina Declassification Project (1975–1984)." Available at: www.gwu.edu/~nsarchiv/NSAEBB/NSAEBB104/Doc4%20761004.pdf.

U.S. Department of State. 2006a. "Subject: Secretary's Meeting with Argentine Foreign Minister Guzzetti, Memorandum of Conversation, October 7, 1976." Available at: www.gwu.edu/%7Ensarchiv/NSAEBB/NSAEBB104/Doc6%20761007.pdf.

U.S. Department of State. 2006b. "March 26, 1976, Secretary of State Henry Kissinger, Chairman." Available at: www.gwu.edu/~nsarchiv/NSAEBB/NSAEBB185/19760326%20Secretary%20of%20State%20kissinger%20Chariman%20pages%2019-23.pdf.

Vila, Pablo. 1987. "Rock Nacional and Dictatorship in Argentina." *Popular Music*. 6.2:129–148.

Wilson, Timothy. 2008. "Starmakers: Dictators, Songwriters, and the Negotiation of Censorship in the Argentine Dirty War." *A Contracorriente*. 6:50–75. Available at: www.ncsu.edu/project/acontracorriente.

Walsh, Rodolfo. 2006. "Historica condena por genocidio: Fallo completo contra Etchecolatz." Available at: www.rodolfowalsh.org/spip.php?article2378.

Wright, Thomas. 2007. *State Terrorism in Latin America: Chile, Argentina, and International Human Rights*. Lanham, M.D: Rowman & Littlefield.

CHAPTER 3

Successes and Limitations of the CONADEP Experience in the Determination of Responsibilities for Human Rights Violations in Argentina

EMILIO CRENZEL

Introduction

This chapter examines the successes and limitations of the investigation of Argentina's National Commission on the Disappearance of Persons (CONADEP) in clarifying human rights violations described in Chapter 2 and identifying responsible parties. CONADEP was established by President Raul Alfonsin in 1983 upon the restoration of democracy in Argentina to investigate the fate of thousands of people who had been disappeared during the 1976–1983 military regime. Over the course of nine months, between December 1983 and September 1984, CONADEP heard testimonies from relatives of the disappeared, survivors, and other witnesses; gathered evidence; and inspected the clandestine detention centers where the disappeared were held. The commission's final report, entitled *Nunca Mas* (*Never Again*), published in November 1984, revealed the characteristics and extent of the system of forced disappearances and established the state as responsible for this act. The report became an unprecedented bestseller on the subject. It was translated into English, Italian, Portuguese, German, and Hebrew and was also published abroad, with 503,830 copies sold as of March 2009 (Crenzel 2008a).

CONADEP's investigation gained greater significance when its findings were used as the key resource in the subsequent prosecution and conviction of the military juntas. It was then adopted as a model by various truth commissions established in Latin America to investigate human rights violations in the context of the region's democratization process from the 1970s to the 1990s (Sikkink 2008). This chapter analyzes CONADEP's creation and the relationship this commission established with the executive branch, the judicial system, and human rights organizations. It examines the main results of its investigation and its role as a provider of transitional justice in Argentina.

Who Should Investigate Human Rights Violations? The Creation of CONADEP

Argentina's military dictatorship (1976–1983) differed from previous military regimes in that it carried out the state's decision to exterminate its opponents through the systematic practice of forced disappearances. This strategy set it apart even from the dictatorships that ruled other countries of the Southern Cone during the same period.[1] Disappearances, already common in 1975 under the constitutional government of Maria Estela Martinez de Peron, were perpetrated by military or police officers who abducted individuals generally in front of witnesses and took them to clandestine detention centers where the abducted people were tortured and, in most cases, murdered. The dictatorship first denied the disappearances and later relativized and justified them as a result of the "war against subversion." It successfully censored the claims made by domestic human rights organizations and the reports from international bodies, like Amnesty International in 1976 and the Organization of American States' Inter-American Commission on Human Rights (IACHR) in 1979, condemning its crimes (Mignone 1991).

During the country's political transition in 1983, the dictatorship issued the "Final Document of the Military Junta on the War against Subversion," discrediting the allegations and leaving to "divine judgment" to examine its actions. Human rights organizations in Argentina including the Asamblea Permanente por los Derechos Humanos (Permanent Assembly for Human Rights or APDH), Centro de Estudios Legales y Sociales (Center for Legal and Social Studies or CELS), Servicio Paz y Justicia (Service for Peace and Justice or SERPAJ), Madres de Plaza de Mayo (Mothers of Plaza de Mayo), Abuelas de Plaza de Mayo (Grandmothers of Plaza de Mayo), Liga Argentina por los Derechos del Hombre (Argentine Human Rights League), Familiares de Detenidos y Desaparecidos por Razones Politicas (Relatives of the Detained-Disappeared for Political Reasons), and Movimiento Ecumenico por los Derechos Humanos (Ecumenical Movement for Human Rights) stepped up their call for "trial and punishment for all perpetrators" and demanded that a bicameral commission be set up to investigate state terrorism, with their assistance (Conviccin 1983; Frente 1983). Human rights organizations believed that only a bicameral commission could coerce the military and might condemn state terrorism politically. However, in September 1983, one month before the democratic elections of October 30, the dictatorship passed the National Pacification Act (Law No. 22.924), known as the "self-amnesty" law, preventing criminal action arising from the "antisubversive war" (Official Bulletin of Argentina 1983b).

Alfonsin, the candidate of the Radical Civic Union Party, declared that if he became president he would repeal the law on grounds of unconstitutionality and declared that in the prosecution of human rights violations, he would distinguish three categories of perpetrators: "Those who planned the repression and issued the corresponding orders, those who acted beyond the orders, prompted by cruelty, perversion or greed and those who carried out the orders strictly to the letter."[2] This solution, conceived by Alfonsin's human rights advisors Carlos Nino and Jaime Malamud Goti, was part of a policy of limited retroactive justice and was based on the hierarchical structure of the military corps, and the prevailing ideological context, which the advisors argued precluded disobedience among subordinates and prevented them from fully understanding the nature of the orders (Nino 1997).

Upon taking office in December 1983, Alfonsin repealed the self-amnesty law and issued decrees 157 and 158/83 ordering the prosecution of seven guerrilla leaders and the dictatorship's first three military juntas. This was known as "the theory of the two evils" because it limited accountability for political violence to two sets of leaders and explained state violence, although not the illegal forms it adopted, as a response to guerrilla violence. Alfonsin also proposed that perpetrators be tried in military courts in the first instance, with the possibility of appeal in civilian courts, and supported the principle of presumption of obedience for all but high-ranking officers in the actions planned by the military juntas. This renewed calls from human rights organizations for a bicameral commission as they anticipated that the military courts would not impose any legal sanctions. Both Peronists and official sectors supported this demand (Official Bulletin of Argentina 1983; Jelin 1995).

This situation worried the president. Nino would later explain that Alfonsin feared that a bicameral commission would lead legislators to competing against each other to impose harsher punishments on the armed forces, thus creating an extremely tense situation. He wished to create instead an instance over which he could have political control, which would not undermine his relationship with the armed forces, would be above party differences, and would have widespread public credibility (Nino 1997). Thus, while legally addressing human rights violations was central to Alfonsin's strategy, the construction of a public truth about these violations was shaped by the demands of both human rights organizations and the opposition. That is, the two key mechanisms of transitional justice of Alfonsin's administration had different origins.

It is not clear where the idea for creating CONADEP came from or what it was modeled on. Alfonsin claimed it was his idea and was not based on any earlier model. Eduardo Rabossi, presidential advisor, said it drew on the experiences of the special commissions formed by the U.S. Congress comprising legislators and civil society personalities to deal with specific issues. In fact, during the congressional debate for the creation of CONADEP, legislators of the governing party referred to this precedent, giving examples of commissions created to "expand Capitol grounds," "establish national forest reserves," and "build Gettysburg Boulevard," all of which incidentally were quite removed from CONADEP's intended purpose.[3]

To form a commission of "notables," Alfonsin invited members of human rights organizations, which had been the leading promoters of the bicameral idea, in the hope of legitimizing his proposal and deterring the establishment of a congressional commission. Because of their opposition to the involvement of the military courts, Adolfo Perez Esquivel (1980 Nobel Peace laureate and head of Service for Peace and Justice) and Augusto Conte, and Emilio Mignone (both directors of the Center for Legal and Social Studies), turned down the invitation.[4] Alfonsin then invited writer Ernesto Sabato, who during the dictatorship had met with and praised General Jorge Rafael Videla but had later gone on to lead the Movimiento para la Recuperacion de Ninos Desaparecidos (Movement for the Recovery of Disappeared Children) with Perez Esquivel. Nino, minister of Interior, Antonio Troccoli, and Jose Lopez, one of Alfonsin's spokesmen, selected Rabossi. The CONADEP also included Gregorio Klimovsky, Marshall Meyer (rabbi), Carlos Gattinoni (protestant pastor), and Monsignor de Nevares (bishop), all members of the Permanent Assembly for Human Rights or APDH; Hilario Fernandez Long, former president of the University of Buenos Aires; Ricardo Colombres, former Supreme Court justice, Magdalena Ruiz Guinazu, journalist and human rights advocator, and Rene Favaloro, heart surgeon. They were all prestigious public figures from a range of fields, including journalism, law, culture, and science and the three largest religious communities—Roman Catholic, Protestant, and Jewish. Most had been human rights advocates to various extents or, like Sabato, had changed their stance toward the dictatorship when it started evidencing signs of crisis. Three legislators from each chamber were also invited to join CONADEP in an attempt to overcome pressures within official sectors in favor of a bicameral commission (Brisk 1994). Thus, the CONADEP was finally composed of thirteen commissioners.

The commission was given an initial timeframe of six months to investigate all forms of state terrorism committed under the military dictatorship, with the possibility of extending its timeframe "for as long as it deems necessary to fulfill its mandate."[5] Only three Radical Party congressmen accepted the invitation to join CONADEP and the Senate seats, which the government reserved for Peronist senators, were not filled.[6] With the exception of APDH, all the human rights organizations in Argentina rejected CONADEP, maintaining that parliament was the "natural" sphere of investigation and that only a bicameral commission would have coercive powers to subpoena the military, conduct inspections without warning, and politically condemn state terrorism. Peronist and center-left representatives also continued to insist on a bicameral commission made up of legislators representing every political group and "advised by human rights organizations and relatives of the victims of repression."

CONADEP, the Government, and the Justice System

The creation of CONADEP turned the investigation of disappearances into a state issue. At the same time, the presence of part of the human rights movement in the commission, especially the APDH, reflected the political power that these organizations had gained in the public sphere. The executive decree that created CONADEP set the six-month term "to prevent the painful need to investigate these events from dominating beyond a reasonable timeframe the efforts towards consolidating democracy in the future." Thus, the mandate subordinated the need to investigate the past to the immediate goal of consolidating democracy. The decree stipulated that the commission's mandate was to "clarify events and facts connected with the disappearance of persons in the country," not specifying, however, the chronological or institutional scope of this investigation. It established that its functions would be to receive depositions and evidence and immediately pass them on to the courts; inquire into the fate or whereabouts of disappeared persons, as well as any other circumstances relating to their location; find abducted children; report to the courts any attempt to conceal or destroy evidence and issue a final report (Official Bulletin of Argentina 1983a). By limiting the scope of the commission's investigation to the disappearances, the government set goals that were more specific than the human rights organizations' call for an investigation into all violations committed by the state. Thus, the murders committed by the armed forces in real or staged confrontations, the political exiling of opponents, or any torture that did not end in a disappearance would not be investigated (Hayner 2001).

The CONADEP began activities on December 22, 1983. Its members unanimously elected Sabato as its president and approved the regulations for its internal operation, which established that in the event of deadlock in a discussion, the matter would be decided by Sabato in his capacity as president.[7] One week later, Graciela Fernandez Meijide, APDH member and mother of a disappeared person, was appointed secretary of depositions; Raul Aragon, lawyer and APDH member, was appointed secretary of procedures, and Radical Party leaders Daniel Salvador and Leopoldo Silgueira were appointed documentation secretary and administrative matters secretary, respectively. Peronist lawyer Alberto Mansur, who, like Aragon and Silgueira, had been exiled during the dictatorship, was appointed legal affairs secretary. Interior ministry employees were initially assigned to work for the commission, but they were unprepared for the harsh testimonies they would hear and quit after only one week. Fernandez Meijide then asked the human rights organizations to send volunteers who were up to the task.[8] Although some survivors and relatives of the disappeared refused to declare before the commission because they distrusted it and the government, most human rights organizations realized it might be their only chance for an investigation and decided to collaborate even if they harbored some hesitations. While Abuelas de Plaza de Mayo (Grandmothers of Plaza de Mayo) worked with CONADEP in the search for the missing children, APDH, Argentine Human Rights League, Relatives of the Detained-Disappeared for Political Reasons, CELS, SERPAJ, and Ecumenical Movement for Human Rights submitted the testimonies they had collected, provided news, and, except SERPAJ, contributed personnel for the commission.

In the end, ninety people, the total number of personnel of CONADEP, set out to work gathering testimonies and cooperating with the commission's different departments and technical teams. Only Mothers of Plaza de Mayo called on their members not to testify; although, some mothers decided to gather testimonies anyway and submitted fifteen files to the commission with information on 101 disappeared conscripts and the organization's Mar del Plata chapter contributed 196 testimonies.[9] From that moment on, while continuing to publicly call for a bicameral commission, human rights organizations worked closely with CONADEP.

According to the commission's members, the executive branch provided all the resources they requested and did not interfere with their investigation. It even accepted the commission's request for a three-month extension and authorized the telecast of the partial conclusions of the investigation in form of a documentary by a state television channel, which was also entitled *Nunca Mas*; this program was viewed by 1,640,000 people. Although in the introduction, Interior Minister Troccoli warned viewers that the documentary showed only a partial account of the country's violent past as it omitted the actions of guerrilla groups which he equated to state terrorism; the program depicted the system of disappearances through the testimonies of relatives of disappeared persons, survivors of captivity, and members of Abuelas and Madres de Plaza de Mayo (Feld 2004; Crenzel 2008a).

Differences arose twice among members of CONADEP over the investigation's relationship with the justice system, an issue that also divided the different branches of government. As the reform of the Military Justice Code promoted by the executive branch gave first instance jurisdiction to military courts in matters of human rights violations, the Ministry of Defense asked CONADEP to submit all the evidence gathered to those courts. The decree that created CONADEP was issued before the reform and established the commission's obligations and limitations with respect to the "justice system" or "judicial branch." After the reform, as the creation of CONADEP was being discussed in the Congress, the government guaranteed it would remit the testimonies to civilian courts.[10] After heated discussions, CONADEP, which had been sending the evidence to civilian courts, decided it would also submit the testimonies to the military courts only if it had "prior authorization from the persons that had provided the testimonies."[11] Rabossi, however, acting on behalf of the government, pressured again for CONADEP to submit the evidence to military courts only. As opinions were tied, Sabato acted as arbitrator and decided that they would continue sending the evidence to civilian courts.[12] This was the only time that CONADEP had to put an issue to a vote. With this decision, the commission demonstrated its independence from the executive and, by conditioning the presentation of evidence to the military courts to the will of survivors and relatives, it granted them the power to decide which courts would process their evidence.

The second conflict arose over how the perpetrators would be named in the final report. De Nevares and Gattinoni who were members of human rights organizations (APDH and the Ecumenical Movement for Human Rights) or supported them (Colombres, Long, and Guinazu) wanted to leave the names in the testimonies that were transcribed in the report and include an annex with a list of the perpetrators. In this way, they sought to give greater exposure to the public accusation of the perpetrators. The members who represented the government (Rabossi, Lopez, Klimovsky, Huarte, and Piucill) agreed not to modify the testimonies and *Nunca Mas* does in fact include more than 400 names of military and police personnel identified by witnesses in their depositions. But they were against the annex, arguing that it would entail interfering with the powers of the courts, which was where jurisdiction over determining responsibilities lay. In the end, the list was only presented to Alfonsin for his information.[13] In contrast to these two intense debates, the members of the commission tacitly agreed on two issues. The first agreement, reached after barely any discussion, was on how to present the disappeared in *Nunca Mas*. CONADEP would describe them merely as human beings whose rights had been grossly violated without mentioning any political affiliations, a view shared by the human rights organizations. Political affiliation was an aspect that the human rights organizations had purposely left out when they reported the disappearances because of the dictatorship's stigmatization of such affiliations and the fear that by mentioning them they would alienate the civil society. CONADEP understood that mentioning affiliations in the report exceeded its mandate and could also entail adopting the theory of the two evils, as it had found that many disappeared persons had been active in guerrilla groups.

The second agreement had to do with the fact that the decree that created CONADEP limited the subject of the investigation to disappearances but did not limit these to any given timeframe. This led relatives of hundreds of disappeared persons to report disappearances that had occurred prior to the 1976 coup, especially under Maria Estela Martinez de Peron's administration. Certain CONADEP members admitted that they avoided investigating the responsibilities of the Peronist Party in the disappearances as well as the responsibilities of the political and economic establishment and the Church, fearing that extending accountability to so many would only serve to weaken the accusations against the material perpetrators. Alfonsin encouraged this position for political reasons.[14] At the time, Martinez de Peron was president of the Peronists, the most important opposition party, and the government, facing both conflicts with the armed forces and an economic crisis, issued decree 1301, known as the "historic reparation" decree, whereby it dropped the case against Peron's widow for the sake of achieving "the unity of the Argentine people" (Clarin 1984a, 8). This decree, far from blaming her for the state violence, presented her as a victim and contributed indirectly to the allegation that the CONADEP was focusing exclusively on those responsible for the disappearances that happened after the coup in 1976 (Crenzel 2008b). However, confronting other powers in addition to the military demanded more political power than the government had. So CONADEP received the testimonies of disappearances that had occurred before the coup and included them in its final report, but omitted any mention of the responsibility that the Peronist Party or other actors could have had in them.

Opportunities and Constraints of the CONADEP Experience

Despite being a governmental commission, CONADEP quickly exceeded the government's intention that it limit its investigation, as stated in decree 187/1983, to "inquiring into the fate of the disappeared" and "receiving depositions and evidence to immediately refer them to the courts" (Official Bulletin of Argentina 1983c). When CONADEP was established, despite testimonies of survivors and reports by international bodies ascertaining that the disappeared had almost certainly been killed, many relatives firmly believed that some could still be found alive. In fact, around that time, human rights organizations were demanding that the executive inspect prisons and hospitals in search of survivors.[15] Several CONADEP members shared this belief and for that reason the first measure of the commission was to organize inspections to try to locate them, all of which proved unsuccessful. These initiatives revealed that CONADEP lacked an investigation strategy. Meijide then argued that this was only serving to sidetrack the investigation and that given the little time it had the commission could not look for every single disappeared person, but that neither could it limit its action to merely drawing up a "list of the disappeared" as the government had apparently informally suggested.[16]

CONADEP issued a press release stating that it "had come to the conclusion that the best way to find out what had happened to the disappeared was to identify those responsible for the disappearances so that they would explain their actions in court" and asked Alfonsin to guarantee that some forty military officers believed to be involved in disappearances not be allowed to leave the country.[17] The executive granted CONADEP's request. This measure boosted the organizations' trust and a week later, in the first days of February 1984, the commission had to extend its work hours to hear the large number of testimonies it received. The commission's decision to make all the information gathered available to human rights organizations contributed to this new atmosphere.[18] The testimonies that until then had been scattered throughout the country and abroad were concentrated and centralized by CONADEP. The commission received 5,580 testimonies that APDH had gathered in Argentina during the dictatorship and thousands of complaints filed with the IACHR, the International Committee of the Red Cross, the United Nations Human Rights Division, Amnesty International, and organizations of various denominations. Upon examining and classifying the testimonies, CONADEP had to define what it considered a case of disappearance. It established that a disappeared person was anyone who had been arrested or abducted and whose whereabouts were unknown. This definition excluded from the disappeared person category anyone who had disappeared but whose body had later been found and identified as well as anyone who, having disappeared, survived (Hayner 2001).

Most of the reports that existed prior to CONADEP had been filed by relatives who lived in Buenos Aires and other large cities and the information they provided was basically about the abductions. In contrast, human rights organizations only had approximately seventy testimonies from survivors, which limited the evidence available on the clandestine captivity, torture, and murder of thousands of disappeared persons. Consequently, the possibility of identifying the guilty parties beyond the juntas and a handful of perpetrators was severely constrained. To deal with this situation, the commission created local delegations throughout the country. Human rights organizations offered their facilities and personnel to these delegations and cooperated with them in Cordoba, Bahia Blanca, and Mar del Plata (where even a member of

Madres de Plaza de Mayo participated) and helped gather testimonies in the country's northeast, northwest, and south regions.[19]

These initiatives expanded the body of testimonies provided by relatives, witnesses, and survivors and modified its characteristics. People living in urban peripheries and far from the large cities had had nowhere to report the disappearance of their loved ones or had been too poor or isolated to know what to do. Of the new testimonies provided to the CONADEP by relatives and witnesses, 64 percent came from such places while 85 percent of the testimonies from large cities came from reports filed immediately after the abductions (Izaguirre 1992). By shedding light on the large number of disappeared trade unionists, these testimonies also modified the class profile of the disappeared. Many of the disappeared were living away from home at the time of their abduction and their relatives had no information on how, when, and where they were abducted. For such cases, CONADEP formed "field teams" that went out to find witnesses among neighbors, colleagues, or fellow students of the disappeared and asked them if they would be willing to testify. CONADEP also asked relatives to provide physical descriptions, forensic data, and photographs of the disappeared to help survivors identify them, include them in the testimonies, and form a file; this file eventually contained over 3,000 photographs.[20] The new testimonies by more survivors who came forward also changed the quality of the existing data. Some of the survivors had been disappeared for days or weeks, others had spent years in captivity in a single place, and still others had been detained in several clandestine detention centers. Some survivors had collaborated with their captors and because their imprisonment conditions had been relatively better, they knew what their captors looked like. Others, in contrast, did not remember many details and could only draw on the abuse that their bodies endured while in captivity. Some gave their testimonies in the country as CONADEP traveled abroad to gather the testimony of others who were exiled or received their testimony in consulates or embassies.

With the assistance of both domestic and international fact-finding delegations, CONADEP was able to increase the number of testimonies provided by survivors to 1,500. Because of its heterogeneity, this body of testimonies greatly enriched the existing evidence. Hundreds of military, police, and civilian facilities located throughout the country were added to the already-known, large clandestine detention centers that had contained the majority of the disappeared, like Escuela de Mecanica de la Armada and Club Atletico in the capital, Campo de Mayo and El Vesubio in Buenos Aires, and La Perla in Cordoba. Following the testimony by survivors, CONADEP also expanded the information available on some of the most important centers, like Campo de Mayo, on which there was only one testimony before the commission was established. The new testimonies also helped map the movement of disappeared persons from one center to another, thereby proving that these centers had been part of a system.[21]

The commission also received statements from some individuals who had been involved in the disappearances (officers, sub-officers, border patrolmen, and policemen) who confirmed the existence of clandestine detention centers and the violations reported (Clarin 1984b). Lastly, the commission gathered a set of previously unheard testimonies from people who had been indirect witnesses to the disappearances: neighbors who had seen the abductions, people who lived near clandestine centers and could confirm the presence of military personnel in them, nurses who had assisted pregnant disappeared women, and cemetery workers who confirmed the existence of unmarked graves. Most prominent among these was a group of morgue workers from Cordoba who in 1980 had sent a letter to then de facto president Videla demanding better pay. To strengthen their demands, the workers included an account of how they had received dozens of corpses of "subversive elements" showing evident signs of violence and how they had participated in their clandestine burial. According to Sabato, this was "one of the most shocking pieces of evidence" obtained by CONADEP, for it confirmed that Videla was aware of such practices (Crenzel 2005).

CONADEP classified the evidence it gathered according to the clandestine detention center. With this decision, the commission fully inverted the nature of the strategic space of the disappearances. The nonplace that the clandestine detention centers had constituted became the focal center around which the disappearances were reconstructed. Through these initiatives and despite the obstacles it faced, like the systematic lack of response from military and police authorities to its requests, CONADEP was able to reconstruct the materiality of the disappearances with the thousands of testimonies gathered around the country, which coincided both in general aspects and in details.

This methodology enabled the commission to focus on any facility where disappeared persons had been held captive, even if only for a few hours, thus taking into account the experience of survivors who were held for a short time in police stations and other facilities before being moved to the large centers and of others who were held there throughout their brief disappearance. This decision revealed "that any police or military facility could merely by virtue of their condition be turned into a clandestine detention center by decision of military officers, thus proving the national scope and the systematic nature of the practice of disappearances."[22] By organizing the evidence in this way, the commission was also able to find out details of certain centers, like Automotores Orletti, where individuals from neighboring countries had been held, thus proving that the dictatorships in the region along with the Argentine military junta had coordinated their repressive actions.

CONADEP also identified and inspected dozens of clandestine detention centers. These inspections, unlike those carried out in 1979 by IACHR, received wide coverage in the press, encompassed almost fifty centers throughout most of the country and, for the first time, involved former captives. When faced with an inspection from the commission, the military and police personnel either tried to stop it, denied any knowledge of the existence of the material infrastructure that was reported, or withheld information. In other cases, witnesses were threatened so they would not testify.[23] In most cases, survivors identified these facilities as their places of captivity. After each inspection, the commission drew up a notarized record to validate it as legal evidence and held a press conference detailing its findings with the participation of survivors. This established a new public truth about these centers and raised a key question: "How could ordinary civilians know the general characteristics of military or police facilities, as well as insignificant details like the location of an electric socket, unless they had really been there?"[24]

In addition to the testimony of survivors and the inspection of clandestine detention centers, CONADEP also checked public cemetery records and found accounts of night burials of young people with evident signs of violence in their bodies. It examined data from the military's own sources, such as draft service records, which refuted the military's claims that the conscripts reported as disappeared had actually escaped or deserted. This was the first investigation of its kind to employ advanced technology, with assistance from international scientific bodies, that would later be used by other truth commissions: a computerized system for recording the disappearances and determining changes in the features of abducted children in order to identify them; tests to determine kinship even without the parents' genetic information, and forensic anthropology techniques used to identify any remains found.[25] All the evidence collected on a clandestine detention center was compiled in a "dossier" to be submitted to the courts. CONADEP classified the crimes committed in each center, attached the corresponding testimonies and documentary evidence along with lists of confirmed victims and personnel involved in the crimes and identified by at least three concurring witnesses, and established the criminal charges under which they were to be filed in court. These dossiers amounted to a true pretrial legal inquest. When CONADEP concluded its investigation, the human rights movement, with the exception of Madres de Plaza de Mayo and the parties of the opposition, all valued the commission's efforts declaring that it had "worked with independence and effectiveness and maintained an autonomous profile," and praised *Nunca Mas* as a body of "irrefutable evidence" that constituted an "accusatory document of immense ethical value and critical for the attainment of justice."[26]

Nunca Mas: The Results of CONADEP's Investigation

A number of factors affected the quality of CONADEP'S investigation and final report, most notably the limited time it had to investigate and receive testimonies, particularly in remote areas, and the refusal of a group of victims to testify and of the military to cooperate (Wright, 2007). However, CONADEP's investigation in 1984 shed light on the quantitative dimension of the practice of forced disappearances placing the number of disappeared persons at 8,961. It also restored the personal identity of the disappeared by including their full name, age, and gender. It revealed the predominantly young and male profile of the disappeared (almost 82 percent were between the ages of sixteen and thirty-five and 70 percent were men) and, by identifying their occupations or activities, revealed that 30 percent were workers and 21 percent were students, thus evidencing that the practice of disappearances amounted to an attempt at extermination.[27] It detected 340 clandestine detention centers, a figure previously unknown even to human rights organizations, thus reconstructing the magnitude and extent of the clandestine system, while the simple fact that most centers were located in military or police facilities refuted the military's denial of any responsibility in the disappearances.

CONADEP confirmed the repressive coordination of the region's dictatorships, the existence of disappeared children appropriated by perpetrators or people close to them, and the many ordinary crimes committed together with the repressive actions. It established the physical elimination of the majority of the disappeared, presenting the forms of their extermination. Its *Nunca Mas* report provided a detailed reconstruction and integrated account of the public and clandestine stages of the disappearances. Its account drew primarily on the testimonies of survivors and relatives of the disappeared, whose depositions represented 15 and 70 percent, respectively, of the approximately 379 that are included in *Nunca Mas.*[28] In this way, CONADEP legitimized the voices that had denounced these crimes and had been stigmatized by the dictatorship.

In line with the executive decrees ordering the guerrilla and military trials, the *Nunca Mas* prologue prepared by CONADEP presented political violence as resulting from these two actors, without offering any explanation as to its causes and connections with the political conflicts of the time. It also attributed responsibility for the disappearances exclusively to the dictatorship, even though 10 percent of the testimonies it heard referred to cases that occurred prior to the coup (CONADEP 1984). This institutional periodization of violence silenced the political and moral responsibilities of the constitutional Peronist government and of political and civil society as a whole in the pre-1976 disappearances, an omission that CONADEP extended by positing society's innocence in the exercise of state terror after the coup, either because it was not involved or was a victim. *Nunca Mas* makes no mention of the institutional and economic causes of the military's intervention (Grandin 2005). This dehistoricization and depoliticization of *Nunca Mas*' account is mirrored in the portrayal of the disappeared. The victims' activism is only mentioned in 3 percent of the cases and all of them are unrelated to political and guerrilla groups (Corralini, Di Iorio, Lobo, and Pigliapochi 2003). Like the human rights organizations during the dictatorship, CONADEP based its denunciation on the specific crimes committed rather than on the universal character of the rights violated.

Moreover, during its investigation, CONADEP did not discuss whether it should voice an opinion regarding the distinction made of different levels of responsibility proposed by Alfonsin for the prosecution of human rights violators and the principle of presumption of obedience it rested on. On the one hand, in *Nunca Mas*, CONADEP established the responsibility of the military juntas in planning the system of disappearances and noted that the members of the armed forces were not free to disagree with the methods of repression.[29] These considerations could imply that the report supports the official position on this matter. However, that position had been seriously undermined by the Senate, when it denied the defense of due obedience for cases of "atrocious and abhorrent acts."[30] *Nunca Mas*, on the other hand, states that "the especially atrocious acts numbered in the thousands." Rather than special they were the "norm" and the commission recommended that "the task groups be criminally investigated."[31] This inquiry entailed investigating middle and lower-ranking officers whom the government intended to exclude from the legal inquiries. Lastly, CONADEP made the following recommendations: Reparation for the relatives of the disappeared, that a forced disappearance be declared a crime against humanity, that all repressive laws be repealed; that justice be made and that human rights be incorporated as a subject in school curricula to educate the younger generations.[32]

In synthesis, *Nunca Mas* presented an explanation that toppled the interpretative monopoly held until then by the perpetrators of the disappearances. It represented the official declaration of a public truth that had a greater legitimacy than the victims' denunciations, thus demonstrating that "the power of words does not come from words themselves but rather from the institutions that legitimize them" (Bourdieu 2001, 50). *Nunca Mas* also placed this truth in the context of a new official reading of the past that did not historicize the violence, its motives and causes, attributed the responsibility for the disappearances solely to the dictatorship, and presented the victims and society itself as innocent for their lack of involvement in violence and politics.

Conclusions

Through CONADEP's work, the state turned the disappearances into a subject of investigation. In doing so, it simultaneously excluded from the investigation the examination of all other human rights violations. CONADEP operated as a mechanism of transitional justice in more than one way. First, it offered immediately after the end of the dictatorship an official channel for survivors and relatives of the disappeared to report the disappearances and legitimized their claims as never before. Second, by gathering the existing testimonies and producing new evidence, it constructed a new public truth about the dimension and scope of the disappearances and the responsible parties, refuting the dictatorship's stance that denied or justified the very existence of the disappeared. Lastly, it collected an unprecedented body of evidence for the prosecution of the material perpetrators of these crimes. To achieve this objective, it employed investigative techniques that would later be used by other truth commissions as important aids in their investigations. The organization of this vast and comprehensive body of testimonies and documents into judicial evidence and its presentation to the courts turned CONADEP's investigation into a true pretrial instance. In fact, the state prosecutor used this evidentiary corpus as the key resource in the trial against the military juntas that would follow.

However, by limiting the responsibility of the disappearances to the dictatorship, CONADEP presented an account of state violence that was dehistoricized. This was complemented by the depoliticization of the identities of the disappeared, as the report omitted any details of their activism. These limitations were the result of constraints inherent in an investigation aimed at producing a legal truth of the violations to the detriment of a historical interpretation. But they also resulted from the decisions that CONADEP adopted to guide its investigation in line with government goals.

However, far from being solely the effort of the government or of a group of renowned civil society notables, as described in transitional justice writings, CONADEP's investigation involved the majority of the human rights movement. These organizations participated in CONADEP's direction, departments, and staff, provided any information they had and collected new evidence, lent their facilities for the commission's offices outside the capital, offered their experience to guide the investigation, participated in the film that disseminated the findings, and contributed to the drafting of the report. That enabled CONADEP to break its initial isolation and exceed by far the goals set for it by the government. This alliance was only shaken when CONADEP discussed the scope of the judicial proceedings and whether the evidence should be submitted to civilian or military courts. The limitations of *Nunca Mas*' account of the political violence and its presentation of the identity of the disappeared arose from a belief shared by the government and the human rights movement. The canonical status that this reading of the past acquired in Argentina reveals the country's persistent difficulties in coming to terms with the complexity of the political violence that tore it apart thirty years ago.

CONADEP's investigation had highly significant political and legal effects: it proposed a new public truth about the disappearances, it formed an unprecedented body of evidence used to prosecute the parties responsible for atrocities, its *Nunca Mas* report became the most widely known and accepted interpretation of the human rights violations, and both the report and the investigation became international models in the field of transitional justice.

Notes

1. Prolonged imprisonment prevailed in Uruguay and disappearances represented a third of the total deaths in Chile. See SERPAJ Uruguay (1989).
2. See Alfonsin's speech, September 30, 1983. Available at: www.ucr.org.ar/discursospresidenciales.
3. House of Representatives minutes, fourth meeting, third extraordinary session, December 22, 1983, 347. Raul Alfonsin (former president), interview with author, July 19, 2007, Buenos Aires and Eduardo Rabossi (member of CONADEP), interview with author, August 19, 2004, Buenos Aires, Based on the testimony of a member of the Forensic Anthropology Team, Hayner (1994) maintains instead that CONADEP was inspired by Bolivia's National Commission for the Investigation of Disappeared Persons created in 1982 by President Hernan Siles Suazo. This precedent, however, was not mentioned by any of the people interviewed.
4. House of Representative minutes, second meeting, first extraordinary session, December 16, 1983, 144–145; draft declaration 275-D-83, December 15, 1983; Adolfo Perez Esquivel (Service for Peace and Justice), interview with author, December 13, 2004, Buenos Aires.
5. House of Representative minutes, second meeting, first extraordinary session, December 16, 1983, 144–145; draft declaration 275-D-83, December 15, 1983.
6. The congressmen were Santiago Lopez, defense attorney for political prisoners and representative for Chubut, Hugo Piucill, APDH member, and representative for Rio Negro and Horacio Huarte, lawyer and representative for the province of Buenos Aires.
7. CONADEP, minutes 3, December 29, 1983, 5 and 6, and minutes 4, January 3, 1984, 9 and 10).
8. Graciela Fernandez Meijide (member of CONADEP), interview with author, August 26, 2004, Buenos Aires.

9. CONADEP, minutes 2, December 27, 1983, 3 and 4; minutes 4, January 3, 1984, 8; minutes 5, January 5, 1984, 13; minutes 6, January 10, 1984, 16; minutes 8, January 24, 1984, 22 and minutes 11, February 14, 1984, 32.
10. House of Representatives minutes, fourth meeting, third extraordinary session, December 22, 1983, 345–367.
11. CONADEP, minutes 9, January 31, 1984, 24; minutes 14, March 6, 1984, 47, and minutes 19, April 10, 1984, 75.
12. CONADEP, minutes 33, July 17, 1984; 128–132.
13. CONADEP, minutes 41, September 4, 1984, 164–170.
14. Raul Aragon (member of APDH), interview with author, December 3, 2003, Buenos Aires; Graciela Fernandez Meijide (member of CONADEP), interview with author, August 26, 2004, Buenos Aires; Alberto Mansur (secretary of legal affairs), interview with author, September 1, 2004, Buenos Aires and Gregorio Klimovsky (member of CONADEP), interview with author, September 6, 2004, Buenos Aires.
15. Mabel Gutierrez (leader of *Familiares de Detenidos y Desaparecidos por Razones Politicas*) interview with author, October 26, 2004, Buenos Aires.
16. Magdalena Ruiz Guinazu (member of CONADEP), e-mail communication with author, August 24, 2004 and Graciela Fernandez Meijide (member of CONADEP), interview with author, August 26, 2004, Buenos Aires.
17. CONADEP, minutes 7, Janauray 17, 1984, 19; minutes 9, January 31, 1984.
18. *Memoria Abierta* archive, APDH, doc. B7.489, n.d., 5.
19. CONADEP minutes 7, January 17, 1984, 20; minutes 10, February 7, 1984, 29; minutes 12, February 21, 1984, 36; minutes 18, April 3, 1984, 67 and 69; minutes 19, April 10, 1984, 74–76.
20. CONADEP, minutes 33, July 17, 1984, 134–135.
21. Interview with Graciela Fernandez Meijide, Buenos Aires, August 26, 2004.
22. Alberto Mansur (secretary of legal affairs), interview with author, September 1, 2004, Buenos Aires.
23. Raul Aragon (member of APDH), interview with author, December 3, 2003, Buenos Aires and Gregorio Klimovsky (member of CONADEP), interview with author, September 6, 2004, Buenos Aires.
24. Santiago Lopez (defense attorney for political prisoners and representative for Chubut), interview with author, October 18, 2004, Buenos Aires.
25. CONADEP 1984, 25, 29, 55, 56, 184, 275–279, 293–300, 322, 361, 365, 367, 375, 402, 474, 475.
26. House of Representatives minutes, twenty-ninth meeting, twenty-first ordinary session, September 28–29, 1984, 5025–5028.
27. CONADEP 1984, 63, 137, 224–226, 234–246, 293, 303, and 479–480.
28. My calculation based on Corralini et al. (2003).
29. CONADEP 1984, 253–259, 300.
30. Senate minutes, February 9, 1984, 318.
31. CONADEP 1984, 15, 16, 223, 256 and 481.
32. CONADEP 1984, 477 and 478.

References

Bourdieu, Pierre. 2001. ¿Que significa hablar? Madrid: Akal.

Brisk, Alison. 1994. *The Politics of Human Rights in Argentina: Protest, Change and Democratization.* Stanford, CA: Stanford University Press.

Clarin. 1984a. "Dicto el PEN un decreto que beneficia a Isabel Peron." May 2:8.

Clarin. 1984b. "Denuncia de militares sobre desaparecidos." March 14:6.

Comision Nacional de Verdad y Reconciliacion. 1991. Informe de la Comision Nacional de Verdad y Reconciliacion. Santiago: Ediciones del Ornitorrinco.

Comision Nacional sobre la Desaparicion de Personas (CONADEP). 1984. Nunca Mas. Informe de la Comision Nacional sobre la Desaparicion de Personas. Buenos Aires: EUDEBA.

Conviccin. 1983 (April 29, special supplement:1–4).

Corralini, Juan, Ana Lobo, Emiliano Di Iorio, and Javier Pigliapochi, eds. 2003. Politicas de memoria: el Nunca Mas. Buenos Aires: Unpublished.

Crenzel, Emilio. 2008a. La historia política del Nunca Mas. La memoria de las desapariciones en Argentina. Buenos Aires: Siglo XXI Editores.

Crenzel, Emilio 2008b. "The National Commission on the Disappearance of Persons: Contributions to Transitional Justice." *The International Journal of Transitional Justice* 2:173–191.

Crenzel, Emilio. 2005. "Cartas a Videla: una exploracion sobre el miedo, el terror y la memoria," Telar, year II, nos. 2 and 3. Facultad de Filosofía y Letras. Universidad Nacional de Tucuman.

Feld, Claudia. 2004. "La television comme scene de la memoire de la dictature en Argentine. Une etude sur les recits et les representations de la disparition forcee de personnes," PhD dissertation, Universite de Paris VIII.

Frente. 1983. April 6.

Grandin, Greg. 2005. "The Instruction of Great Catastrophe: Truth Commissions, National History, and State Formation in Argentina, Chile and Guatemala," American Historical Review 110:46–67.

Hayner, Priscilla. 1994. "Fifteen Truth Commissions—1974 to 1994: A Comparative Study," *Human Rights Quarterly* 16:597–655.

Hayner, Priscilla. 2001. *Unspeakable Truth. Confronting State Terror and Atrocity.* New York: Routledge.

Izaguirre, Ines. 1992. "Los desaparecidos, recuperacion de una identidad expropiada," Cuaderno 9, Instituto de Investigaciones Gino Germani. Universidad de Buenos Aires.

Jelin, Elizabeth. 1995. "La politica de la memoria: El movimiento de derechos humanos y la construccion de la democracia en Argentina." In Juicio, castigos y memorias, derechos humanos y justicia en la política Argentina, ed. Carlos Acuna, et al. Buenos Aires: Nueva Vision.

Mignone, Emilio. 1991. Derechos humanos y sociedad: El caso argentino. Buenos Aires: CELS.

Nino, Carlos. 1997. Juicio al mal absoluto.Los fundamentos y la historia del juicio a las juntas del proceso. Buenos Aires: Emece.

Official Bulletin of Argentina. 1983a. December 19.

Official Bulletin of Argentina. 1983b. September 27.

Official Bulletin of Argentina. 1983c. September 19.

SERPAJ Uruguay. 1989. Nunca Mas. Montevideo: SERPAJ.

Sikkink, Kathryn. 2008. "From Pariah State to Global Protagonist: Argentina and the Struggle for International Human Rights." *Latin American Politics and Society* 50:1–29.

Wright, Thomas. 2007. *State Terrorism in Latin America: Chile, Argentina, and International Human Rights.* Lanham, MD: Rowman & Littlefield.

CHAPTER 4

Recalling the Legacy of the 1985 Trial of the Military in Argentina

Mario Di Paolantonio

Introduction

As Argentina moved toward democracy in 1983, a legal process was also set in motion to account for the dictatorship's repressive strategy and to symbolically mark the turn to democracy. In 1985, this process led to the so-called "Trial of the Military," which remarkably brought before the law the nine junta leaders deemed responsible for violations committed during the 1976–1983 military regime, which were discussed in Chapter 2. In light of the social divisions and conflicts that the Trial of the Military brought to the fore, igniting various military rebellions, the trial appears to illustrate why domestically prosecuting perpetrators of a prior regime is fraught with conflict, provides no clear benefits, and should be avoided. However, rather than dismiss the trial as an inevitably flawed enterprise, I want to propose that the legacy of the trials is both instructive and formative. In this chapter, I consider how the very failure and betrayed hopes of the 1985 Trial of the Military in Argentina provided civil society with the impetus for the ongoing work of righting past wrongs and restructuring the normative dimension of democracy in Argentina.

In the first part of the chapter, I present the various ways in which the state sought to rewrite Argentinean law in order to structure its vision of reconciliation. I discuss the selective strategy of prosecution, the amnesty laws enacted to contain further trials, and the pardons issued by executive decree. My purpose in this section is to illustrate how the state, amid the instability and inconsistency of the transition to democracy, utilized a legal strategy of containment that ultimately compromised the law. However, in the second part of the chapter, I discuss how, despite the restrictions imposed by the state, the 1985 trial nevertheless sets a political precedent, engendering a residual memory of "what could be." Through a consideration of the normative aspirations created by the legacy of the 1985 trial, we can come to appreciate recent events in Argentina where the possibility of prosecuting former military personnel accused of past violations has again gained momentum in the courts.

Alfonsin's Legal Strategy: The Politics of Reconciliation

The transition from the dictatorship to a democratically elected government at the end of 1983 was at the outset marked by a popular desire to "know" and to bring to "justice" those responsible for the past violations. We can appreciate the determination here; for in a society where disappearances were once part of the strategy employed by the state, where literally there is no institutional body to confirm death—for there is no physical body, nor any body of the state willing to verify such a death—the struggle to legally account for the remains provided a means to restore the social significance of political institutions such as the judiciary. While most of the parties competing in the electoral process at the time took note of the growing public determination for accountability, it was the leader of the Union Civica Radical, Raul Alfonsin, who was able to articulate and politically harness its force. Largely running on a campaign that promised to address the past violations, an unprecedented (for a non-Peronist party) 52 percent of the electorate handed Alfonsin a decisive victory on October 30, 1983. Upon taking office, President Alfonsin and the rights community concurred with the first step in redressing the past violations, agreeing to an impartial inquiry that would establish the facts about the disappeared and educate the public about the past violence. As discussed in Chapter 3, the task for this investigation was assigned to a special commission (the National Commission on the Disappeared or CONADEP) set up under Decree 187 on December 15, 1983. The commission produced a two-volume report entitled *Nunca Mas* that included various survivor testimonies and a list of some of the disappeared. The promise to seek legal accountability was, however, a more difficult issue that eventually positioned Alfonsin in opposition to the demands of most human rights groups.

In his introduction to the 1986 English version of *Nunca Mas*, Dworkin writes that "Argentina needed to bury its past as well as to condemn it, and many citizens felt that years of trials would undermine the fresh sense of community Alfonsin's victory had produced" (*Nunca Mas* 1986, 18). It is debatable as to whether "many citizens" felt as Dworkin suggests, given the public resolve for a legal endeavour that could provide answers to the fate and remains of the disappeared, answers that the military was not willing to divulge voluntarily, and which CONADEP was for the most part incapable of garnering. However, Dworkin's suggestion does parallel the unease expressed by Alfonsin and his advisers to mark the transition, as promised, with an explicit display of the rule of law while containing a potential wave of trials against the military. Although the military's tactic of disappearances was a mechanism that scattered responsibility widely throughout the ranks, the initial idea voiced within Alfonsin's circle was to bring to trial only a handful of high-ranking officers (Osiel 1986, 154).

Once in office, Alfonsin and his advisers, namely the legal philosophers Carlos Nino and Jaime Malamud, drafted a comprehensive statute (Law 23.049) that formally established jurisdiction for the trials and a reinterpretation of the military's due obedience clause. Jurisdiction for the trials was allocated to the highest military court, the Supreme Military Council, with a broad right of appeal to the civilian courts. This initial strategy sought to give the military an internal process for "self-purification." It was hoped that this would garner legitimacy for the transition's commitment to the law and maintain the path toward reconciliation by avoiding a massive purge and public humiliation of the whole military institution. The desire to include the military within the "fresh sense of community" thus depended on carefully limiting the issue of criminal responsibility. To this end, the reinterpretation of the norm of due obedience proposed that "a rebuttable presumption was to be created for those who followed orders that ultimately violated human rights and erred about the legitimacy of the orders. This presumption was not to be available to those who had decision-making capacity" (Nino 1996, 69). The legislative package that initiated the criminal proceedings against the military thus focused on the nine commanders of the first three military juntas from 1976 to 1983. In accordance with Alfonsin's cautious steps to provide justice, the legislative strategy prevented further trials against the military as it sanctioned, for those who did not occupy its commanding offices, an automatic presumption of due obedience, the so-called "taking orders" defence. However, some modifications were made to draft Law 23.049—the most significant one taking place in the Senate where a small regional party (whose leader, Senator Elias Sapag, had two of his sons disappeared) introduced an exception to the defence of due obedience, excluding anyone who committed "abhorrent" or "atrocious" acts. This qualification, which more or less exceeded the cautious path favoured by Alfonsin for democratic consolidation, began to complicate the legal process.

In the aftermath of several extensions, it was evident that the Supreme Military Council was unwilling to carry out the prosecutions against the nine junta-commanders. As the Buenos Aires Federal Appeals Court intervened and transferred jurisdiction to the civilian courts, the failed strategy of promoting an institutional purge gave way to a public trial. The pedagogical benefits of having the procedures of the trial exposed to the public are widely proposed by many. According to Nino "public inquiry into the truth is much more precise and much more dramatic when done through a trial, with the accused contributing to the development of the story. In fact, the quality of narration in an adversarial trial cannot be fully replicated by other means" (1996, 146). But the narratives that the trial brought forth were not connotative of any more "precise" or transparent "truth." Rather, the "truth" effects depended on the situation that provided the narratives and their possible public reading. As the narratives of the 1985 Trial of the Military became more public, they consequently became more entangled with the *political*—a more complex and unpredictable system that inevitably threatened the precariously regained "fresh sense of community" that Alfonsin sought to pursue.

Necessarily then, the public narratives surrounding the trial were punctuated with "official" reminders about the need for restraint and consolidation.

The trial was thus framed by the Alfonsin administration as an educational medium that could, if limited to prosecuting only certain officers, "objectively" settle the divisions and conflicts that existed during the transitional period. In this sense, the law was presented by Alfonsin as a pure principle and neutral procedure, without force or explicit interest, which could inculcate a collective and objective lesson on the founding values of the nation.

Containing the Public Demand for Rule of Law: The Judicial Decision

On December 9, 1985, the court delivered its verdict. Since the court attributed responsibility for the proven criminal acts to individual commanders, the sentences varied. Out of the nine defendants, four were acquitted (Graffigna, Galtieri, Anaya, and Lami Dozo), and only two were given life sentences (Videla and Massera). Agosti was sentenced to four-and-a-half years, Viola received seventeen years, and Lambruschini was sentenced to eight years. Aware that the ruling would establish a precedent regarding the issue of how far to prosecute beyond this trial, concern was also expressed on how the due obedience defense might be circumscribed in the future. While the court was preparing its decision, Alfonsin and his strategists remained concerned with democratic consolidation. Despite a request by Alfonsin to resolve the issue of due obedience (Verbitsky 1987), the court's verdict concerning itself only with the commanders could not properly settle the matter of subordinate responsibility. On the one hand, the court dealt with the issue of responsibility by implementing the "control over the act" theory. This theory states that "the criminal acts perpetrated by the subordinate officers were always under the control of the defendants; hence they must answer as indirect perpetrators even if some of the direct perpetrators can be exempt from criminal responsibility" (Nino 1996, 89).

On the other hand, the court qualified this reading with a reminder that the trial had not adjudicated the question of the criminal responsibility of lower-ranking military personnel for the crimes considered. Hence, the court noted that "the Supreme Council retains the obligation under Law 23.049 to investigate the criminal culpability of subordinates" (Gray 1986, 696). Much to the chagrin of those proposing strategies for consolidation, the trial's inability to decisively interpret the due obedience defence opened the way for further prosecutions. The very trial that was intended to prevent further prosecutions inadvertently provided a loophole for further prosecutions.

A popular chant that could be heard in the background to the 1985 trial called out "*castigo a todos los culpables*" ("punish all of the guilty"). It was the hope of the executive that the exemplary trial, and its pedagogical showcasing of liberal norms, would end the impulses and sentiments that were, in one way or another, provoked by calling up the divisive past in the present. However, as the possibility for prosecutions widened, it was no longer possible to contain the various impulses and sentiments within the display of an uncontroversial set of legal norms and procedures. The law itself became complicit with these impulses exceeding the prudential consideration for reconciliation. For it now seemed—in the popular imagination—that the law could be asked to go beyond the limits of an exemplary model and in due process "punish all the guilty." In less than a year after the court's ruling on the nine commanders, it was clear that "the scope of the trials had already escaped the control of the Executive and the judicial process had assumed a life of its own" (Brysk 1995, 80). A tide of charges against the military came before the courts. By 1986, at least 3,000 cases before the Supreme Military Council were pending, as others were proceeding in civilian courts.

While the prosecutions continued to come before the courts, Alfonsin and his legal team drafted a number of measures to decisively limit further trials. In the attempt to avoid an amnesty, their strategy sought to limit the demand for justice by proposing legislation that marked a cut-off date for all trials. The *Punto Final* law specified a sixty-day limit for submitting charges that were defined in Law 23.049; otherwise, all such charges would once and for all be extinguished. Despite the fact that the first thirty days of the period for submission fell on the traditional vacation season, a large number of indictments were brought forth. However, as military officers and personnel continued to be called before the law, the conciliatory effect that the *Punto Final* law was hoping to generate did not materialize. Some months after the *Punto Final* deadline, in April 1987, a serious military rebellion against the trials developed. The conflicting aspirations and interests within the "fresh sense of community" came to the fore.

Three days before Alfonsin negotiated with the military rebels to end the challenge, he declared to the legislature that "we will reaffirm in concrete actions the criteria of responsibility that will permit national reconciliation" (Mignone 1992, 261). Linking the issue of responsibility with the goal of national reconciliation evidently implied returning to the original legal strategy of allowing most of the officers to claim the "just following orders" defence. The military rebellion, which came to be known as the "Easter Week" crisis, was resolved on Easter Sunday (April 19, 1987) after Alfonsin met directly with the military rebels. Within the following weeks, legislation began to be drafted and was subsequently passed by Congress on June 5, 1987 (under Law 23.521). The law revised the due obedience defence to favor a closure for further trials: It explicitly defined and confined the notion of decision-making capacity only to the high military ranks; it conceded that subordinates were innocent of any criminal violations since they legitimately were following orders that they could not question; this law consequently annulled the legislative exception to the defence that excluded anyone who committed "abhorrent" or "atrocious" acts.

From Amnesty Laws to Pardons

The general demand for law that was unleashed by the 1985 Trial of the Military was not stimulated only by the amnesty laws brought forth by Alfonsin. In October 1989, Alfonsin's successor Carlos Menem began to issue blanket pardons to military officers who were not covered by the amnesty laws and whose cases still remained open. The 213 pardons issued by decree to military officers were not only a definite break with the strategy of legal redress but also demonstrated the resolve of the executive to contain and channel the call for rule of law. Official state discourse and action under Menem would continue—in a more resolute and definite manner than Alfonsin's government to impede the legal means of addressing past violations. Despite considerable international and domestic protest, by the end of 1990, Menem conferred a second set of pardons freeing former junta leaders convicted in the 1985 Trial of Military. At home and abroad, he repeatedly claimed that the pardons sought to promote national reconciliation, an effort to put the past to rest and address the more pressing concerns of the present.

While not a response to the same type of "foundational crisis" faced in the immediate phase of the transition to democracy in 1983, the pardons issued by Menem can still be understood as operating under a type of "state of exception" rather than any state of political normalcy. Argentina was still negotiating the transition as mid-level military officers were (even after the legislative concessions put in place by Alfonsin) defying the chain of command and threatening civil order in the attempt to register their version of the past. Ironically, the pardons display the strong interventionist role adopted by the state in order to manage the divisive tendencies that were brought to the fore by the law's attempt to provide the foundation for the general norms and legitimacy of the democratic transition. The very basis upon which the Alfonsin administration had attempted to direct the transition was now actively managed by Menem for the purpose of "institutional stability." Of course, the Alfonsin administration paved the way for this strategy of containment, but Menem's endeavor represents a more aggressive phase of attempting to contain the demand for justice. In this sense, Menem's pardons appear to be a "creative act" undertaken in the name of stability, reconciliation, or even in the name of securing (for posterity) the rule of law.

The well-respected TV anchorperson, Mariano Grondona, captured the popular sentiment of post-pardon Argentina when he stated that "you can imagine the indignation and outrage of those affected [by the violent repression] as they faced the impunity and double standard of legality...If a citizen steals a chicken he goes to jail. If a member of the armed forces kills serially he stays home" (Roniger and Sznajder 1998, 148). The anecdote displays the crux of the matter here: The very basis of the rule of law, the very grounds of the transition, is explicitly debilitated amidst such an interventionist state policy of reconciliation. The stability that is fostered through the public appreciation for general norms of fairness through the application of the law is potentially forfeited by claims to be acting in the name of securing stability, reconciliation, and the future conditions of the rule of law. The "creative intervention" of the state, which in this regard grants specific concessions to representatives of powerful sectors of society (such as the military) while enforcing the law upon a citizen "for stealing a chicken," risks rendering the function of government into an arbitrary and ultimately indefensible guarantor of law. This ultimately threatens the social allegiance, especially required during a democratic transition, which grants the state its very basis to write, enforce, and protect the law.

The amnesty laws and pardons thus reveal a paradox perhaps typical of the state of exception. On the one hand, the interventionist state's ability to render decisions that are unprecedented in order to forge stability and social cohesion appears to be a necessary and fundamental maneuver in order to regulate the state of exception. On the other hand, this very act, in compromising the general norms and principles that are claimed (even if only symbolically) to be the basis of the democratic transition, erodes the social legitimacy and allegiance necessitated by this new order. It appears that the law is ultimately determined by power, by the state safeguarding its interest of self-preservation, granting whatever "legal" compromises and concessions to those deemed powerful or threatening enough to register their interests. Consequently, it seems that in this context, there is a "failure to implement effectively the "ethical model" of democracy envisioned during the first period of democratic rule" giving way to "another model of democracy," namely, one that is "less attentive to the demands of civil society and more concentrated at the level of decision-makers" (Roniger and Sznajder 1999, 195).

A Memory of Justice: Invoking the Legacy of the Trial

The public character of the Trial of the Military—as both Osiel (1997) and Nino (1996) aptly recognize—provided an educational opportunity, furnishing the emerging collective with a formative event. By placing the trial at the center of the legitimizing process of the democratic transition, the regime ensured that the law became central to the emerging democratic aspirations. Smulovitz (2002, 252) acknowledges that:

> The spectacular character of the trial, in which weak citizens held powerful individuals accountable for past violations, helped to build an image of a judiciary that could discipline the powerful and defend the rights of the weak.... The legal discourse was able to order the past and to give credibility to the witnesses' stories, becoming, in turn, an effective mechanism for a historical and political judgment of the dictatorial regime. Therefore, the decision of the Buenos Aires Federal Court [that opened the way for further prosecution] made the courts the stage upon which the promise of the newborn democracy was to be fulfilled. The political impact and high visibility of this decision began to transform perceptions of the traditionally subordinate role of the judiciary. As a result of this "spectacular" and "unexpected" public event, the conservative judiciary appeared to become a place where the rights [and democratic aspirations] of citizens could be realized.

When we remind ourselves that the 1985 trial represented the first time that a democratic government in Latin America prosecuted (in accordance with the rule of law) its military predecessors for its past violations, we can come to appreciate the radical act of seeking justice for the past so that it may alter the social terms for instituting the present. In a symbolic sense, the trial aimed not simply to preserve, register, or re-inscribe the past (wronged), but to set an institutional precedent for that yet to come. But what happens to this public awareness in the face of the politics of containment and compromise that enforces the terms/settlement of the state? What remains of that aspiration for democracy and law forged through the now barred trials? If we were to exclusively focus on negotiations brokered between prime institutional players (between military and state-officials) we risk moving too quickly away from these questions, hastily dismissing the legacy of the trial.

Although we must admit that the process for writing and righting the past through the verification of the facts through legal accountability is strictly undermined by the politics of containment discussed above, we must explain the enduring desire to seek justice. That is, we must account for the persistence of the democratic aspiration that remains widespread in the society in memory of the 1985 trial. It is not so much the precise content or procedures of the trial that are at issue here. Rather, the issue is how the trial failed to deliver on the promises and aspirations that established a legacy widely circulated throughout the society—a legacy that remains despite the compromises. The sustained demand for legal action in Argentina needs to be appreciated amidst a set of unsettled issues that erupted and consequently disrupted the politics of social containment. More specifically, we need to note how the public desire and momentum for overturning the amnesty laws took shape in response to certain "eruption of memories."

The Disruption of Confessions

In its summary report on human rights in Argentina, the Center for Legal and Social Studies (CELS) describes the situation of the early 1990s in this way: "Once the amnesty laws were sanctioned, public debate [regarding the unsettled past] went through a period of withdrawal that was the product, to a large extent, of the politics of forgetfulness imposed by the State" (CELS 2002). However, the sense of dissatisfaction and frustration lurking within this period bursts to the fore in form of a public discourse through an unprecedented and macabre episode. Amid this period of "public withdrawal" with the unsettled past, a series of former military executioners and torturers began to confess to the criminal methods systematically employed by the military during its Dirty War.

In 1995, the confession by retired naval officer Adolfo Scaling, given to journalist Horace Frisky, was the most infamous. Scaling was the first to publicly confess and launch a lawsuit against his commanding officers for lying about their issuing orders that grossly violated human rights. What is termed the "Scaling effect" unleashed a series of public confessions, usually given to reporters by former military executioners and torturers. By 1998, eight officers had come forward to confess. While the media often showcased these confessions through the moral discourse of "reconciliation," "atonement," or "dialogue" (Kaiser 2002, 503), the motivating factor behind the confessions by perpetrators had less lofty goals. Shielded from prosecution by the amnesty laws, those engaged in the confessional enterprise appeared to risk very little while potentially placing themselves in a profitable position as they brokered monetary contracts for their confessions and courted sympathy from a public that previously shunned them.

What made these confessions unusual was that, for the first time, the military's unified stance (which steadfastly refused to reveal any information to the public other than that which substantiated their claim of having fought a righteous Christian war) began to come apart. A vast amount of "difficult knowledge" was suddenly unleashed on the public by violators with varying agendas. The eruption of fragmented details about the traumatic past caused disturbing ripples, bringing to the fore memories and unsettled issues that were supposed to have been put to rest by the state's strategy of containment. While a majority in society desired details denied over the years, it became vexing to hear the extensive nature and the list of characters that operated within the repressive apparatus, while being unable (given the amnesty laws) to prosecute or further investigate those implicated. Public frustration and dissatisfaction, rather than "acknowledgement," "truth," or "atonement," was the result of hearing these confessions that were literally beyond the law's reach.

By 1995, "it was evident from the beginning that Scaling's words had reached many ears, and little by little the surprising conversations that could be heard in bars and shops filtered through to the various institutions which until then had remained excessively silent" (CELS 1996, 85). It is important to note that the memories unleashed by the confessions took place in a highly volatile social environment, when Menem's neoliberal policies were underway, and consequently a sense of the betrayal of the public interest by the state was already in place. In this strained atmosphere, the social discontent with the neoliberal course adopted by the state readily transformed into anger with the state refusing to investigate and prosecute those implicated through the confessions. Human rights groups were able to draw together the general dissatisfaction and uncertainty erupting at this time through a politics of memory and legal recall. As Roniger and Sznajder note "against this background of a civil society traumatized by the experiences of economic catastrophe and disappointment with the shifts in policies since the initial stages of redemocratization, the frustrated hopes for justice [economics and rights based] were channeled into the struggle over the politics of memory and oblivion" (1998, 149).

The awareness and consequent disapproval of the state's threat to the rule of law offered a focus for public indignation. Human rights groups committed to reactivating the promise of the 1985 trial were thus poised to give direction to that general dissatisfaction, exposing "the legal and moral contradictions of Argentine democracy" (Feitlowitz 1998, 194–195). Through the prevalent human rights concern to revisit the unfinished and thus interrupted work of the 1985 trial, public discourse focused on the contested role of law in the transition, asking: "Why did the armed forces continue to refuse to provide information on the fate of the disappeared? How could the search for truth and justice continue in the courts when the amnesty laws prevented prosecutions?" (Human Rights Watch 2001). Both the military and the state were thus explicitly identified as frustrating the pursuit of democracy and justice. As these questions gained currency through public dissemination, it made "good sense" (to those identifying with the need to expand democracy) to overturn the amnesty laws in order to recover a more ethical sense of democratic legitimacy promised through the trial. Consequently, "given the renewed public interest in legal action, CELS decided [in 1995] to press the courts to investigate a few emblematic cases" (Human Rights Watch 2001). The *juicios por la verdad* (truth trials) were thus crafted within the general momentum and dissatisfaction of the time.

Juicios por la verdad

The persistent aspiration for democracy and law evoked by civil society against the state's politics of containment needs to be understood as a world-building normative activity. This is an activity, as Peruzzotti notes, which strives to "re-introduce a normative narrative about political institutions, narratives lost after decades of strategic praetorian struggles" (2002, 86). Consider the example of such normative regeneration offered by the work of CELS. During the eruptions of confessions, CELS brought before the courts a case that sought to overturn the amnesty laws put in place by Alfonsin, laws that not only effectively closed down further legal investigations and prosecutions of the military's involvement in the disappearances, but also consequently closed any institutionally sanctioned effort that would compel the military to provide information and confirmation about the death of the disappeared and the location of their remains. CELS based their case on "the inalienable right to the truth, the obligation to respect the body, and the right to mourn the dead. The suit also cites the right to definitively establish the identity of the children born in captivity" (Feitlowitz 1998, 242–243). These are all claims that were violated under the dictatorship, and—given the closing down of further trials and the short tenure of the CONADEP Commission—never properly redressed with the return to democracy.

The case of legal recall constructed by CELS—which would become known as *juicios por la verdad*—drew on evidence gathered from the Trial of the Military and international human rights conventions that held precedence over domestic laws. Significantly, CELS sought to build the thrust of their argument on various narratives that explicitly described the normative role of institutions regarding the "rights of the dead" and the "right to bury and mourn the dead." While the *juicios por la verdad* were restricted to judicial investigations that could not lead to prosecution due to the amnesty laws, they were an effective means of accumulating evidence and sustaining the momentum for legal recall, ultimately setting the stage for overturning the amnesty laws. Presently, such "truth trials" continue to take place across Argentina since they are able to garner significant information and public attention.

The initial case crafted by CELS that would launch these "truth trials" argued that social institutions establish their symbolic basis and legitimacy on the ability to provide and maintain intergenerational links (Braun and Pelento 1989). This recognizes that a social obligation is owed to the dead and to the facilitation of the mourning process, since the ground on which different generations link together in order to foster communal institutions is determined by the need to tend to the dead. The inability to locate the dead (the disappeared) in Argentina ruptures this link, placing the significance and function of societal institutions at risk when remains are desecrated and information is withheld from those seeking to know and mourn. The courts—as the exemplar of institutional memory and societal continuity—are thus shown to have an obligation to the relatives and society as a whole in reasserting and continuing the legal process that was begun with the Trial of the Military. In building this case, Feitlowitz reports how CELS resuscitated legal precedents and narratives of symbolic importance in order to press the issue in the courts and throughout society. She writes that:

> in addition to legal sources, CELS' argument brings to bear world history and literature as support for the essential human need for funeral rites: the burial ceremonies developed by the Neanderthals; Sophocles's *Antigone* (a work frequently adapted by Latin American playwrights in the 1970s and early 1980s); and Philippe Aries's *Death in the West*, which argues that funerals are the one sacred rite common to Judaism, Christianity, and Islam, and the one observance that binds atheists, agnostics, and believers. (1998, 243)

Here, we witness CELS striving to repair and engender the sense of belonging to a normative community. That is, a community with functioning institutions that can honor and protect the intergenerational link. Emilio Mignone—the director of CELS who headed the suit, and whose daughter Monica Candelaria Mignone disappeared in May 1976—explained that, in spite of the limitations of the amnesty laws, the federal judges who heard the case, "explicitly acknowledged the rights to know and mourn, and that is extremely important. In fact, it was a first for our courts" (Feitlowitz 1998, 243). In April 1995, the courts ordered the naval chief of staff to make available files and any relevant information that could contribute to the knowledge of the remains, hence ensuring the right and possibility of mourning.

This public discourse surrounding rights and institutions is thus related to the regeneration of social significance that can challenge the force of containment wielded by the state, recovering lost and suppressed normative possibilities that challenge the present settlements. We are dealing here not with some static transcendental injunction (an abstract rule) that issues from the concept of the "human," but with the social impact of a legacy that re-generates itself into an aspiration for rights; an aspiration that keeps transferring its claim to new generations, expanding the normative efficacy of democracy and civil society. The symbolic significance of democracy and justice—which the Trial of the Military was fundamental in unleashing—is not depleted of its force, but continues to provide momentum to the needs and struggles of the present in Argentina.

Conclusions

In 2001, almost a decade after the presidential pardons, various Argentine courts began initiating criminal procedures against officers who committed human rights violations during the military's Dirty War. The courts summoned the same military officers who were formerly pardoned by Menem or granted immunity through the two amnesty laws issued by Alfonsin. In March 2001, weeks before the twenty-fifth anniversary of the 1976 military coup, Federal Judge Gabriel Cavallo revoked, as unconstitutional, the two amnesty laws (the *Punto Final* and the *Obediencia Debida*) that were preventing junior and mid-level officers from being prosecuted for crimes committed during the military's Dirty War. The wider social significance of Cavallo's ruling can be discerned in how it effectively opened the way to pursue other cases—which are still presently underway—against military officers accused of similar crimes.

Given that Cavallo's ruling required "a persistent demand for justice" insofar as "judges can only rule on cases that are brought before them" (Skaar 2001, 2), we need to appreciate how the memory of justice played a crucial role in nourishing and sustaining the demand. Hence, rather than dismiss the 1985 trial as an inevitably failed enterprise that requires us to seek better means to achieve reconciliation after a transition to democracy, we can find in its legacy a resource for sustaining the demand for justice, for providing normative sense, and direction in the opening to democracy. Although lower courts drawing on Cavallo's precedent repeatedly struck down the amnesty laws, appeals were still pending before the Supreme Court, which until 2005 remained hesitant in delivering a ruling on the constitutionality of the amnesty laws. The reluctance to issue a ruling in a timely manner was publicly seen as a cynical attempt by the court to bargain with a government that sought to impeach certain of its members for corruption and political bias. As the public legitimacy of the Supreme Court eroded, a series of dismissals and new appointments occurred. It is significant that the June 14, 2005 declaration of the unconstitutionality of the amnesty laws (by a vote of seven to one) was one of the first major rulings of the (reformed) Supreme Court, effectively asserting the significance of law and democracy in addressing the unsettled past. However, the present trials in Argentina proceed in a precarious context as certain witnesses have been intimidated and even disappeared, as, for example, in the case of Jorge Julio Lopez, the main witness in the 2006 trial of Miguel Etchecolatz, a former police commissioner sentenced to life imprisonment for his participation in torture and disappearances.

While this chapter accounts for the conciliatory evasions, compromises, and containment of the law by the state, it explicitly resists the temptation to view the dynamics of the law through this actor alone. To this end, I have been implicitly critical of any account that would minimize the impact that the 1985 Trial of the Military had on societal demands. Clearly the state compromises and the public dissatisfaction with the trial do not result in the debilitation of civil society or in a turning away from the "ethical model" of democracy and law inherently promised by the democratic transition. Rather, the memory of the trial's promise for justice plays a key role in forging and sustaining a normative demand to overturn a set of positive laws for the sake and possibility of furthering law and democracy.

References

Braun, Julia, and Maria Lucila Pelento. 1989. "Les vicissitudes de la pulsion de savoir dans certains deuils speciaux." In *Violence d' e'tat et psychanalyse*, ed. Janine Puget. Paris: Bordas.

Brysk, Alison. 1995. *The Politics of Human Rights in Argentina: Protest, Change, and Democratization*. Stanford, CA: Stanford University Press.

CELS. 1996. *Informe anual sobre la situacion de los derechos humanos en la Argentina 1995*. Buenos Aires: CELS.

CELS. 2000. *Derechos humanos Argentina informe anual 2000*. Buenos Aires: ELS/EUDEBA.

Nunca Mas: The Report of the Argentine National Commission on the Disappeared. 1986. New York: Farrar Straus Giroux.

Feitlowitz, Marguerite. 1998. *A Lexicon of Terror: Argentina and the Legacies of Torture*. New York: Oxford University Press.

Gray, Evan. 1986. "Human Rights: Conviction of Former Argentine Military Commanders for Human Rights Abuses Committed by Subordinates: Decision of the Argentine National Chamber of Federal Criminal and Correctional Appeals." *Harvard International Law Journal* 27:688–698.

Human Rights Watch. 2001. *Argentina: Reluctant Partner*. Available at: www.nuncamas.org/investig/hrw_121201_08.htm.

Kaiser, Susana. 2002. "*Escraches*: Demonstrations, Communication and Political Memory in Post-Dictatorial Argentina." *Media, Culture & Society* 24:499–516.

Mignone, Emilio. F. 1992. "Beyond Fear: Forms of Justice and Compensation." In *Fear at the Edge: State Terror and Resistance in Latin America*, ed. Juan Corradi, Patricia Weiss Fagen, and Manuel Antornio Garreton. Berkeley, CA: University of California Press.

Nino, Carlos Santiago. 1996. *Radical Evil on Trial*. New Haven, CT: Yale University Press.

Osiel, Mark. 1997. *Mass Atrocity, Collective Memory, and the Law*. New Brunswick, NJ: Transaction Publishers.

Osiel, Mark. 1986. "The Making of Human Rights Policy in Argentina: The Impact of Ideas and Interests on a Legal Conflict." *Journal of Latin American Studies* 18:135–80.

Peruzzotti, Enrique. 2002. "Towards a New Politics: Citizenship and Rights in Contemporary Argentina." *Citizenship Studies* 16:77–93.

Roniger, Luis, and Mario Sznajder. 1999. *The Legacy of Human-Rights Violations in the Southern Cone: Argentina, Chile, and Uruguay*. New York: Oxford University Press.

Roniger, Luis, and Mario Sznajder. 1998. "The Politics of Memory and Oblivion in Redemocratized Argentina and Uruguay." *History and Memory* 10:133–169.

Skaar, Elin. 2001. "Judicial Independence and Human Rights Policies in Argentina and Chile." Working Paper 15. Bergen: C. Michelsen Institute.

Smulovitz, Catalina. 2002. "The Discovery of Law: Political Consequences in the Argentine Case. In *Global Prescriptions: The Production, Exportation, and Importation of a New Legal Orthodoxy*, eds. Yves Dezalay and Bryant G. Garth. Ann Arbor, MI: University of Michigan Press.

Verbitsky, Horacio. 1987. *Civiles y militares: Memoria secreta de la transicion*. Buenos Aires: Editorial Contrapunto.

PART III

Bosnia-Herzegovina

Map from the United States Central Intelligence Agency's World Factbook.

Map from Wikimedia Commons and licensed into the public domain

CHAPTER 5

Violence Born of History/History Born of Violence: A Brief Context for Understanding the Bosnian War

CHRISTINA M. MORUS

Introduction: A Necessary Prologue

In 1943, Josip Broz Tito's Partisans drove Axis forces from present-day Bosnia and declared the Socialist Federation of Yugoslavia. Tito envisioned a nation of "brotherhood and unity" where pan-Slavic cooperation transcended ethno-national loyalties. To this end, Yugoslavia was comprised of six equal republics (*e.g.*, Croatia, Montenegro, Serbia, Slovenia, Bosnia-Herzegovina [BiH], and Macedonia) whose citizens were expected to reject their ethnonational identities and embrace broader Yugoslav identity. Fifty years later, Yugoslavia crumbled, leaving in its wake the physical and social rubble of Tito's pan-Slavic dream. Yugoslavia's wars of secession propelled the term "ethnic cleansing" into global consciousness. How all this came to pass is worth filling many volumes. The concern of this chapter is the historical, social, and political context for the Bosnian War. Beginning in March 1992 when BiH declared independence and ending in December 1995 with the Dayton Agreement, the Bosnian War left as many as 50 percent of Bosnian homes destroyed, 2 million people displaced, and 100,000 dead (Malcolm 1996, 252). Yet, these numbers neither explain the war's causes, nor why even today, the war is so difficult for outsiders to understand.

An evenhanded account of the Bosnian War inevitably resists brevity as the ways various parties used history in the build-up to war complicates any recounting. To accurately convey even basic details requires a multitude of considerations. Initially, the issue of time is a consideration: How far back does one go? The choice of an historical entry point suggests one's point-of-view and shapes the way an audience will understand BiH's past and present. For the region's nationalist politicians, and for many non-regional journalists and scholars, the events that set the war in motion began over a thousand years ago. Yet, rooting this contemporary conflict in a distant past risks reinforcing the mythologies of inevitability that surround it. Still, because nationalist politicians used historical narratives to sell war as the inexorable zenith of history, it is essential to account for those historical moments that punctuated nationalist discourses. This leads to the second important consideration: Whose history to tell?

In many ways, the context for the Bosnian War is intertwined with the region's history such that the story of BiH is not complete without considering Croatia, Serbia, and Yugoslavia. Given that history was itself a legitimizing rationale for nationalist agendas as well as for the international community's response, deciding which perspective to pay closest attention begs careful consideration. To echo Burke (1945), every narrative is a selection of reality. At the same time, it is a deflection of reality in that selecting what story to tell and how to punctuate it both reflects a way of understanding an event and precludes (or deflects) other interpretations. There are various ways that the historical and contemporary events associated with the Bosnian War can be narrated. As such, understanding this conflict necessitates attention to the roles played by multiple selections of history. Further, as Burke states "[e]very way of seeing is also a way of not seeing" (1935, 70). Any recounting of the war in the present context encourages one way of seeing history, necessarily precluding others.

Associated with history's complexities, the atmosphere of misperception surrounding this war and region should be taken into consideration. Beyond those scholars and analysts who are regional specialists lies narrow familiarity. As Mertus (1999) suggests, American public understanding of the Balkans is mired in complexity and misinformation. Public awareness of the Bosnian War is often reduced to glib generalizations of "age-old ethnic hatreds" in a "far-off land" that "seemed to go on forever" (Rhine *et al.* 2001, 593). In fact in their study of American public knowledge regarding Bosnia, Rhine et al. found that, even in 1994, when the war was a daily media feature, just 32 percent of American adults could name the warring groups. Further while most had heard of "ethnic cleansing," fewer than 40 percent could define it (2001, 597).

While Western media ethnocentricity is a factor, the Bosnian War is a complex event in history involving many actors and factions that cannot be treated easily in a news story and hence often oversimplified. Western media has tended to characterize the war as an inevitable manifestation of "age-old ethnic hatred," an interpretation encouraged by regional nationalist politicians. Yet, this categorization obfuscates understanding in two ways. First, accepting this conflict as an historical inevitability disguises the fact that this war was the result of modern human choices in response to contemporary material conditions. While opportunistic politicians promoted a historical trajectory punctuated to suggest the inevitable culmination of past events in the present moment, the Bosnian War was not a historically predetermined *fait accompli*. For 2,000 years, the Balkan region intermittently suffered and flourished under various rulers. While the region's timeline is punctuated by episodic conflicts, it is also heavily peppered with periods of peace. Contemporary politicians could have selected narratives that reflected ethnic cooperation, yet these aspects of history were subordinated to a story riddled by conflict.

Second, the idea that the warring factions were clear-cut ethnic groups is misleading, and to treat these exaggerated categories as immutable feeds myths of inevitability. Although it is broadly true that there were three warring ethno-religious groups, these groups are not homogenous. Within each group exists subfactions with various goals, strategies, and beliefs. Yet, essential ethnic categorization was critical to politics and choices of both the warring factions and the international community, so it is crucial to understand ethnic constitution in this context.

Understanding Ethnicity

Unlike in the United States where "ethnicity" implies distinctive cultural traditions, physical traits, language, and history shared in unique combination, the ethnic groups in BiH (*e.g.*, Serbs, Croats, and Bosniaks) all share a common language, customs, and culture. Further, as all three groups are descendants of the same Slavic European racial stock, their ethnicity is physically indistinguishable, even to one another. So what distinguishes ethnicity? In some instances, each group's name or accent of speech, but even these are not absolute ethnic indicators. The definitive characteristic of ethnicity among these groups is religion. Although terms like "Serb" and "Croat" can shield the integration of religion and ethnicity (concealing religious overtones of nationalist reiterations of history), "Serbian" is synonymous with Orthodox Christianity and "Croatian" with Catholicism. While the immutable fixity of these categories is largely a contemporary phenomenon, many regional people believe the distinction is essential and timeless. It makes no difference if citizens do not practice their faith or their family has lived in Croatia for hundreds of years or even if an individual possesses Bosnian citizenship. A citizen is categorized as Croatian if Catholic and is not Catholic if Serbian. For example, orthodox Christians have lived in Croatia's Krajina region for over 600 years, yet they are still "Serbs."

In BiH, identity is slightly more complicated. Although ethnic identification waxed and waned throughout the centuries, Riedlmayer (1993) points out that until the late nineteenth century, people of all faiths were identified as Bosnian. However, as ethnic consciousness gained force in Croatia and Serbia, the situation in BiH changed. By the time of the Bosnian War, Catholic Bosnians identified as "Bosnian-Croats," and orthodox Bosnians as "Bosnian-Serbs." The third major ethnic group comprises Bosnians whose ancestors converted to Islam during the Ottomans. Formerly known as "Bosnian-Muslims," today the term "Bosniak" is often used to distance religion from ethno-national affiliation.

Still, people in BiH have lived in peaceful tolerance for most of the past 500 years (Riedlmayer 1993). Even as late as 1990, as war that consumed Croatia and Yugoslavia imploded, ethnic war in BiH was inconceivable to many. While it is disingenuous to claim that ethnic consciousness or tension was nonexistent before 1990, it is fair to say that ethnicity was rarely foremost for most individuals. People of all ethnicities shared schools and places of employment, mixing socially, professionally, and romantically. While other republics had clear ethnic majorities, BiH represented Yugoslavia's multi-ethnic essence where, according to a 1991 population census, nearly 44 percent of the population were identified as "Bosnian-Muslim," slightly over 30 percent as Serbs, around 7 percent as Croats, and the rest as "other" (Snyder *et al.* 2006). In fact, Riedlmayer (1993) reports that about one-third of urban marriages in twentieth-century BiH were between partners of different ethnic/religious backgrounds. In the build-up to and execution of the war, religion and history melded in polarizing ethno-nationalist discourses, exaggerating ethnic difference. With this in mind, I lay out the historical events relevant to the Bosnian War and offer details about the conflict, starting with early regional history.

Early History

Like the rest of the region, BiH was part of the Roman Empire, divided between Byzantium and other successors after Rome's decline. Croat and Serb kingdoms appeared in the ninth century, and after the split of the Church in 1054 AD, Serbs followed Orthodox Christianity, while Slovenes and Croats became Roman Catholics (Malcolm 1996). Emerging around 1200 AD, the first Bosnian independent state lasted over 250 years. During this time, the atmosphere was largely tolerant despite three vying Christian churches (e.g., Catholic, Orthodox, and a schismatic Bosnian Church). The first independent Serb state evolved at the end of the twelfth century and lasted for two centuries (Nikolic 2002). This period marks the emergence of modern Serbian national consciousness through legends of a glorious Serb nation savagely interrupted by invading Turk barbarians. Of primary legendary importance is the tale of the Battle of Kosovo of June 28, 1389 (St. Vitus Day).

The story of this battle is an epic struggle against hopeless odds, followed by betrayal and defeat. Yet, there is also a promise of rebirth and triumph. According to the myth, on the eve of battle, the prophet Elijah offered the Serbs a choice: Victory and an earthly kingdom or defeat but an eternal kingdom in heaven (Doder and Branson 1999). Choosing the heavenly kingdom, the Serbs then suffered 500 years of Turkish domination. But the story does not end there. The heroic Milos Obilic gives the subjugated Serbs a glimmer of hope. Feigning Turkish loyalty, he gains access to their camp. Obilic then bows to kiss the feet of Sultan Murad only to reveal a hidden dagger, killing the sultan and sacrificing his life for Serbian honor. This legend, from early oral tradition through nineteenth century literary standardization, is a precious subject of Serbian poetry, myth, and history, and forms the core of Serb nationalism (Nikolic 2002, 21).

Meanwhile, under Turkish rule, many Bosnians willingly converted to Islam and were rewarded with subsidized education, social programs, libraries, schools, and mosques. Modern Serbian hostility toward Bosniaks stems in part from an interpretation of this period as Bosnian treachery against Christianity and their Serbian brethren. Still, even under the Turkish rule, Bosnia was hardly an Islamic state (Malcom 1996). Some Bosnians chose Orthodoxy, some chose Catholicism, and those choosing Islam did so in a broad-minded way.

In 1878, the Bulgarians drove the vestiges of Turkish rule from the Balkans. Slovenia, Croatia, and much of modern-day BiH stayed under the Hapsburgs. Serbia again became independent. In response to the recurrent subjugation and division of the region's people came nineteenth-century politician Ilija Garasanin's dream of "Greater Serbia." He envisioned a unified nation for all Serbs, more akin to "Yugoslavia" than to its polarizing contemporary manifestation. In the 1980s and 1990s, the idea of Greater Serbia was abused by Serb nationalists to justify wars in Croatia and BiH, and by Serbia's enemies who demonized Garasanin as the founder of Serb nationalism. As two brief wars again reshuffled the territory in 1912 and 1913, a regional movement to realize Greater Serbia gathered strength. To thwart any potential uprising, Austro-Hungarian Archduke Franz Ferdinand traveled to Sarajevo. On June 28, 1914 (again St. Vitus Day), Greater Serbia activist, Gavorillo Princip, assassinated Ferdinand, heir to the Austrian throne. The struggle for Bosnia had provided the infamous spark that ignited World War I.

Two World Wars and the First Yugoslavia

The Serbs fought World War I with the Allies and, upon the signing of the Treaty of Corfu on January 6, 1919, Serbia led the new kingdom of the Slovenes, Croats, and Serbs—soon renamed the kingdom of Yugoslavia. In this state, Bosnians were not recognized "people." Catholic-Bosnians aligned with Croats, Orthodox-Bosnians with Serbs, and everyone else was forced to declare themselves as either a Serb or a Croat. This policy marked the beginning of divisive ethnic consciousness among Bosnians. It also bolstered the Serbian and Croatian nationalist demands in the 1990s to split BiH between them.

In 1941, the Nazis invading Yugoslavia were welcomed by the Ustase (Fascist Croatian nationalists). The Nazi policy viewed Serbs as *untermenschen* (subhuman), and Ustase proved to be willing executioners, imprisoning and murdering Serbs, Jews, Gypsies, and anti-fascist Croats with a zeal that shocked even the Nazis (Williams and Scharf 2002, 42). Memories of Ustase crimes resonated for decades, figuring prominently in nationalist politics of 1990s (Denitch 1994). Even with a brutal Ustase/Nazi campaign to exterminate Serbs, contemporary World War II narratives situating all Serbs as innocent lambs-to-slaughter are reductionist. Despite Serbia's official Allied association, a nationalist group loyal to Serbia's king, the Chetniks, fought for Serbian regional supremacy. Although the extent and degree of Ustase atrocities significantly eclipse Chetnik crimes, this does not mean Chetniks lacked a desire or capacity for viciousness. No less violent than Ustase and no less dogmatic, Chetniks committed their share of atrocities. Notably, Chetnik mayhem is not part of Serbian World War II narratives. A third regional force, Tito's communist Partisans, fought the Ustase and Chetniks to establish a unified nation for all South Slavs. In the war's later years, volunteers from all ethnic groups swelled the Partisans' ranks. In 1943, before the end of World War II in Europe, Partisan liberation gave birth to Tito's Socialist Federation of Yugoslavia.

Tito's Yugoslavia

Tito dealt quickly and harshly with Ustase criminals as well as some Chetniks and suspected "anti-Partisans," executing as many as 250,000 people between 1945 and 1946 (Malcolm 1996, 193). After this execution, public memory was cleansed of the war's atrocities and the Partisan struggle took precedence in World War II history: A narrative that sacrificed accuracy to foster broader national unity. From that point, people were expected to identify themselves as Yugoslavs, and "brotherhood and unity" was encouraged, if not enforced. Although Tito imposed restrictions on open religious displays, especially for Muslims, BiH was restored to pre-1918 borders and "Bosnian-Muslim" became a recognized ethnic group (neither Serb nor Croat). After adjusting to communism's restrictions, most Bosnians found that pan-Slavism suited their multi-ethnic society. Under Tito, tolerance was widespread and BiH thrived culturally, even hosting the 1984 Winter Olympics in Sarajevo.

Tito's constitution provided a system of checks and balances among the six republics to ensure peace and equality. He placed the seat of government in Belgrade but balanced the large Serbian Republic's power with the formation of two autonomous provinces, each with strong non-Slavic minorities (Vojvodina in North Serbia and Kosovo in South Serbia). In the 1980s, nationalists pointed to this decision as evidence of Serbia's historic victimization, subjugated by Turks, then Ustase, and then within Yugoslavia.

Tito died in 1980 at the age of eighty-eight, leaving no successor. Many people thought this was the end of Yugoslavia, but Yugoslavia lasted ten more years. According to the revised 1974 Constitution, post-Tito leadership would proceed with an annually rotating eight-member presidency (one from each republic and province). But when the Soviet Bloc disintegrated and Yugoslavia lost its strategic importance, the country faced an economic crisis without a strong leadership. Pan-Slavic "brotherhood and unity" dissolved as nationalism became a strategy for acquiring power. Yugoslav leaders quarreled over how the country should proceed. Republican and provincial leaders put ethnic interests above the collective interests of Yugoslavia (Judah 2000, 156). As Serbian nationalism percolated, "Yugoslavism came to be perceived as a Serbian attempt to blur the distinction between Yugoslavia and Serbia at the expense of the other republics" (Guzina 2003, 92). In the meantime, each of the Croatian and Serbian nationalists fed the other's paranoid fantasies, reinterpreting history for evidence of a present threat that the other posed.

This nationalism, predicated on impending victimization, caught on among Kosovo Serbs. The pro-nationalist Serbian press exacerbated instability with frequent reports of "persecution of the Kosovo Serbs" (Judah 2000, 156). Meanwhile, Orthodox clergy in conjunction with nationalist intellectuals claimed "that Kosovar Albanians were plotting to 'ethnically cleanse' Serbs from Kosovo" and were "plotting an Islamic state" (Sells 2003, 311). Furthering this fervor, in 1986 the Serbian Academy of Arts and Sciences (SANU) leaked to the Serbian press a memorandum claiming that Tito had purposely subordinated Serbs within Yugoslavia, that Kosovar-Albanians were plotting genocide, and that Croats were plotting a Ustase rerun. Hence the need for Greater Serbia was stronger than ever. Serbian president Ivan Stambolic, a staunch Titoist, condemned the memorandum's chauvinistic tendencies but the document's criticism of Serbian leaders had led the public to mistrust his leadership. The memorandum proved substantially divisive, later guiding the policies of Slobodan Milosevic–a significant actor in any account of the Bosnian War.

The Rise of Milosevic

Born in 1941 during the Nazi occupation, Milosevic grew up in Tito's Yugoslavia (Scharf and Schabas 2002, 5). At university, Milosevic met his closest friend and most crucial political contact, Ivan Stambolic (Judah 2000, 161). Stambolic brought Milosevic with him at every step of his career. By 1985, Stambolic was Serbia's president and Milosevic was Serbia's Communist Party leader. Throughout 1986, public controversy over the SANU memorandum raged, coloring Serbian impressions of the problems in Kosovo. By 1987, the Serbian press "exposed" creeping Islamic fundamentalism in BiH while sensational reports of forced exodus and discrimination against the Serbs in Kosovo increased tensions between Kosovo Serbs and the ethnic Albanian majority. Stambolic sent his protege to stabilize Kosovo (Sell 2002). This was the defining moment of Milosevic's political career and the beginning of Stambolic's end.

Upon arriving in Kosovo, a group of Serbs confronted Milosevic, alleging that Albanian police had mistreated and beat them. Milosevic assured that "no one will be allowed to beat the Serbs again . . . no one." Taken out of context and rebroadcast on Serbian television ad nauseam, this line catapulted Milosevic into public favor of the Serbs. Re-contextualized in the tenor of the Kosovo myth, this allusion to historic victimization was not lost on Serbian audiences, many of whom were feeling drawn to nationalist ideas. Riding this wave of media attention, in a September 1987 televised session of parliament, Milosevic called for a "vote of no confidence" on Stambolic's presidency, dismissing his lifelong mentor on national television.

Immediately after Stambolic's ousting, Serbian media intensified its stories of history's injustices against Serbs, framing stories in the tenor of the SANU memorandum. Milosevic seized the opportunity to solidify power. Staging rallies throughout Serbia, he encouraged ethno-national consciousness and promoted the idea of Greater Serbia (Silber and Little 1995). Milosevic "promised to unite Serbs dispersed throughout Yugoslavia whose fate he claimed Croat or Muslim majorities threatened" (Duffy and Lindstrom 2002, 78). By March 1989, Serbia was the strongest of the republics. Milosevic put allies in office in Kosovo and Vojvodina and was soon able to change the constitution to revoke the autonomic status of both the provinces. When allies assumed the Montenegrin and Macedonian presidencies, Milosevic controlled the Federation. He celebrated his new power with a grand televised display of nationalism and an inflammatory speech delivered at the 600th anniversary of the Battle of Kosovo. In 1990 under popular pressure, Croatia and Slovenia held their first democratic elections. Slovenia formed a multi-party coalition with former communist, Milan Kucan, as president. In Croatia, nationalist Democratic Union leader Franjo Tudjman won a decisive victory.

Franjo Tudjman and the Road to War in Croatia

Born in 1922, Tudjman served Tito's Partisans, becoming one of the youngest soldiers in Yugoslavia's National Army (JNA). Beginning in the 1970s, Tudjman often spoke against Serbian nationalism, was an outspoken anti-Semite, and expressed sympathies with the Ustase. Tudjman became Croatia's president, and he "mobilized Croats around a historic quest for self-determination," rallying nationalism with "the promise that he would restore Croatian national pride and reverse the discrimination that Croats allegedly suffered in Yugoslavia" (Duffy and Lindstrom 2002, 73–74). Extending his appeal, Tudjman fostered Croatia's image as "the buttress for Europe against the barbaric forces of the East, Orthodoxy and Islam" (Sells 2003, 314).

In many ways, Tudjman was Milosevic's nationalist counterpart. Both the leaders strategically employed media to advance their agenda. Also mirroring Milosevic, Tudjman reinterpreted Croatian history as a grand narrative of continuous struggle, positing "historical developments of the twentieth century in a monotonous and monolithic line of events that logically ends with the proclamation of the independence of Croatia" (Brkljacic 2003, 42). Intensified by threatening discourse toward Krajina-Serbs, Croatian nationalism fed Serbian nationalism.

Yugoslavia Disintegrates into War

By 1990, Milosevic's popularity in Serbia spurred nationalism in other republics (Scharf and Schabas 2002). Slovenia and Croatia resisted Milosevic's efforts to keep Yugoslavia unified under his control, advocating instead for loosely confederated republics and diffused Serb power. Ironically, in this period, BiH alone strove to preserve Yugoslavia's multi-ethnic balance (Judah 2000, 165). The elections in BiH in 1990 resulted in a government with all major ethnic groups represented in approximate proportion to the population.

In the spring of 1991, Milosevic blocked Croat Stipe Mesic's presidential rotation, deepening republican rifts beyond repair. Recognizing the futility of continuing in a unified Yugoslavia, Croatia and Slovenia declared independence on June 25, 1991 (Croatia provocatively adopted the Ustase flag.) As few Serbs lived in Slovenia, their struggle for independence lasted just ten days. Macedonia declared independence in September, seceding peacefully. Milosevic could handle losing Slovenia, even Macedonia, as neither contained large Serbian populations. Croatia, as part of Greater Serbia, was another story. "Serbian attention turned to . . . Croatia, where ethnic Serbs comprised a significant minority" (Duffy and Lindstrom 2002, 75).

The War in Croatia

In the month following the declaration of Croatian independence, Croatia's Krajina-Serbs, claiming that they were threatened by the Croatian nationalist system, declared an independent state. The Croats battled to control the region but Milosevic sent the JNA to defend Krajina's Serbs. The conflict expanded and "by September 1991, Croatia and the Serb-controlled JNA were at war" (Duffy and Lindstrom 2002, 75). The poorly armed and organized Croat forces were no match for the Serbs who, under the auspices of the JNA, were better armed and organized. Following heavy casualties, Croat forces quickly ceded a third of Croatian territory. In addition to the violence in Krajina and the siege of border towns like Vukovar, the JNA's characteristic strategy involved extensive shelling, as in the seven-month siege on the ancient city of Dubrovnik. Croatian War officially ended in 1992 but fighting persisted in Krajina until 1995, with civilian atrocities on both sides continuing in alternating cycles of ethnic cleansing. In all, Amnesty International estimates as many as 20,000 people from both sides were killed, and as many as 600,000 were displaced from 1991 to 1995. More than 20,000 Croats and 150,000 Serbs are still missing or displaced.

Throughout the Croatian War, Tudjman and Milosevic escalated their symbiotic nationalism. Tudjman's treatment of Krajina-Serbs fed Milosevic's assertions of Serbs under threat. Milosevic's call for Greater Serbia intensified as Tudjman dismissed Serbs from official positions and prohibited the Cyrillic script. Moreover, Tudjman's "resurrection of symbols that Croatia had used during World War II, when it was a Nazi quisling state, aided Milosevic's efforts to mobilize constituents" (Duffy and Lindstrom 2002, 79).

The Bosnian War 1992–1995

The Croatian War was horrific, but the most excessive brutality was yet to come. "By the time the violence reached BiH, the Serb forces were initiated into killing on the basis of religious identity" (Sells 2003, 314). Mass rape, forced deportation, and concentration camps were norms of the Bosnian War.

Serbs, Croats, and Bosniaks each committed atrocities to varying degrees and the international community also played a part. Even after the secession of Slovenia and Croatia, BiH naively imagined a place in a multi-ethnic Yugoslav Federation. Yet with the escalating violence in Croatia and increasingly vocal demands for Greater Serbia, the situation in BiH grew progressively tenuous. With the promise of international support, on March 1, 1992, the BiH people overwhelmingly voted for independence, and on April 6, 1992, the United States and the European Union recognized BiH's statehood under Bosniak president Alija Izetbegovic.

Bosnia under Alija Izetbegovic

Born in 1925, Izetbegovic was a lawyer, activist, author, and politician. He did not take part in World War II and was jailed for three years in 1946 as "anti-communist." Although his family upheld many Muslim traditions, his upbringing and mentality were secular, and he felt that Islamic cultural principles could enrich secular life. Still, even though Izetbegovic openly advocated multi-ethnic tolerance, nationalists used his ethno-religious identity and secular Islamic writing as evidence that he led a dangerous fundamentalist movement. In 1988, Izetbegovic founded the largely Bosniak Party of Democratic Action (SDA). In 1989, the SDA won the largest share of parliamentary votes in the Socialist BiH Republic, followed by the Bosnian-Serb and Bosnian-Croat parties. Together, they organized a presidency in which two representatives from each ethnic group and a seventh self-identified "Yugoslav" would serve, rotating the leadership. As Yugoslavia disintegrated, the Serbian and Croatian representatives abdicated. Izetbegovic remained president, hoping to preserve a multi-ethnic BiH. When the chauvinistic agenda of Serb-dominated Yugoslavia showed no signs of yielding, Izetbegovic ordered the independence referendum. Bosnian-Serbs resisted the split, abstaining from the vote. Upon BiH's declaration of independence, the Bosnian-Serbs under the leadership of Radovan Karadzic proclaimed an independent *Republika Srpska.*

Bosnian-Serb Leadership

Radovan Karadzic was a successful Freudian-trained psychiatrist prior to his political career. He was a master of myth and propaganda, fostering ethnic division and intolerance. In the early 1990s, before his presidency, Karadzic held meetings in which he warned the thousands of attendees of an impending Bosniak genocidal conspiracy against Serbs. He was as well-known for explicit threats against Bosniaks as he was for his desire to be perceived positively in Western media. He speaks excellent English and talked freely to the international press, though often his interviews were outright lies.

Karadzic had two political partners in crime, Biljana Plavsic and Momcilo Krajisnik. Known more for cruelty than intellectual prowess, Krajisnik was one of two vice-presidents under Karadzic. Despite indictment for war crimes, Krajisnik was a member of the post-war Bosnian presidency from

1996 to 1998. Karadzic's other vice-president, Plavsic, was the least powerful of the three but in some ways the most interesting. Known as the "Serbian Iron Lady," Plavsic was a geneticist and Sarajevo University professor before becoming the first female BiH president in the period 1990–1992. After the war, she assumed the presidency of *Republika Srpska* from 1996 to 1998.

There is little evidence of Plavsic's nationalism before1986. Still, her later nationalist discourse was regarded excessive even by infamous paramilitary commander and Serbian Radical Party (SRS) leader, Vojislav Seslj. Invoking her scientific background, Plavsic demonized Bosniaks through references to a fundamentalist threat genetically inherent in their "race." While Plavsic's arguments were "preposterous by the standards of the scientific discipline that she had long practiced," they were accepted as truth in the phantasmagoric environment of Serb nationalism (Sells 2003, 312). Further to incendiary statements, Plavsic was well known for publicly praising the "heroism" of paramilitary leader and ostentatious war profiteer "Arkan" (Zeljko Raznatovic) whose excessive violence against Croats and Bosniaks is nearly as notorious as his reputation in Serbia's organized crime underworld.

The Theater of War

Sporadic violence punctuated the month between the referendum and international recognition of BiH sovereignty. On March 2, 1992, as the referendum's results were announced, Serb paramilitary forces surrounded Sarajevo, retreating when thousands of citizens braved sniper fire to protest (Malcolm 1996, 235). While some of Sarajevo's citizens celebrated this sign of hope, Eastern Bosnia was already enveloped in violence. By the end of March, a Serbian paramilitary group known as "Arkan's Tigers" seized the town of Banja Luka. By April, they had laid siege to the town of Bijeljina, cutting off water and electricity and indiscriminately slaughtering Bosniaks. Other paramilitary groups like "Seslj's Chetniks" and "Jovic's White Eagles" subjected more towns to the same treatment (Malcolm 1995, 236). Their cleansing tactics were as ruthless as the propaganda of their political counterparts. Radio Television Belgrade (and eventually the media in Banja Luka) portrayed Croat bodies and burning Bosniak villages as Serbian victims, rather than victims of the Serbs, thus supporting claims of impending Ustase and fundamentalist Muslim terror. This manipulation ensured that a radicalized and fearful population stood behind Serb forces, framed as heroic defenders of the Serb people.

On April 5, 1992, Serb forces again surrounded Sarajevo and were confronted by 50,000 to 100,000 multi-ethnic protestors (Malcolm 1996, 235). This time, Serb forces opened fire on the demonstrators, marking Sarajevo's first casualty and the beginning of the four-year siege of Sarajevo. In the meantime, JNA forces were bombing various Bosnian towns into surrender while paramilitary forces took care of the "clean-up." By the end of April 1992, 95 percent of Bosniaks had been cleansed from Kupres, Doboj, Tuzla, Zvornik, Visegrad, and Foca, giving Serbs control of 60 to 70 percent of BiH (Malcolm 1996, 237).

In the first month of conflict, Milosevic claimed that JNA troops were defending Yugoslavia. In early May, Milosevic declared a new Yugoslavia consisting of Serbia and Montenegro. The JNA officially withdrew from BiH, leaving behind weapons, supplies, and Bosnian JNA soldiers as well as paramilitary units. General Ratko Mladic commanded the former JNA soldiers who became the Army of *Republika Srpska* (VRS), and Milosevic supplied resources to the JNA throughout the war. Still, the JNA's official withdrawal was enough to placate Western politicians and journalists who were quick to characterize the violence as inevitable civil war among three equally equipped ethnic groups who had been fighting for centuries.

Additionally, because of a United Nations arms embargo, the Army of BiH (ARBiH) and the Bosnian-Croat Army (HVO) were ill-prepared for war. With Serbian support and JNA weapons, the VRS was not affected by the embargo. The HVO could smuggle weapons by sea. The ARBiH was largely defenseless. Though they sometimes captured VRS weapons through ambush, the ARBiH had no heavy artillery. In September 1992, the ARBiH possessed two tanks and two armored personnel carriers to the VRS's "300 tanks, 200 [armored personnel carriers], 800 artillery pieces and 40 aircraft" (Malcolm 1996, 243). Though a year later, the ARBiH had "40 tanks and 30 APCs," the VRS still far out-manned and out-gunned them, as did the HVO's "roughly 50 tanks and more than 100 artillery pieces" (Hoare 2007, 392). Further, even in its early days, the VRS had 80,000 soldiers, while the ARBiH had only 3,500 (Malcolm 1996, 239–40). The HVO was better prepared—15,000 Croat paramilitaries from Herzegovina joined the Croatian Army during the 1991–92 Croatian War. When combined with 15,000 Bosnian-Croats, early resistance to the JNA in Mostar and the VRS in Northern BiH was feasible.

In the war's initial days, the HVO claimed to be fighting for Bosnia and therefore allied with ARBiH. Still, despite early suggestions of Bosniak/Croat cooperation, Izetbegovic was skeptical. Back in 1991, Tudjman had demanded an autonomous state for Bosnian-Croats. Given his open call for Greater Croatia and rumors of collusion with Milosevic to divide BiH, Croatian intentions were suspect. Izetbegovic's suspicions proved to be accurate. By May 1992, the HVO and the VRS were both fighting the ARBiH. At the same time, Bosnian-Croats abandoned large areas to Serbs in apparent support of the dual chauvinistic dreams of Greater Serbia and Greater Croatia. This agreement was short lived, however, as the Croats vacillated between pursuing Greater Croatia and defending their territory against the VRS. Before long, a tripartite war raged.

Casualties of War

Within the first year, VRS forces gained a large part of BiH and Serb atrocities against Bosniaks and Croats were widespread. In spring 1992, three notorious Serbian-run concentration camps emerged—Keraterm, Omarska, and Trnoplje. At these camps, Bosniaks and Croats, often civilians, were imprisoned in appalling conditions, and subjected to torture, starvation, and sometimes execution. Furthermore, in 1992 Bosniak women "arriving in refugee camps in Croatia began reporting that they had been raped by Serbian men…Eighty percent of the rapes are said to have occurred in detention camps" (Engle 2005, 784–785).

While men and women in all camps suffered sexual violence, specific camps were dedicated to mass rape, most notably in Foca. The International Criminal Tribunal for the former Yugoslavia (ICTY) estimates that from 1992 to 1995, VRS and paramilitary soldiers raped between 20,000 and 50,000 women and girls, some as young as twelve, as part of a systematic plan to terrorize and destroy the Bosniak community (Ramet 2002, 67). Moreover, as Serbian culture is patrilineal, women were often impregnated (with "Serb babies") and held until it was too late to terminate pregnancy. Adding to their humiliation, the women were domestic slaves to the soldiers. Survivors continue to carry psychological trauma and physical health problems to this day.

Early in the war, Serb soldiers committed the lion's share of atrocities, but soon HVO and ARBiH soldiers became equally vicious. All three sides set up detention/concentration camps in schools, hospitals, and churches. By 1993, reports of HVO camps for Serbs and Bosniaks had surfaced. Most notoriously, after cleansing several towns and destroying all remnants of non-Croat culture, HVO forces imprisoned and massacred Serb and Bosniak civilians at camps in Ahmici and Stupni Do (Hoare 2007, 373). While Serbs were the most frequent perpetrators of systemic war rape, HVO and ARBiH soldiers also used "rape warfare."

There are also many reported ARBiH atrocities against Croats and Serbs (most famously under Naser Oric). During 1992–93, ARBiH forces brutally attacked Konjic, Visoko, Bratunac, and Srebrenica burning villages, and expelling and torturing civilians. These rogue elements of the ARBiH were brought under control in 1993 but by that autumn other ARBiH factions had perpetrated similar atrocities in Central Bosnia and Northern Herzegovina (Hoare 2007, 383). As they became better organized, more frequent reports of ARBiH crimes emerged. By the end of 1994, all sides were committing atrocities, though the extent to which this was an organized command mandate seems less clear for ARBiH soldiers than for the VRS and HVO.

Throughout 1993, the ARBiH managed to drive back the VRS in a few spots, most notably in the Bihac pocket (Malcolm 1996, 254). This was made possible partly through their year of combat experience, partly through weapons captured in ambushes and partly through clandestine foreign assistance. Sequestered under siege in Sarajevo, Izetbegovic became impatient with Western promises of assistance. With plenty of able-bodied men but no money or weapons, Izetbegovic appealed for help to Muslim nations, which sent limited weapons and supplies, and some uninvited volunteers. While actual numbers are disputed (the ICTY estimates between 300 to 1,500), it is clear that none of the warring parties were happy to see the foreign fighters, whose presence created strategic control problems for Izetbegovic. Meanwhile, Serb media reports of "mujahedeen jihad" fanned the flames of an already thriving bonfire of fear.

In 1993, the Vance-Owen Peace plan proposed dividing BiH: Forty-three percent to Serbs, 25 percent to Croats, and 23 percent to Bosniaks (with the remaining 9 percent designated as multi-ethnic). After much negotiation, the plan failed (Hoare 2007). Another round of negotiations were held in summer of 1993. It was decided that BiH's 2 million Bosniaks would be concentrated into "safe-areas" protected by a UN Protection Force (UNPROFOR) with a mandate to fire only when deliberately attacked. The rest of BiH was divided between Serbs and Croats. Both Tudjman on behalf of the Croats and Milosevic for the Serbs agreed to the arrangement. Izetbegovic was not even consulted.

Meanwhile, Serb forces had surrounded Sarajevo for nearly four years, cutting off water, electricity, and contact with the outside world. Although Serb forces never fully captured the city, sporadic bombing and indiscriminate sniper fire were daily happenings for Sarajevo's citizens. A particularly gruesome attack in May 1992 killed sixteen civilians who had queued for bread, but the VRS adamantly denied responsibility for the attack. Finally, when a February 1994 attack on Sarajevo's open-air market killed sixty-eight people, North Atlantic Treaty Organization (NATO) took a more proactive role, threatening air strikes on Serb positions.

In March 1994, the United States mediated an agreement between the HVO and ARBiH to join forces against the VRS (Hoare 2007, 383). Now there was an UNPROFOR presence, NATO air strikes, and a Bosniak-Croat coalition. Everything pointed to the beginning of the end. Yet the war's final year saw some of the worst atrocities. The siege of Sarajevo intensified and towns throughout BiH forcibly changed hands (most for a second or third time). Furthermore, despite promises, neither the UN nor NATO protected the safe areas. Their inaction allowed for the only officially recognized "genocide" in Europe since the 1948 UN Convention. More than a powerful testimony to war's cruelty, the events of the 1995 Srebrenica massacre are a microcosm of the Bosnian War.

In March 1994, as part of UNPROFOR, 600 Dutch soldiers (DutchBat) were dispatched to protect safe-area Srebrenica where as many as 60,000 Bosniak refugees had expanded the town's pre-war population by 10,000-fold (Rohde 1998). By winter 1995, Serbian forces controlled the surrounding territory, cutting off Srebrenica from rest of the world. On July 7, 1995, Mladic led troops into Srebrenica. When the UN denied requests for air support, DutchBat commander, Lieutenant-Colonel Thom Karremans, negotiated with Mladic. On July 10, they reached an agreement—the Serbs would evacuate the Bosniaks on buses, and the UN would pay for gasoline. Realizing that DutchBat would not protect them, 15,000 Bosniak men fled through the mountains (Feher 2000). Through that night and the next day, Mladic's soldiers separated the remaining men from the women and children. DutchBat soldiers maintained calm, kept Bosniaks separated, and loaded the buses. The women were taken to Bosniak territory only to wait in vain for their men. From July 12 to 17, 8,000 to 10,000 Bosniak men were slaughtered and thrown into mass graves. For the next two weeks, those who had fled were hunted and killed.

The International Community and the Final Toll

The Srebrenica massacre points to a crucial role played by the international community. Throughout most of the war, Western media misunderstood and misrepresented the conflict. At the same time, leaders who could have intervened were as clueless about the situation and region as their publics, often taking Milosevic's rhetoric at face value. As such, the international community perceived the warring factions as equal, primitive, and irrationally violent, and failed to lift the arms embargo.

Moreover, the decisions and (in)actions of the UN exacerbated the crisis in many instances. In 1992, a UN headquarters was in place in Sarajevo to direct peacekeeping in Croatia. However, when the Bosnian War began, Secretary-General Boutros-Ghali declined to send a peacekeeping operation and by May 1992, UN presence had evaporated. Although UNPROFOR was eventually deployed, their mandate was largely observational and humanitarian, and they were not permitted to engage unless explicitly provoked. This meant that UNPROFOR were often bystanders to the worst atrocities. Even humanitarian efforts were plagued by error and incompetence. Although aid convoys offered some relief, lack of regional knowledge resulted in unfortunate consequences. Local militias "taxed" aid transports, taking as much as 50 percent. UNPROFOR was lightly armed and the VRS easily hijacked aid convoys, confiscating UN weapons and vehicles. Further, when air drops were attempted, the pallets often dropped miles away from their targets, forcing civilians to risk reaching the dropped pallets through rough terrain, landmines, and snipers.

Overall, throughout the conflict the West stood impotent, offering ineffectual diplomatic solutions and weak military assistance. From the arms embargo to botched peacekeeping and bungled attempts to broker peace, the international community vacillated from bystander to peace obstacle. Still, the international community did disable Serb forces in late 1995 and after several years of negotiation, finally brokered the Dayton Agreement, which ended the Bosnian War in December 1995. While no one was fully satisfied, the United States pressured leaders of Serbia, Croatia, and the three Bosnian entities to agree. BiH would be a single state divided into two nations: A Muslim-Croat Federation containing 51 percent of BiH (including Sarajevo) and *Republika Srpska* with 49 percent (Hoare 2007, 398).

Conclusions

By the end of the war, hundreds of thousands of innocent civilians were traumatized. ICTY estimates as many as 50 percent of Muslim-Croat Federation homes were damaged and 6 percent decimated. Twenty-five percent of *Republika Srpska* homes were damaged and 5 percent decimated. Additionally, more than half of the 2 million displaced civilians have not returned. The Documentation Center in Sarajevo reports the figures as 93,837 for dead, of which 63,687 are Bosniaks (30,514 civilians), 24,216 Serbs (1,978 civilians), 5,057 Croats (2,076 civilians), and 877 others (Hoare 2007, 398). ICTY figures differ slightly, claiming 102,622 deaths—28,000 ARBiH, 6,000 HVO, and 4,000 VRS as well as 38,000 Bosniak and Croat civilians, and 16,700 Serb civilians. Add the 326 UNPROFOR casualties and one thing is clear: There were no winners in this war.

Today, an uneasy peace exists in BiH between the two states within one nation, and the physical, emotional, and social scars of war still mar the landscape. Many refugees are afraid to return to their pre-war homes. Bosnian schools often maintain a "two schools under one roof" policy, separating children of different ethnic backgrounds. Further, people's views are still frequently shaped by ethnically biased local media. In the Muslim-Croat Federation, there is some physical restoration and social repair, only evident when juxtaposed with the extreme poverty and lack of physical and social regeneration in *Republika Srpska*. Still, the region fumbles toward recovery, and purging war-time political and military leaders is important to this process. While nationalists can still garner some support, their power is limited at best, and as discussed in Chapter 6, the ICTY has dealt with the "biggest fish" on all sides.

References

Brkljacic, Maja. 2003. "What Past Is Present?" *International Journal of Politics, Culture, and Society* 17:41–52.

Burke, Kenneth. 1945. *A Grammar of Motives*. Berkeley, CA: University of California Press.

Burke, Kenneth. 1935. *Permanence and Change: An Anatomy of Purpose*. New York: New Republic, Inc.

Denitch, Bogdan. 1994. *Ethnic Nationalism: The Tragic Death of Yugoslavia*. Minneapolis, MN: University of Minnesota Press.

Doder, Dusko, and Louise Branson. 1999. *Milosevic: Portrait of a Tyrant*. New York: Free Press.

Duffy, Gavin, and Nicole Lindstrom. 2002. "Conflicting Identities: Solidary Incentives in the Serbo-Croatian War." *Journal of Peace Research* 39:69–90.

Engle, Karen. 2005. "Feminism and Its (Dis)contents: Criminalizing Wartime Rape in Bosnia and Herzegovina." *The American Journal of International Law* 99:778–816.

Feher, Michael. 2000. *Powerless by Design: The Age of the International Community*. Durham, NC: Duke University Press.

Guzina, Dejan. 2003. "Socialist Serbia's Narratives: From Yugoslavia to a Greater Serbia." *International Journal of Politics, Culture, and Society* 17:91–111.

Hoare, Marko A. 2007. *The History of Bosnia: From the Middle Ages to the Present Day*. London: Saqi Books.

Judah, Tim. 2000. *The Serbs: History, myth and the destruction of Yugoslavia*. New Haven, CT: Yale University Press.

Kurspahic, Kemal. 2003. *Prime Time Crime: Balkan Media in War and Peace*. Washington, D.C.: Institute of Peace Press.

Malcolm, Noel. 1996. *Bosnia: A Short History*. London: Macmillan.

Mertus, Julie. 1999. *Kosovo: How Myths and Truths Started a War*. Berkeley, CA: University of California Press.

Nikolic, Milos. 2002. *The Tragedy of Yugoslavia*. Baden-Baden: European Trade Institute Press.

Ramet, Sabrina. 2002. *Balkan Babel: The Disintegration of Yugoslavia from the Death of Tito to the Fall of Milosevic*. Boulder, CO: Westview Press.

Rhine, Staci L., Stephen E. Bennett, and Richard S. Flickinger. 2001. "Gaps in Americans' Knowledge About the Bosnian Civil War." *American Politics Research* 29:592–607.

Riedlmayer, Andras. 1993. *A Brief History of Bosnia-Herzegovina*. Available at: www.kakarigi.net/manu/briefhis.htm.

Rieff, David. 1995. *Slaughterhouse: Bosnia and the Failure of the West*. New York: Touchstone.

Rohde, David. 1998. *Endgame: The Betrayal and Fall of Srebrenica, Europe's Worst Massacre since World War II*. Boulder, CO: Westview Press.

Scharf, Michael. P. 2002. *Slobodan Milosevic on Trial: A Companion*. New York: Continuum.

Sell, Louis. 2002. *Slobodan Milosevic and the Destruction of Yugoslavia.* Durham, NC: Duke University Press.

Sells, Michael. 2003. "Crosses of Blood: Sacred Space, Religion, and Violence in Bosnia-Hercegovina." *Sociology of Religion* 64:309–331.

Silber, Laura, and Alan Little. 1996. *The Death of Yugoslavia.* London: BBC/Penguin Books.

Snyder, Cindy. S., Wesley J. Gabbard, J. Dean May, and Nihada Zulcic. 2006. "On the Battleground of Women's Bodies: Mass Rape in Bosnia-Herzegovina." *Affilia* 21:184–195.

Williams, Paul R. 2002. *Peace with Justice? War Crimes and Accountability in Former Yugoslavia.* Oxford: Rowman & Littlefield.

CHAPTER 6

Transitional Justice in Bosnia: The International Criminal Tribunal for the Former Yugoslavia

JANINE NATALYA CLARK

Introduction

Since the mid-1990s, criminal prosecutions have become an increasingly common international response to the complex and vexed question of how to deal with human rights violations. Whereas amnesia and amnesty were in the past considered acceptable and in some cases necessary as remedies for human rights violations, today the emphasis is very strongly on individual accountability. Criminal trials have thus become a core transitional justice mechanism, to which the steady proliferation of war crimes tribunals attests. The spread of these tribunals, in turn, reflects the growing expectations of retributive justice and its role in post-conflict societies. It must, however, be emphasized that while the virtues of criminal trials have been widely extolled, "seldom are such assertions grounded in empirical data" (Weinstein and Stover 2004, 4). Empirical research in this area is thus essential: The imputed merits of war crimes tribunals cannot be simply assumed.

This chapter focuses on the first international tribunal created since Nuremberg, the International Criminal Tribunal for the former Yugoslavia (ICTY). It explores and analyzes the ICTY's impact in the country that has been the focus of so much of its work, Bosnia and Herzegovina (BiH), and draws upon the author's extensive fieldwork in the country.[1] This chapter's central argument is that while the tribunal is an important transitional justice mechanism for BiH, it also has significant limitations, thus underscoring that we should not rely too heavily upon criminal trials and retributive justice. Trials have a fundamental role to play in post-conflict societies, yet they "should not be held up as some kind of panacea for righting past wrongs or as a 'magic bullet' for 'healing' victims and war-torn societies" (Weinstein and Stover 2004, 5).

Background to the ICTY

As Yugoslavia disintegrated, unable to withstand the pressure of so many centrifugal forces tearing it apart, a lone voice called for the creation of an international war crimes tribunal. In an article entitled "Nuremberg Now?" published in the Serbian newspaper *Borba* on May 16, 1991, Mirko Klarin, the co-founder and editor-in-chief of the South East News Service Europe news agency, argued that it was necessary to establish such a tribunal before the outbreak of an armed conflict. If some people were planning and preparing for war, he maintained, it was necessary to set up the tribunal sooner rather than later (Klarin 2001, 97). Klarin's appeals, however, went unheeded and the following month, Slovenia and Croatia declared their independence from Yugoslavia. War had begun.

As discussed in Chapter 5, BiH was a microcosm of Yugoslavia itself, epitomizing Tito's "brotherhood and unity." BiH is most ethnically mixed of all the former Yugoslav republics[2]; inter-ethnic marriages were common, and few people expected the war to spread to BiH. After Slovenia and Croatia seceded from Yugoslavia, however, Bosnia's leadership feared being left in a rump Yugoslavia dominated by Serbia and its president, Slobodan Milosevic. After a referendum on independence in February 1992, BiH declared independence on April 6, 1992. It was the start of a bloody three-year war that claimed thousands of victims[3] and forced 2.2 million people to flee their prewar homes (BiH Ministry for Human Rights and Refugees 2005, 21).

"Something Must be Done"

In the summer of 1992, amid growing calls for "something to be done" in BiH, the idea of establishing an international tribunal for the former Yugoslavia began to take shape. The United Nations Security Council Resolution 764 (July 13, 1992) warned that violations of international humanitarian law in the former Yugoslavia would result in the perpetrators being held individually responsible. The next month, following the broadcast of an ITN footage on August 6, 1992 showing emaciated Bosnian Muslim prisoners interned in the Omarska concentration camp in Northwest BiH, UN Security Council Resolution 771 (13 August 1992) called upon states and international human rights organizations to submit to the Security Council any "substantiated information" of war crimes in the former Yugoslavia. At the London Conference on August 26, 1992, the German minister of foreign affairs, Klaus Kinkel, opined that an international court must be created. The French government strongly concurred with this opinion and subsequently sponsored the UN Security Council Resolution 780 (October 6, 1992), which set up a Commission of Experts, headed by M. Cherif Bassiouni, to provide its conclusions on the evidence of war crimes in the former Yugoslavia.

It was during this period that the U.S. government also began to advocate the creation of a war crimes tribunal. In mid-December 1992, Secretary of State Lawrence Eagleburger delivered his "Naming of Names" speech in Geneva, in which he announced that the U.S. government had identified ten suspected war criminals (including Milosevic, Radovan Karadzic, the

Bosnian Serb leader, and Ratko Mladic, the commander of the Bosnian Serb Army) who should stand trial for war crimes. In its preliminary report, submitted on January 26, 1993, the Commission of Experts similarly expressed the need for an international criminal tribunal. The ultimate decision to establish a tribunal was made on February 22, 1993 with the adoption of UN Security Council Resolution 808. Article One of this resolution declared that the tribunal would prosecute "persons responsible for serious violations of international law, committed in the territory of the former Yugoslavia since 1991." The ICTY was officially established and its statute adopted on May 25, 1993 (UN Security Council Resolution 827).

The traditional mode of creating an international body is based on a treaty but this "was discarded as being too slow (possibly taking many years to reach full ratification) and insufficiently effective as Member States could not be forced to ratify such a treaty against their wishes" (Cassese 1994, 7). Instead, the ICTY was set up under Chapter VII of the UN Charter, on the basis that the UN Security Council judged the situation in the former Yugoslavia to constitute a threat to international peace and security. However, since the Security Council is an executive body with no authority to establish courts, however, questions were immediately raised regarding the tribunal's legitimacy (Johnstone 2002; Dickson and Jokic 2006; Laughland 2007). Some ICTY defendants have themselves challenged its legality, most notably the late Milosevic, who consistently refused to recognize the tribunal's authority.

When the ICTY was first set up, it also faced considerable skepticism. It was not taken seriously and few imagined that it would become a fully functioning institution (Goldstone 2000, 77; Klarin 2004, 547). This lack of confidence in the tribunal, moreover, was not wholly unfounded. To cite Cassese, the ICTY's first president: "Our borrowed robes symbolized the total lack of infrastructures or facilities at our disposal. We had no seat, no courtroom, no prison, no budget, no computers, no law clerks, no secretaries and no set of rules governing the criminal procedure" (2004, 585). No comprehensive assessment of the ICTY can therefore overlook just how far it has come since its inception. Ultimately, what it has demonstrated is that "an international criminal justice system is feasible" (Jorda 2004, 584).

Structure and Jurisdiction

The tribunal, which is located in The Hague in the Netherlands, consists of three main organs. The Office of the Prosecutor (OTP) is responsible for preparing indictments and investigating and prosecuting cases. It is led by the chief prosecutor, currently Serge Brammertz, who is elected by the UN Security Council for a renewable four-year term. The Chambers hear the evidence presented by the prosecution and defense, issue judgments, and impose custodial sentences on those accused who are found guilty. The ICTY has a detention unit where defendants are held prior to and during their trials. It does not, however, have its own prison. Once sentenced, therefore, defendants are transferred to prisons in countries that have signed agreements with the tribunal on the enforcement of sentences, including Britain, Italy, France,

Germany, Spain, and Sweden. The maximum sentence that the ICTY judges can impose is life imprisonment. There is no death penalty. The Chambers have sixteen permanent judges and a maximum of twelve *ad litem* judges who are appointed to hear particular, more specialized cases. ICTY trials do not involve a jury. Three judges sit in each case, one of whom is the presiding judge and is responsible for overseeing the proceedings. Five judges hear appeals. The ICTY has three trial chambers and one appeals chamber. The judges, all of whom are from outside the former Yugoslavia, are appointed by the UN General Assembly. The tribunal's permanent judges, in turn, elect the ICTY's president, currently Judge Patrick Robinson from Jamaica, who presides over all appeals proceedings and plenary sessions. Finally, the Registry is responsible for public information, security, and management of the tribunal, including interpretation and translation, protection of witnesses, and supervision of detainees. As of January 13, 2009, 1,129 people were employed at the ICTY, representing eighty-four different nationalities.

The ICTY has jurisdiction to prosecute four categories of crimes, namely (1) grave breaches of the 1949 Geneva Conventions, including willful killing, torture, and willfully causing great suffering or serious injury to body or health, (2) violations of the wars and customs of war, which encompass the use of weapons calculated to cause unnecessary suffering and the wanton destruction of cities, towns, or villages, (3) crimes against humanity, which include murder, torture, and rape, and (4) genocide as defined in the 1948 Convention on the Prevention and Punishment of Genocide.[4] These categories are not mutually exclusive, and there is considerable overlap between them. Torture, for example, can be prosecuted as a grave breach of the Geneva Conventions and/or as a crime against humanity. Crimes against humanity, however, can only be committed as part of a systematic or widespread attack on a civilian population, which is not a requirement for breaches of the Geneva Conventions. Unlike the Nuremberg Tribunal, the ICTY is not mandated to prosecute crimes against peace. It has primacy of jurisdiction over national courts but its jurisdiction is concurrent rather than exclusive, which means that national authorities, in cooperation with the ICTY, are expected to continue their own war crimes investigations and prosecutions. Defendants can be charged with personal responsibility or, if they are in positions of authority, command responsibility. The tribunal is only concerned with individuals and does not have jurisdiction over states or organizations. The ICTY is not a permanent court but an *ad hoc* tribunal with a finite life span. On June 10, 2002, the ICTY's then president Judge Claude Jorda submitted the Tribunal's Completion Strategy, which UN Security Council Resolution 1503 (August 28, 2003) subsequently endorsed. It is anticipated that the ICTY will complete all first instance trials by 2010 and all appeals by the end of 2013.

Prosecutions at the ICTY

The ICTY has issued 161 indictments and to date has completed cases involving 120 individuals. According to one legal commentator, "as a matter of policy, international prosecutions should be limited to leaders, policy-makers and senior executors; however, this does not preclude prosecutions of other persons at the national level" (Bassiouni 1996, 20). Indeed, the ICTY was established precisely to prosecute such "big fish." The tribunal's first indictments, however, were driven by far more immediate practical considerations: "The initial indictments were issued under tremendous pressure to obtain crucial funding from the United Nations" (Goldstone 2002, 281). When the ICTY was created it had no budget. Prior to his first meeting with the UN Advisory Committee on Administrative and Budgetary Questions, therefore, the tribunal's first chief prosecutor, Justice Richard Goldstone, needed to issue an indictment to prove to the UN committee that the tribunal was working and merited financial support. Hence, the first person that the tribunal indicted (on 4 November 1994) was not Milosevic, Mladic, or someone of their ilk. It was Dragan Nikolic, the former commander of the Susica detention camp in the municipality of Vlasenica in Eastern BiH. According to Goldstone, Nikolic "was not an appropriate first person for an indictment by the first international war crimes tribunal but we had no option. In order for the work to continue, we had to get out an indictment quickly" (2002, 281).

By starting with the "small fish," however, and by using a pyramidal approach, the tribunal was thereby able to build up an evidence base against high-level perpetrators. In July 1995, the ICTY issued indictments against Karadzic and Mladic, and in 1997 the OTP's strategy clearly shifted, focussing on leadership figures. Milosevic himself was indicted in May 1999 during the NATO bombing campaign. Part of the ICTY's Completion Strategy, moreover, is to concentrate on the most senior leaders. In effect, "[t]he broad approach of the ICTY Completion Strategy may be summarized as 'senior perpetrators for the International Tribunal, minor offenders for national courts' " (Takemura 2007, 680). Hence, at the time of writing this chapter in 2009, ICTY proceedings are underway or ongoing against Karadzic, Ljubisa Beara (the former colonel and chief of staff of the Bosnian Serb Army main staff), Momcilo Krajisnik (a former member of the Bosnian Serb leadership), Nebojsa Pavkovic (the former chief of staff of the Yugoslav Army), Momcilo Perisic (a former chief of general staff of the Yugoslav Army), Nikola Sainovic (the former deputy prime minister of the Federal Republic of Yugoslavia), and Vojislav Seselj (the president of the Serbian Radical Party). Among those that the tribunal has found guilty are Tihomir Blaskic (the former commander of the Bosnian-Croat Army or HVO, Miodrag Jokic, (a former commander of the Yugoslav Navy) and Biljana Plavsic (former co-president of the *Republika Srpska* in BiH).[5]

Until recently, the ICTY's two most-wanted indictees, Mladic and Karadzic, remained at large. However in July 2008, Karadzic was arrested in Belgrade and is now in custody at the tribunal's detention unit in Scheveningen. For Bosnian Muslims, there can be no real justice until these two men are brought to justice.[6] The ICTY is widely criticized in BiH for failing to capture them. However, such criticism overlooks the critical fact that the tribunal itself has no powers of arrest. In essence, the tribunal "remains very much like a giant without arms and legs—it needs artificial limbs to walk and work" (Cassese 1998, 13). It is entirely dependent on states, and if they fail to cooperate "the ICTY cannot fulfil its functions" (Cassese 1998, 13).[7] According to a former chief prosecutor, this lack of enforcement powers necessarily thrusts the tribunal into the realm of politics (Del Ponte 2008, 42). This in turn inevitably raises questions about the neutrality of the justice that it is dispensing. Bosnian Serbs and Bosnian Croats widely regard the ICTY as biased against their ethnic groups, an important factor in assessing the tribunal's impact in BiH.

The ICTY's Impact in BiH

Without the ICTY, war criminals in BiH may never have been brought to justice. Through its trials, the tribunal has documented and acknowledged the suffering of thousands of victims, given some of them the opportunity to tell their stories, and has comprehensively established a historical record of the crimes and atrocities committed in BiH between 1992 and 1995. It also provided the momentum for creating the State Court of BiH (created in 2005), and its intensive capacity-building work with judges and prosecutors in BiH will allow local courts to continue prosecuting war crimes long after the ICTY has completed its mandate. Notwithstanding the importance of the tribunal's work, however, it is submitted that in many respects its impact in BiH has in fact been minimal. In particular, the problem of denial still exists, victims are dissatisfied, and sixteen years after its creation, the tribunal has fundamentally failed to connect with BiH's citizens.

Denial and Competing Truths

Although UN Security Council Resolution 827 does not actually refer to reconciliation, one part of the ICTY's mandate[8] is to contribute to the restoration and maintenance of peace, which arguably encompasses reconciliation. Furthermore, the tribunal itself has often made an explicit linkage between its work and reconciliation (Cassese 1994; Kirk McDonald 1999; Del Ponte 2007). According to this argument, an important way in which the ICTY, and indeed criminal trials more generally, can aid reconciliation is by establishing the truth. In reality, however, "there is not only one truth but many truths about the past" (Hamber 1998, 3). Truth is an inherently contested concept and nowhere is this more evident than in BiH itself, where essentially three competing versions of truth exist (*e.g.*, the Bosnian Muslim, Bosnian Serb, and Bosnian Croat).

While conducting fieldwork in BiH during the summer of 2008,[9] the author was repeatedly told to "write the truth." What the interviewees actually meant by this was *their* truth. For example, there were interviewees on all three sides who insisted that it would not be worthwhile to speak to people from other ethnic groups because "they" are not ready to face the truth. It is difficult to envisage how reconciliation in BiH can take place unless and until these competing versions of truth are themselves reconciled. While the ICTY is helping to establish a historical record of what happened in BiH during the war, the notion that "revealing is healing" is premised on the assumption that the truths it is documenting will be accepted and internalized by those who need to be reconciled. In BiH, this is a flawed assumption, as evidenced by the prevalence of denial. According to the ICTY's website:

> Determining the facts of the crimes committed in the former Yugoslavia is crucial in order to combat denial and prevent attempts at revisionism. The detail in which the ICTY's judgments describe the crimes and the involvement of those convicted makes it impossible for anyone to dispute the reality of the horrors that took place in and around Bratunac, Brcko, Celebici, Dubrovnik, Foca, Prijedor, Sarajevo, Srebrenica and Zvornik, to name but a few.[10]

Yet this is a naive and oversimplistic argument because however thorough and meticulous the tribunal's judgments are, the reality is that there are many people in BiH who are unwilling or unable to accept them, particularly among the Bosnian Serbs and Bosnian Croats. As one example, Srebrenica has been a strong focus of the ICTY's work and in 2001, Radislav Krstic was found guilty of aiding and abetting the crime of genocide. Krstic, the deputy commander of the Drina Corps, was the first person convicted at the ICTY of genocide. During fieldwork in BiH, however, the author frequently encountered Bosnian Serbs, from Srebrenica and nearby Bratunac to Prijedor in Northwestern BiH, who continue to deny that genocide occurred in Srebrenica. While acknowledging that Bosnian Muslims were killed in this eastern Bosnian town, they variously maintained that it was not genocide because only men were targeted and not women and children, because only soldiers died, not civilians or because there were far fewer victims than the Muslims allege. Halfway between Srebrenica and Bratunac is Potocari and the Memorial Center, which opened in 2003, where the victims of Srebrenica are buried (those whose bodies have been recovered and identified). While Serbs living in Srebrenica and Bratunac regularly drive past the center, where row upon row of white tombstones stretch as far as the eye can see, many persist in arguing that there was no genocide here, an example of what Cohen terms "interpretative denial." That is to say that, "it is not the raw facts (something happened) that are being denied but they are given a different meaning from what seems obvious to others" (Cohen 2001, 7).

To take a second example, early on the morning of April 16, 1993, the HVO and a special unit of the military police, known as "the Jokers," launched a surprise assault on the village of Ahmici in Central BiH. During the attack, 116 Bosnian Muslims were killed, including thirty-two women and eleven children. Several defendants have been tried and convicted for their involvement in this massacre, including Blaskic, Dario Kordic, and Mario Cerkez. In Ahmici however, "there is no indication that these proceedings have in any way transformed the way in which Croats in the village interpret what happened" (Stover 2007, 143–144). Croat interviewees in Ahmici and nearby Vitez thus variously insisted that the Bosnian Muslims had provoked the attack, that no civilians were killed, and that it had been a "fair fight."

That Bosnian Serbs and Bosnian Croats widely view the ICTY as a political and biased institution can help to explain their refusal to accept its judgments (Zoglin 2005, 73). For the former, the ultimate proof of the tribunal's partiality was its acquittal of Naser Oric, a Bosnian Muslim.[11] These negative perceptions of the ICTY, however, cannot alone account for the prevalence of denial, which also exists among the Bosnian Muslims. While generally accepting that there was suffering on all three sides, the Bosnian Muslim interviewees were typically very dismissive of crimes committed by their own side, for example in Kravica, Celebici, Krizancevo Selo, and Buhine Kuce. They maintained that their army was simply acting in defense and that any crimes committed were insignificant in relation to Serb and Croat crimes. In short, each side is locked in its own sense of victimhood and it is this that ultimately explains the persistence of denial. Despite claims to the contrary (Wilson 2005, 942), the reality is that denial remains a significant problem in BiH and a crucial obstacle to the reconciliation process, wherein "guilt needs to be recognized with the acceptance of responsibility for atrocities or other events symbolizing intercommunal and interpersonal relations" (Jeong 2005, 156). In short, the ICTY has had little success in combating denial in BiH and as long as there are large numbers of people unwilling to accept its judgments, this will inevitably limit the potential impact of its work.

Dissatisfaction among Victims

According to one commentator "[m]ore than the judges, prosecutors, defense counsel or journalists, it is the victims who have the right to decide whether the Tribunal has been a success or failure" (Klarin 2004, 557). What is very clear from speaking to victims on all three sides, however, is that while they are generally happy that the ICTY exists, their high expectations of the tribunal have not been met. The result is that many victims have been left feeling disappointed and dissatisfied. The tribunal's website maintains that "[b]y holding individuals responsible for crimes committed in the former Yugoslavia, the Tribunal is bringing justice to victims."[12]

Yet for victims, there is no justice when thousands of (potential) war criminals are still free. The ICTY's 161 indictments only scratch the surface of culpability, thus underscoring the limitations of criminal trials in societies where wide scale atrocities have been committed (Humphrey 2003, 498; Amstutz 2005, 553). More fundamentally victims, particularly Bosnian Muslim victims, regard ICTY prison sentences as unacceptably lenient. In Prijedor and Kozarac in northwestern BiH, the Bosnian Muslim interviewees, almost all of whom had been interned in one or more of the three concentration camps set up in this area (Keraterm, Omarska, and Trnopolje), angrily asked how they can feel satisfied that justice has been done when defendants such as Dragan Kolundzija, Damir Dosen, and Predrag Banovic (all of whom held positions in the Keraterm camp) have received prison sentences of three, five, and eight years, respectively.[13]

Undoubtedly, it will always be extremely difficult to satisfy victims. What is an adequate punishment for somebody who has committed rape and murder? To date, however, the ICTY has only issued two life sentences, and it has no clear sentencing policy. Sentences are ultimately a discretional issue for the tribunal's judges but because the latter come from a variety of legal systems and cultures: "[T]here is a broad discrepancy between the sentences passed by some Chambers and those passed by others" (Cassese 2004, 596). To take one example, Drazen Erdemovic, a soldier in the 10th Sabotage Detachment of the Bosnian Serb Army and the first person to be convicted by the tribunal, was sentenced to five years' imprisonment in March 1998. Erdemovic had personally killed approximately seventy people. In November 2001, Dosen, a shift leader at the Keraterm camp who did not actually kill anyone, was also sentenced to five years' imprisonment for crimes against humanity.

In some cases, even the sentences handed down by the same judges are difficult to rationalize. Since genocide is the most heinous of all crimes, one might have expected that the one ICTY defendant currently serving a life sentence would be Krstic, the only defendant convicted of aiding and abetting genocide in Srebrenica. Yet in April 2004, the Appeals Chamber sentenced Krstic to thirty-five years' imprisonment, thus reducing his original sentence of forty-five years. Conversely in November 2006, the Appeals Chamber sentenced Stanislav Galic, the commander of the Sarajevo Romanija Corps of the Bosnian Serb Army, to life imprisonment for crimes against humanity, thus significantly increasing his original sentence of imprisonment for twenty years.[14]

These are extremely complex cases, and the ICTY's judges must take into consideration a wide variety of factors when sentencing a defendant, including family circumstances, prior good conduct, and expressions of remorse. Whether or not justice has actually been done in these cases, however, is not the fundamental issue and is beyond the scope of this chapter. What is critical is that justice must be *seen* to be done (Clark 2009a). What impact the tribunal ultimately has in BiH will partly depend upon how the country's citizens perceive it. "[T]hese perceptions may negatively affect the ability of the court to fulfil the social and political aspects of its mission" (Fletcher and Weinstein 2004, 40). How people view the ICTY, in turn, is strongly linked to how much they understand it. Victims will continue to criticize the tribunal's sentences as long as they cannot make sense of them, and they will not be able to do so unless and until the tribunal makes a concerted and systematic effort to reach out to BiH's citizens.

ICTY Outreach—Too Little Too Late

When the ICTY was created in 1993, war was raging in BiH. For practical and security reasons, therefore, it would not have been feasible to establish the tribunal within the former Yugoslavia. However, by setting it up in The Hague, over 900 miles from the Balkans, the founders ensured that outreach work would be imperative from the outset. From its very inception, the ICTY needed to reach out to and engage with people in the former Yugoslavia. It is not only the tribunal's geographical distance from the region that made early outreach essential. Since its official languages are English and French, it is also linguistically removed from BiH and the former Yugoslavia, where the principal languages spoken are Bosnian, Croatian, and Serbian. Not until the year 2000, however, could somebody officially speak on behalf of the ICTY in these languages. Further contributing to its remoteness from the region, the tribunal combines elements of the adversarial common law system and the inquisitorial civil law legal systems yet leans disproportionately toward the former, which is largely alien to people in the former Yugoslavia, even to its best-trained lawyers (Tolbert 2002, 7).

Outreach, it is argued, "is crucial to a tribunal's success" (Del Ponte 2008, 376). Yet, it was not until six years after the ICTY was created that an outreach program was established. Judge Gabrielle Kirk McDonald had been "devastated" to learn that after months of work on the *Dusko Tadic* case, culminating in an extremely detailed judgment in which the defendant was sentenced to twenty years' imprisonment for grave breaches of the 1949 Geneva Conventions, crimes against humanity, and violations of the laws or customs of war in Kozarac and Prijedor, Serbs in and around Prijedor continued to deny that crimes had been committed in this area (XY Films 2004). She thus came to realize that "there was a need—a necessity, really—for the Tribunal to do more: to actually communicate with the people of the former Yugoslavia" (Kirk McDonald 2004, 569). It was on Kirk McDonald's initiative, therefore, that the ICTY's outreach section was established in 1999. That it has not succeeded in overcoming the very denial that proved the catalyst for its creation, however, necessarily raises important questions about the effectiveness of the tribunal's outreach work.[15]

One significant problem is that for the first six years of the tribunal's existence, it was (and still is) the object of highly negative propaganda. This helped to turn public opinion, particularly Serb public opinion, decisively against the ICTY, and it has been extremely difficult for its outreach section to counter this. According to one commentator, "[p]olitical unity is rare in the formerly Yugoslav republics but the ICTY has achieved it: majorities of all of the major national groups reject the Tribunal" (Hayden 2006, 398).

A second major problem is that the tribunal's outreach section has always been understaffed and underfunded, which has necessarily impacted the outreach work that it has been able to undertake. While the ICTY has a staff of approximately 1,100, just two people work in its outreach section in The Hague, and its regional outreach offices (in Belgrade, Pristina, Sarajevo, and Zagreb) are similarly understaffed. There are just two people working in each regional office, only one of whom is able to speak on the record, and the office in Zagreb has for many years been staffed by just one person. Furthermore, the tribunal's outreach program has never received funding from the UN and has needed to rely exclusively on donations, mainly from the European Commission. According to a former deputy prosecutor, what this illustrates is that "the tribunal's impact in the region in general . . . is of marginal interest to UN policymakers" (Tolbert 2002, 13). That the tribunal is now under pressure to complete its mandate has further limited its outreach work. Since the adoption of the ICTY's Completion Strategy in 2003, its outreach activities have primarily focused on what is called capacity-building work, such as training for local judiciaries in the former Yugoslavia (as will be discussed in Chapter 7). While such work is extremely valuable and will arguably form one of the tribunal's most important legacies, it will be unfortunate if it takes place at the expense of reaching out to and communicating with local communities in the former Yugoslavia.

The consequences of the tribunal's geographical, linguistic, and legal/procedural remoteness from the former Yugoslavia and of the tardiness and shortcomings of its outreach work are significant. Strong prejudice against the ICTY persists, particularly but not exclusively among Serbs (Saxon 2005; Hayden 2006), and the ICTY remains a source of misunderstanding and confusion (Saxon 2005, 564). In BiH, the author regularly met people who make no distinction between the ICTY and the International Court of Justice (ICJ), erroneously attributing to the former the latter's 2007 judgment that Serbia was not responsible for the genocide in Srebrenica. Even more frequently, the author encountered individuals who criticize the tribunal—which has no powers of arrest—for failing to arraign war criminals, and who completely fail to realize that the tribunal is *ad hoc* with a finite mandate, as a result of which it can only indict and prosecute a limited number of suspected war criminals. In short, "[t]he outreach of the ICTY to the victim societies has evidently failed to bridge the gap in knowledge and appreciation of its work at the grassroots level" (Zacklin 2004, 544).

Most problematically, because so few people understand the ICTY and its work, a fundamental disconnect exists. The tribunal has not succeeded in reaching "hearts and minds" (Wald 2006, 336), and hence there is no local ownership for the ICTY process. This has necessarily limited the ICTY's impact in BiH. If the ICTY is to realize its goals of deterrence, justice, and contributing to the restoration and maintenance of peace, its work must be understood, viewed as legitimate, and it must engage local communities (Kirk McDonald 2004, 571; Artz 2006, 227). Yet with so many people still searching for the bodies of their missing loved ones, thousands of people still internally displaced and large numbers of people living in very poor conditions,[16] for some the tribunal is simply a distant institution with little relevance to their difficult everyday lives.

To conclude, it can be argued that "the relationship between a tribunal and the local populace is a critical dimension of its success" (Fletcher and Weinstein 2004, 44). The ICTY's relationship with local people in BiH, however, is characterized by prejudice, confusion, misunderstanding, apathy, and indifference. While public support for criminal trials is extremely high in BiH (UNDP 2005, 17), the continued prevalence of denial and competing truths, the dissatisfaction of victims, and popular attitudes toward the tribunal all suggest that it has had only a limited impact in the country. This in turn, it is submitted, underscores the confines of retributive justice in post-conflict societies and the importance of embracing other forms of transitional justice (Boraine 2006, 27). In BiH, there is a strong case to be made for a form of truth and reconciliation commission (TRC). Based in BiH itself, such a commission would potentially create a far greater sense of local ownership and interest in the truth-finding process, and its immediacy would arguably make it more successful in tackling the problem of denial than a distant and poorly understood judicial body (Clark 2009c, 17–19). What is more, there is considerable public support in BiH for a TRC.[17]

Conclusions

The ICTY has made huge strides since its creation in 1993, and in terms of its jurisprudence, its instrumental role in the development of international criminal law and its capacity-building work in the former Yugoslavia, and thus its achievements are significant. Notwithstanding the importance of retributive justice, however, its merits are often simply assumed rather than proven (Fletcher and Weinstein 2002, 585). Any comprehensive assessment of international criminal tribunals like the ICTY must systematically explore the effects their work is having on the ground. This analysis of the ICTY's impact in BiH has not only highlighted the limits of retributive justice but has also explored some common, yet untested claims, including the contention that criminal trials establish the truth. Perhaps one of the greatest legacies of the tribunal will be its ability to strengthen the local judiciary as discussed in the next chapter.

Notes

1. Between May and August 2008, the author conducted semi-structured interviews with 171 people (109 men and sixty-two women) in twenty-five different places in BiH, including Bratunac, Potocari, and Srebrenica (Eastern BiH), Kozarac, Prijedor, and Trnopolje (Northwestern BiH), Ahmici and Vitez (Central BiH), Mostar and Stolac (Western Herzegovina), and the country's capital, Sarajevo. Of the total 171 interviewees, ninety-eight were ordinary people, the majority of whom could be described as victims. They included concentration camp survivors, men and women who had lost close family members, internally displaced persons, and women who had been raped. Of the remaining seventy-three interviewees, twenty-eight were non-governmental organization leaders; twenty were religious figures; fifteen worked for international/European bodies (including the NATO), and ten were officials. Eighty-eight interviewees were Bosnian Muslims (Bosniaks), forty Bosnian Serbs, twenty-nine Bosnian Croats, one Jew, and the remaining thirteen were with other nationalities. Only forty-five interviewees were English-speaking. The author interviewed the remaining 126 interviewees in their own language (Bosnian/Croatian/Serbian). A combination of purposive, opportunistic, and snowball sampling strategies were used.
2. BiH had a pre-war population of 4.3 million, of which 44 percent were Bosnian Muslims, 31 percent were Bosnian Serbs, and 17 percent were Bosnian Croats. Just over 5 percent of the population declared themselves as "Yugoslavs."
3. By December 31, 1995, after a bloody three-year war, over 150,000 people in BiH were registered as killed, dead from starvation or hypothermia, or missing, and at least 170,000 were recorded as injured (United Nations Development Program 2005, 7).
4. Article II of the Convention defines genocide as: "[m]any of the following acts committed with the intent to destroy, in whole or in part, a national, ethnical, racial or religious group, as such: (a) Killing members of the group; (b) Causing serious bodily or mental harm to members of the group; (c) Deliberately inflicting on the group conditions of life calculated to bring about its physical destruction in whole or in part; (d) Imposing measures intended to prevent births within the group; [and] (e) Forcibly transferring children of the group to another group."
5. Under the 1995 Dayton Agreement, BiH was divided into two entities, the Federation and *Republika Srpska*.

6. Of the 161 individuals that the ICTY has indicted, only Mladic and Goran Hadzic (the former president of the *Republika Srpska Krajina* in Croatia) remain at large.
7. Although all states are under an obligation to cooperate with the ICTY, by virtue of Article 25 of the UN Charter, the ICTY can do no more than to report acts of noncompliance to the UN Security Council which has often "failed to respond in a meaningful way" (Kirk McDonald 2004, 562).
8. The ICTY's mandate is threefold: To deter further crimes, to deliver justice, and to contribute to the restoration and maintenance of peace.
9. See note 1.
10. Available at: www.icty.org/sid/324.
11. Oric was the senior commander of Bosnian Muslim forces in parts of Eastern BiH, including Srebrenica, and he was indicted by the ICTY in 2003 for wanton destruction of cities, towns, or villages and murder and cruel treatment. On May 30, 2006, the ICTY Trial Chamber found him guilty of failing to discharge his duty as a superior to take necessary and reasonable measures to prevent the occurrence of murder and cruel treatment. It sentenced him to two years' imprisonment, but as he had already spent three years in detention, the judges ordered his immediate release. Oric's defense team immediately filed an appeal and on July 3, 2008, the Appeals Chamber found him not guilty, on the basis that his effective control over his subordinates had not been proven beyond reasonable doubt.
12. Available at: www.icty.org/sid/324.
13. Kolundzija was a shift commander at the Keraterm camp; Dosen was a shift leader, and Banovic was a guard at the camp.
14. The second defendant sentenced to life imprisonment, in July 2003, was Milomir Stakic, the former head of the Municipal Council for National Defense in Prijedor. In March 2006, however, the ICTY Appeals Chamber reduced his sentence to forty years' imprisonment.
15. All of the Serb interviewees in Prijedor, for example, insisted that Keraterm, Trnopolje, and Omarska were not concentration camps at all but rather "collective centers," which the Bosnian Muslims had entered of their own free will, feeling safer in these "centers" than they did in their own homes.
16. According to the International Commission on Missing Persons (ICMP) in Sarajevo, an estimated 30,000 persons in BiH were unaccounted for at the end of the war and approximately 13,500 people are still missing, most of whom are in mass graves (2007, 11). By March 2008, according to the United Nations High Commission for Refugees (UNHCR) in Sarajevo, 1,025,316 people had returned to their homes in BiH (578,572 internally displaced persons and 446,744 refugees). This means that 1,174,684 people are still internally displaced or living as refugees. Data supplied by the UNHCR office in Sarajevo, June 2008. In 2005, a total of 7,311 people were living in collective centers in BiH, 4,467 in the Federation and 2,844 in *Republika Srpska* (Bosnia and Herzegovina Ministry for Human Rights and Refugees 2005, 130).
17. A public opinion poll by the United Nations Development Program in June 2005, for example "revealed significant support in BiH for a truth commission. Nearly three-fifths of people [just over fifty-five percent] unreservedly recognize the need and desirability of such a forum" (2005, 17).

References

Amstutz, Mark R. 2005. *The Healing of Nations: The Promise and Limits of Political Forgiveness*. Lanham, MD: Rowman and Littlefield.

Arzt, Donna E. 2006. "Views on the Ground: The Local Perceptions of International Criminal Tribunals in the Former Yugoslavia and Sierra Leone." *The Annals of the American Academy of Political and Social Science* 603:226–239.

Bassiouni, M. Cherif. 1996. "Searching for Peace and Achieving Justice: The Need for Accountability." *Law and Contemporary Problems* 59:9–28.

Boraine, Alex. 2006. "Defining Transitional Justice: Tolerance in the Search for Justice and Peace." In *Transitional Justice and Human Security*, ed. Alex Boraine and Sue Valentine. Cape Town: The International Centre for Transitional Justice.

Bosnia and Herzegovina Ministry for Human Rights and Refugees. 2005. *Comparative Analysis on Access to Rights of Refugees and Displaced Persons*. Sarajevo: Ministry for Human Rights and Refugees.

Cassese, Antonio. 2004. "The ICTY: A Living and Vital Reality." *Journal of International Criminal Justice* 2:585–597.

Cassese, Antonio. 1998. "On the Current Trends towards Criminal Prosecution and Punishment of Breaches of International Humanitarian Law." *European Journal of International Law* 9:2–17.

Cassese, Antonio. 1994. *First Annual Report*. UN doc. IT/68.

Clark, Janine N. 2009a. "Judging the ICTY: Has It Achieved Its Objectives?" *Southeast European and Black Sea Studies* 9:123–142.

Clark, Janine N. 2009b. "International War Crimes Tribunals and the Challenge of Outreach." *International Criminal Law Review* 9:99–116.

Clark, Janine N. 2009c. "The Limits of Retributive Justice: Findings of an Empirical Study in Bosnia and Herzegovina." *Journal of International Criminal Justice*. doi:10.1093/jicj/mqp041.

Cohen, Stanley. 2001. *States of Denial: Knowing About Atrocities and Suffering*. Cambridge: Polity Press.

Del Ponte, Carla. 2008. *Madame Prosecutor: Confrontations with Humanity's Worst Criminals and the Culture of Impunity*. New York: Other Press.

Del Ponte, Carla. 2007. "Address by Tribunal Prosecutor Carla Del Ponte to NATO Parliamentary Assembly." Available at: http://www.un.org/icty/pressreal/2007/pr1193e.htm

Dickson, Tiphaine, and Aleksandar Jokic. 2006. "Hear No Evil, See No Evil, Speak No Evil: The Unsightly Milosevic Case." *International Journal for the Semiotics of Law* 19:355–387.

Fletcher, Laurel E., and Harvey M. Weinstein. 2004. "A World unto Itself? The Application of International Justice in the Former Yugoslavia". In *My Neighbor, My Enemy: Justice and Community in the Aftermath of Mass Atrocity*, ed. Eric Stover and Harvey M. Weinstein. Cambridge: Cambridge University Press.

Fletcher, Laurel E., and Harvey M. Weinstein. 2002. "Violence and Social Repair: Rethinking the Contribution of Justice to Reconciliation." *Human Rights Quarterly* 24:573–639.

Goldstone, Richard J. 2002. "Prosecuting Rape as a War Crime." *Case Western Reserve Journal of International Law* 34:277–285.

Hamber, Brandon. 1998. "The Past Imperfect: Exploring Northern Ireland, South Africa and Guatemala". In *Past Imperfect: Dealing With the Past in Northern Ireland and Societies in Transition*, ed. Brandon Hamber. Belfast: INCORE.

Hayden, Robert M. 2006. "Justice Presumed and Assistance Denied: The Yugoslav Tribunal as Obstruction to Economic Recovery." *International Journal for the Semiotics of Law* 19:389–408.

Humphrey, Michael. 2003. "International Intervention, Justice and National Reconciliation: The Role of the ICTY and ICTR in Bosnia and Rwanda." *Journal of Human* Rights 2:495–505.

International Commission on Missing Persons (ICMP). 2007. *Background Document on the Work of the International Commission on Missing Persons*. Sarajevo: ICMP.

Jeong, Ho-Won. 2005. *Peacebuilding in Post-conflict Societies: Strategy and Process*. Boulder, CO: Lynne Rienner.

Johnstone, Diana. 2002. *Fools' Crusade: Yugoslavia, NATO and Western Delusions* London: Pluto Press.

Jorda, Claude. 2004. "The Major Hurdles and Accomplishments of the ICTY: What the ICC Can Learn From Them." *Journal of International Criminal Justice* 2:572–584.

Kirk McDonald, Gabrielle. 2004. "Problems, Obstacles and Achievements of the ICTY." *Journal of International Criminal Justice* 2:558–571.

Kirk McDonald, Gabrielle. 1999. "Remarks at the United States Supreme Court." Available at: http://www.un.orf/icty/pressreal/SPE990405.htm

Klarin, Mirko. 2004. "The Tribunal's Four Battles." *Journal of International Criminal Justice* 2:546–557.

Klarin, Mirko. 2001. "Nirnberg sada!" In *The Path to The Hague: Selected Documents on the Origins of the ICTY*, ed. International Criminal Tribunal for the Former Yugoslavia. The Hague: ICTY.

Laughland, John. 2007. *Travesty: The Trial of Slobodan Milosevic and the Corruption of International Justice*. London: Pluto Press.

Saxon, Dan. 2005. "Exporting Justice: Perceptions of the ICTY among the Serbian, Croatian and Muslim communities in the Former Yugoslavia." *Journal of Human Rights* 4:559–572.

Stover, Eric, and Harvey M. Weinstein. 2004. "Conclusion: A Common Objective, a Universe of Alternatives". In *My Neighbor, My Enemy: Justice and Community in the Aftermath of Mass Atrocity*, ed. Eric Stover and Harvey M. Weinstein. Cambridge: Cambridge University Press.

Stover, Eric. 2007. *The Witnesses: War Crimes and the Promise of Justice in The Hague*. Philadelphia, PA: University of Pennsylvania Press.

Takemura, Hitomi. 2007. "Big Fish and Small Fish Debate—An Examination of the Prosecutorial Discretion." *International Criminal Law Review* 7:677–685.

Tolbert, David. 2002. "The International Criminal Tribunal for the Former Yugoslavia: Unforeseen Successes and Foreseeable Shortcomings." *The Fletcher Forum of World Affairs* 26:5–17.

United Nations Development Program (UNDP). 2005. *Justice and Truth in Bosnia and Herzegovina: Public Perceptions—Early Warning System Special Edition*. Sarajevo: UNDP.

Wald, Patricia M. 2006. "International Criminal Courts—A Stormy Adolescence." *Virginia Journal of International Law* 46:319–346.

Weinstein, Harvey M., and Eric Stover. 2004. "Introduction: Conflict, Justice and Reclamation". In *My Neighbor, My Enemy: Justice and Community in the Aftermath of Mass Atrocity*, ed. Eric Stover and Harvey M. Weinstein. Cambridge: Cambridge University Press.

Wilson, Richard Ashby. 2005. "Judging History: The Historical Record of the International Criminal Tribunal for the Former Yugoslavia." *Human Rights Quarterly* 27:908–942.

XY Films. 2004. *Justice Unseen, slijepa pravda*. Sarajevo: XY Films.

Zacklin, Ralph. 2004. "The Failings of Ad Hoc International Tribunals." *Journal of International Criminal Justice* 2:541–545.

Zoglin, Kate. 2005. "The Future of War Crimes Prosecutions in the Former Yugoslavia: Accountability or Junk Justice?" *Human Rights Quarterly* 27:41–77.

CHAPTER 7

Home Court Advantage? Domestic Trials and Transitional Justice in Bosnia-Herzegovina

Ryan M. Lowy and Patrice C. McMahon

Introduction

Many justifications are made for the use of international criminal prosecution to address mass atrocities and human rights violations in post-conflict societies. Domestic courts are easily politicized; rule of law within these countries is usually weak, and domestic institutions and leaders are generally considered to be less credible than representatives of the international community. As discussed in Chapter 6, these and other arguments led to the creation of the International Criminal Tribunal for the Former Yugoslavia (ICTY) in 1993. This organization was also seen as an evidence of the globalization of democratic norms and the triumph of liberal legalism (Bass 2000, 20; Hagan and Kutnjak Ivkovic 2006). Yet within a decade, the United Nations (UN) Security Council acknowledged the shortcomings of these assumptions and the need for other instruments to lay the foundation for a durable peace in the Balkans. The Completion Strategy adopted by the UN in August 2003 reflected this thinking. By 2010, the ICTY's work would be concluded and remaining cases would be transferred to domestic courts in the Balkans. Thus, domestic trials, rather than an international justice system, would become the primary mechanism to address the past and to encourage justice and reconciliation in the future.

This chapter considers one aspect of transitional justice that has received scant attention. Using Bosnia-Herzegovina (BiH) as a case study, it examines both the opportunities and challenges of the transition from international to domestic prosecution.[1] Much has been written on international criminal prosecution and on the ICTY in particular (Peskin 2008; Drumbl 2007; Meernik 2005; Kerr 2004). Perhaps even more research has focused on the effectiveness of truth commissions (Brahm 2007; Van der Merwe, Baxter, and Chapman 2009). The proliferation of different accountability mechanisms in the 1990s has also encouraged a spate of empirical research (Meernik

2005; McMahon and Forsythe 2008; Fletcher, Weinstein, and Rowen 2009). Most recently, scholars have emphasized the methodological hurdles associated with evaluating transitional justice (Thomas *et al.* 2008; Van der Merwe *et al.* 2009; Fletcher *et al.* 2009).

We fully appreciate the methodological difficulties of evaluation, especially given that domestic trials have only recently been used to promote justice. This exploratory research relies on secondary sources and data from the UN, the ICTY, and BiH institutions as evidence for our argument and interpretative analysis. Fieldwork in the Federation and discussions with international officials and Bosnians working on this specific issue also shaped our tentative claims about the utility and challenges associated with domestic trials.[2] Our main proposition is that despite the international community's extensive involvement in BiH since 1996 and notable legal advancements in the years since, the effectiveness of domestic trials is limited. At the time of this writing in mid-2009, trials in BiH are hampered by ongoing political struggles, economic shortfalls, and cultural obstacles. This domestic instrument may someday fulfill the expectations laid out by transitional justice enthusiasts—domestic courts may help to overcome the psychological distance created by the ICTY, build local legal capacity, and encourage the adoption of liberal norms. In all of these areas, trials may, indeed, prove to be crucial; however, these expectations have not yet arrived.

From International to Domestic Courts

There is much debate on the motivation for the creation of the ICTY in 1993. Supporters of the tribunal saw it as an essential "ingredient of peace building in the former Yugoslavia" (Akhavan 1998, 739; Goldstone 1996). In addition to punishing criminals, the existence of an international tribunal would purportedly help the region rebuild their judicial systems, foster respect for human rights and the rule of law, and establish the conditions for reconciliation (Thomas, Ron, and Paris 2008). For some, the tribunal reflected the world's commitment to both human rights and justice (Hagan 2003). Skeptics of the ICTY and international criminal justice argued that the establishment of this organization instead represented a "fig leaf for inaction," a way for the international community to do something while avoiding a costly war in the Balkans (Hagan 2003, 60). It is well established that international institutions without coercive or economic power hold little sway over states' behavior. Still a third group admits that the use of international courts to address human rights violations reflects different motivations and embodies various short- and long-term goals (Elster 2004; Minow 1998; Kritz 1995).

Regardless of why the ICTY was created, its utility and viability started to wane by the late 1990s, when ICTY judges started to think about its exit strategy and how it would transfer its responsibilities to local authorities. It was pressure from the UN Security Council and the General Assembly, rather than any sudden faith in Balkan domestic institutions that led ICTY officials to devise a Completion Strategy that required cooperation and coordination with local justice systems in the Balkans. Shifting from international to domestic responsibility was complicated because no provision for domestic courts was envisioned when the ICTY was established and domestic trials were politically sensitive and economically costly. Efforts in the early 1990s to arrest, detain, and try war criminals in the region were considered arbitrary and politically motivated (Donlon 2008, 262). In short, trials were regarded as occasions for dispensing ethnic justice or for exacting revenge (Bohlander 2003, 67). To combat capricious activities, Presidents Izetbegovic, Tudjman, and Milosevic agreed in 1996 to cooperate with the ICTY before the apprehension of suspected criminals within their countries. The Rome Agreement, as it is known, states that "[p]ersons, other than those already indicted by the International Tribunal, may be arrested and detained for serious violations of international humanitarian law only pursuant to a previously issued order, warrant, or indictment that has been reviewed or deemed consistent with international legal standards by the International Tribunal" (Office of the High Representative 1996, hereafter OHR). From this point on, officials in BiH were required to have cases reviewed by the Tribunal's Office of the Prosecutor (OTP) before arresting or detaining individuals suspected of war crimes.

This process led to the establishment of the Rules of the Road (RoR) Unit. This office within the ICTY at The Hague was a temporary solution to halt arbitrary arrests by national authorities, to protect those who were displaced during the war, and to encourage freedom of movement throughout the region. In cases where there was no previous indictment from the ICTY, evidence was sent to the OTP for review. After review, the OTP was to determine whether there was sufficient evidence to proceed. The ICTY's RoR Unit reviewed and classified potential cases in three ways: Evidence was sufficient to proceed with arrest and indictment (A); evidence was insufficient to meet international standards (B), and evidence was ambiguous and warranted further investigation (C). Category C cases could be re-submitted once more after evidence became available (Roper and Barria 2006, 73). From 1996 to 2004, the RoR Unit reviewed 1,419 cases involving 4,985 suspects; approval to proceed with arrest was granted for less than 20 percent (848) of the suspects (International Criminal Tribunal for the Former Yugoslavia 2009a).

With the reconstruction of BiH institutions failing to produce the political and social stability the international community had hoped for, the Peace Implementation Council (PIC) developed a plan in 1998 to address the country's failing legal system.[3] The 1998 plan identified several objectives: Strengthening the rule of law; creating independent, impartial, and multi-ethnic judiciaries; establishing judicial institutions at the state level to address criminal offenses by BiH public officials; and increasing efforts to prosecute organized crime, corruption, and other serious criminal behavior (OHR 1998). While the PIC's acknowledgement of the need to strengthen domestic institutions was important, the plan did not specifically address the prosecution of war crimes. The shortcomings of the RoR procedures were evident, and cases that were transferred back to BiH ignored fundamental realities in the country's ethnically divided court system. For example, it was clear that BiH courts did not meet international standards in 1996 when RoR procedures were established and again in 1998 when the PIC called for the creation of new state judicial institutions to deal with public officials who were indicted on criminal charges. Given what many saw as intractable problems with the country's courts, in 2000 Wolfgang Petritsch, the OHR's then High Representative established the State Court.[4] A draft of the law on the State Court was adapted from the law drawn up by the Council of Europe and agreed upon by members of the Ministry of Civil Affairs, Ministries of Justice of the Federation of Bosnia and Herzegovina, and the *Republika Srpska* as well as the OHR.

Within a matter of months, the ICTY and the OHR started to work together to develop the domestic capacity for trying war crimes within BiH's new State Court, creating a working group that decided on the institutional and legal framework for this institution, as well as the type and number of cases that would be tried. Although it took another five years for the first case to be transferred from the ICTY to the State Court, the establishment of this institution put BiH on the path to re-establishing its judicial system and assuming domestic responsibility for human rights violations. This and similar judicial developments in Croatia, Kosovo, and Serbia have simultaneously allowed the ICTY to put into practice its Completion Strategy, transferring authority to domestic officials throughout the Balkans.

The establishment of the State Court's special War Crimes Chamber (WCC) was much debated in BiH. Initial suggestions to re-create a totally international court within BiH were dismissed because of the cost involved and because the twin goals of the Completion Strategy were to end international prosecutions and to transfer the judicial process and authority to domestic courts. Yet, since the State Court was new and untested, there was a great deal of concern over the court's independence and neutrality; in 2003, the OHR and ICTY decided that the best way to counter these and other concerns was to staff the WCC with national and international officials (Donlon 2008, 274–277). Before any cases were transferred, the State Court had to establish that it was ready to handle the cases that would come its way. In January 2004, the High Representative enacted the Criminal Code and Criminal Procedure Code (CPC) for BiH, a set of uniform criminal laws that would enhance the capacity of the State Court to meet "criminal legislation standards existing in international law" (OHR 2003). In a report to the UN in August 2003, ICTY president Theodor Meron concluded that the "establishment of [the War Crimes Chamber within the State Court]...should enable the Tribunal to begin transferring some cases of mid- and lower-level accused by the end of 2004 or early 2005" (ICTY 2003a). That same month, the UN Security Council passed Resolution 1503, which called for a timeline for the completion of ICTY activity. By the end of 2008, all first instance trial activities were to be completed and all activities, including appeals is to be completed by the end of 2010 (United Nations 2003). At last, a deadline was in place for the conclusion of ICTY activity and a full transition to the State Court.

The ICTY and Domestic Trials

Although the ICTY has moved forward with its Completion Strategy, unforeseen complications have forced it to revise its initial timeline, and in

November 2008, the president of the ICTY acknowledged that the completion of court proceedings would not be likely even by 2011 (United Nations 2008). At the time of this writing, there are eight cases at trial, four in pretrial, four on appeal, and two individuals (Goran Hadzic and Ratko Mladic) are still at large (ICTY 2009b). The late arrests of certain individuals, most recently Stojan Zupljanin and Radovan Karadzic, in 2008, as well as two outstanding fugitives have contributed to the readjustment of the timeline. Meanwhile, BiH continues to make substantial changes to their court structure that will allow them to handle the cases being transferred from the ICTY, as well as those that have been initiated by domestic authorities.

The extension of the ICTY beyond the initial 2010 deadline will probably not have much of an impact on the progression of BiH's State Court. However, the ICTY and the State Court are closely intertwined in three ways: Reforms of BiH's judicial system have been pushed along by the imminent conclusion of the ICTY; they have not occurred organically or in response to local impulses. Second, evidence and expertise is concentrated in The Hague and while some recognize that this needs to be transferred to BiH, the existing gap in professional expertise and experience has a direct bearing on legal developments and outcomes in BiH (Stover and Weinstein 2004). Finally, the international community has provided well over $1.5 billion to support the activities of the ICTY (ICTY 2009). Donors who have provided generously for the ICTY's activities need to be persuaded to channel their contributions and in-kind support toward rebuilding and strengthening BiH's judicial system. The hope is that the State Court will carry out or even exceed the ambitious goals of the ICTY, and domestic trials will foster ethnic reconciliation and establish an environment where rule of law and human rights are respected.

It is worthwhile to note that despite the claims made about the ICTY and how it promotes peace and reconciliation in the Balkans, there is little empirical evidence to support such assertions. In fact, research casts considerable doubt on the whether the ICTY has been successful in accomplishing any of these goals, or whether this institution has had a positive bearing on outcomes in BiH or the region (McMahon and Forsythe 2008; Peskin 2008; Meernik 2005; Kerr 2004). The shortcoming of the ICTY, namely, its legitimacy and failure to communicate adequately with people in the Balkans may also limit the success of domestic trials. The ICTY and the prosecution of war criminals have not been viewed in the same way by Bosnians; most Bosnian Serbs are suspicious of the ICTY and transitional justice more broadly. From the very beginning, the work of the ICTY was seen as a way to punish Serbs (Biro *et al.* 2004, 183–203). Although not much data on local perceptions of the ICTY is available, most evidence that exists demonstrates that Bosnian Serbs do not place much faith in the neutrality of the ICTY (Stover and Weinstein 2004). A 2002 poll shows that Bosnians either do not know or do not trust the ICTY; among international organizations, the ICTY is the least trusted, with 51 percent of Bosnians in the BiH but only 4 percent in the *Republika Srpska* indicating that they trusted the ICTY (South East Europe Public Agenda Survey 2002).

Communication regarding the work of the ICTY and domestic trials is also essential; distrust of the ICTY thus may be related to ignorance of its work. Even though the ICTY realized the need and importance of communicating its activities to the people in the Balkans by developing an Outreach Program in 2001, there is still a significant gap in what people know about the ICTY. The Outreach Program emphasizes trial coverage by local media and it places outreach officers in areas most affected by the trials (ICTY 2009c). Both the ICTY and BiH authorities recognize the importance of informing citizens of the former Yugoslavia of what courts are doing to foster greater support. These activities are meant to "leave a lasting legacy and ensure a permanent shift from impunity to a culture of accountability" (ICTY 2009c).

The Home Court Advantage?

The ICTY was initially informed by a "universalistic" notion of international criminal justice: The crimes committed in the former Yugoslavia were so heinous that they were considered crimes committed against the international community and its consequent legal order. The punishment of these crimes thus could not be assumed by a single government or local authority. The ICTY's primacy over local law was never in doubt, and the ICTY was entrusted with absolute control of its case load and framing the narrative that best fitted the goals of the international community. Although this is a positive way to attract international support, it discounts local input and needs. Not surprisingly, as BiH's political and social transition progressed and then regressed, the ICTY's primacy proved to be both short-sighted and problematic. By 2000, a more "transitionalist" view of international criminal justice began to take hold, with the realization that local input was necessary to supplement the work of the ICTY and to help establish the conditions for peace, reconciliation, and rule of law. The State Court provides the country with its best hope that this transitionalist view will be realized.

The State Court

The State Court is a hybrid court consisting of both international and domestic officials. International support was critical to the establishment of the State Court, not only in terms of financial support but also in providing the expertise and personnel for this body. The Court is comprised of three sections: the criminal division, administrative division, and the appellate division. Within the criminal and appellate divisions, the court is further divided. The criminal division includes three sections: War crimes (Section I), organized crime, economic crime, and corruption (Section II), and all other criminal offenses including electoral issues (Section III). The appellate division is divided into three sections, which decide on appeals arising out of the criminal division. The administrative division is headed by the president of the State Court who is elected by all the judges for a five-year term.

The War Crimes Chamber (WCC) was created within the State Court in 2003 for the specific purpose of handling cases that were transferred from the ICTY and because lower courts were deemed either incapable or unwilling to try war criminals. The underlying philosophy for the creation and investment of the WCC was clear: "[A]ccountability for gross violations of human rights that took place during the conflict ultimately remains the responsibility of the people of Bosnia" (Human Rights Watch 2006). The WCC represents an important component of the ICTY's exit strategy because it will be responsible for trying the bulk of the cases transferred from The Hague as well as newly indicted war criminals (Court of Bosnia and Herzegovina 2007). The WCC also represents an important milestone in BiH's institutional development; it may well represent a unique opportunity to hold perpetrators accountable for war crimes and to build respect for the rule of law in the country. Critics of the WCC see it as a short-sighted attempt at the quickest and cheapest solution to facilitate the international community's withdrawal from BiH; skeptics also argue that for the WCC to be effective, the international community needs to invest more in local courts.

Trials in BiH

With the imminent closure of the ICTY, the WCC has had to prove it could handle not only the type of cases that would come its way from The Hague but that it is also capable of managing the large number of cases many expect will come from BiH directly. To ease the burden of the State Court, the Criminal Code introduced by the OHR in 2003 allows for the transfer of cases from the State Court to the entity (regional) authorities, both at the cantonal and district levels. The process allows state prosecutors to review cases and classify them as either "sensitive" or "highly sensitive." Highly sensitive cases are to be processed by the State Court while sensitive cases can be processed by either cantonal or district courts (Human Rights Watch 2008). This process closely resembles the RoR procedures undertaken by the ICTY to review cases. This procedure is expected to strengthen the State Court as well as regional and local courts by creating clearer jurisdictional boundaries and standard processes.

The State Court has issued indictments or amended indictments for ninety-four cases in the WCC since it began operating in 2005. The first year of operations saw a slow start to the process, issuing only six indictments; one year later the number had nearly quadrupled. In 2008, the WCC issued its largest number of indictments to date with thirty-four; thirteen have been issued in the first five months of 2009 (Court of Bosnia and Herzegovina 2009). Verdicts have been handed down in forty-four of these cases: Compared to the progress of the ICTY since it was established (with significantly more financial support), the WCC has performed quite well. The pace of trial proceedings at the state level is also promising; in cases where a verdict was reached, the average trial time was under one year from indictment to first instance verdict. The shortest trial lasted thirty-five days (Court of Bosnia and Herzegovina 2009). The number of cases it has addressed and pace of prosecution are a testament to the State Court's commitment to strengthening the country's judicial system. It also shows the commitment of both BiH and the international community to replace the ICTY.

In accordance with the Completion Strategy, the ICTY began to review cases that would be referred to the State Court in 2003. The first case that was transferred involved Radovan Stankovic, a member of a Bosnian Serb paramilitary unit in the city of Foca. Stankovic was originally indicted in June 1996, but was not apprehended until 2002 when he was arrested by the Stabilization Force (SFOR). In 2005, his case was transferred to the State Court to stand trial for several crimes, including the detention and rape of women and girls by Serb soldiers in what was called the Karaman House. Documents from the BiH OTP show that Stankovic not only repeatedly raped individuals but he would also assign women to be raped by other soldiers; in total, he was indicted on three separate charges of rape. He was also accused of raping a woman at the Miljevina Motel and another he forcibly removed from a hospital in Foca (Court of Bosnia and Herzegovina 2005). The Stankovic case was an important test of the WCC, even though the outcome proved to have mixed results.

Stankovic was convicted of the counts against him involving the forced detention and rape at Karaman's House and was sentenced to sixteen years imprisonment. An appellate decision upheld the initial conviction and amended the sentence to twenty years, and an effective justice system seemed to be well within reach. The State Court had successfully tried and convicted an individual transferred from the ICTY and international standards were met for a fair trial. However, Stankovic was acquitted of the rape in the Foca hospital and charges were dismissed in the case of the rape at the Miljevina Motel, illuminating some of the ongoing problems with the State Court and the country's political environment (Court of Bosnia and Herzegovina 2006). In the charges against Stankovic regarding the incidents at Karaman's House, the State Court used evidence previously collected by the ICTY where he had already been indicted for these crimes. The charges of rape at the Miljevina Motel and removal and rape of a patient at a Foca hospital were later added after the transfer to the State Court on December 7, 2005. In this case, the ICTY had compiled what was deemed sufficient evidence for the prosecution of war criminals while BiH officials were unable to do the same. The first case transferred from the ICTY showed that although the State Court has the ability to conduct criminal proceedings against war criminals, the judicial system might not be sufficiently strong enough to carry out the investigation and prosecution of war criminals alone. In total, five cases (naming ten individuals) have been transferred to the State Court. In these cases, the ICTY has handed sentences ranging between eight-and-a-half to thirty-four years. Other achievements of the WCC should also not be overlooked, including efforts to promote regional cooperation in war crimes cases. In 2004, BiH signed the European Convention on Mutual Assistance in Criminal Matters, and in July 2005, the WCC entered into agreements with the authorities in Croatia and in Serbia and Montenegro to enhance prosecutorial cooperation (Human Rights Watch 2006). BiH also established a video link with a court in Belgrade to ensure that their trials are aired in Serbia.

The Legacies of Dayton Remain

The existence of domestic trials is a positive sign of the country's stability and nascent institutional development; they are also crucial to the creation of effective domestic human rights instruments. However, BiH today is still at a difficult crossroads, and there is a significant gap between international aspirations and local realities. Almost fourteen years of intense international effort to stabilize the country has proven far more challenging than anticipated. In fact, for the first time since the Dayton Agreement was signed, many Bosnians are talking about the possibility of the country's collapse (McMahon and Western 2009). In the past three years, ethnic nationalist rhetoric from leaders of the country's three constituent ethnic groups has intensified, bringing reform to a standstill. As the Sarajevo-based Democratization Policy Council warned, the promises of Dayton are unraveling just as the guardrails that prevented the re-emergence of violence are being dismantled (Basseuner *et. al* 2008). In sum, the efficacy of domestic trials must be considered in light of BiH's broader political environment; we contend that political tensions and institutional complexities, as well as economic and culture challenges, prevent domestic trials from acting as an effective mechanism of accountability and justice.

The political structures created by Dayton created what some have called "a house of cards in Bosnia" (Chandler 2000). The country's constitution is a complex, inconsistent document plagued by ambiguity and highly dependent on the will of the international community. The country's federal system of governance is based on consociational rules, cooperation among political leaders, a minority veto, proportionality of political representation, and a significant amount of autonomy for groups in society. This system depends on a fragile compromise that has both kept the country together while dividing it into two largely mono-ethnic entities, the Federation and the *Republika Srpska*. This means that the Federation and the *Republika Srpska*, rather than the state government, have vast responsibilities, including primary control over the collection of taxes, education, and justice. To accommodate Bosnian Croats, power is further devolved within the Federation and most power resides in the hands of local, rather than Federation, officials. To prevent any one ethnic group from dominating, power sharing among the country's three main ethnic groups was institutionalized by the use of ethnic and regional quotas in all state institutions.

Like all other institutions in BiH, the country's legal system is infused with ethnic politics, and regional courts are staffed with individuals based on their ethnicity and political leanings rather than expertise (Donlon 2008, 264). The justice system has been further delayed by rampant corruption that has meant that any individuals in positions of influence are closely tied to politicians who have an ability to remove them from office. Even if judges are inclined to conduct fair trials, there are many incentives to follow the will of powerful politicians who are bent on engaging in ethnic nationalism. Because of ethnic politics and corruption, many of the cases that have been tried before regional courts have been compromised and some convictions overturned (Donlon 2008, 262). The establishment of the State Court was in response to this ethnically charged environment in BiH, which hinders fair trials. The State Court takes "the final and legally binding position in terms of the implementation of BiH laws and international treaties," but it does so *only* upon request from the lower courts, leaving a legal vacuum (Barria and Roper 2008, 321). In a 2005 assessment of local trials, the Organization for Security and Co-operation in Europe (OSCE) concluded that domestic trials were limited by both the painfully slow turnaround time and by domestic institutions that contained judges and prosecutors who were politically appointed and were vulnerable to political influences (Donlon 2008, 264).[5]

With this said, significant resources have gone into strengthening the rule of law in BiH, and a new, if highly complex court structure currently exists, with national level courts, regional courts, as well as the Brcko District courts (Barria and Roper 2008). This complicated structure still reflects the misguided efforts of Dayton, and the country's judicial system suffers from numerous and intense structural problems, with competing legal authorities undermining their ability to conduct fair and effective war crimes trials (Human Rights Watch 2006). A great deal of emphasis has also gone into establishing fair and transparent procedures for transferring cases to the entities and local courts; nonetheless, these logistical problems remain. Local prosecutors, for example, are unable to determine how many cases will be returned back to their jurisdiction under this referral process. Without knowing how many cases will ultimately need to be processed or when they will be returned by the state prosecutor, local officials have trouble ensuring adequate staffing. Additionally, because of ethnic tensions, there is considerable distrust of local courts and their ability to prosecute war criminals (Human Rights Watch 2008).

Lawyers and judges, moreover, must work with other elements of the society that are even less inclined to doling out justice and may be indifferent or hostile to this process. Complications with effective investigations were noted by Human Rights Watch (2006) in a report on the WCC. The War Crimes Unit (WCU) of the BiH State Investigation and Protection Agency is the main investigating body and in additional to political and ethnic issues that may hamper their work, it also suffers from personnel and equipment shortages. The work of the WCU is nonetheless vital to obtaining evidence in existing cases and could prove to be invaluable to regional courts as well provided they increase the number of qualified investigators and receive the necessary equipment.

The Stankovic case highlights another important area of concern for the state judicial system, the need to properly staff the country's prison system, and ensure the support of the country's police. In May 2007, Stankovic escaped from the prison in Foca where he was detained and is currently still on the run. Following the escape, High Representative Christian Schwartz-Schilling noted that establishing proper prisons run by responsible individuals was a priority for BiH (Office of the High Representative 2007). He called for a state prison that would house criminals convicted by the Court. Undertaking this project would require time and substantial financial resources. In the meantime Schwartz-Schilling suggested prisoners not be sent to prisons that are located and run by individuals of the same ethnic group. That is to say, Serbs should not be sent to prisons in the *Republika Srpska*, Croats to prisons in Herzegovina, and Bosniaks to prisons in Central BiH. Though he noted the issue was about security rather than ethnicity, it is clear that ethnicity was a major concern in placing inmates in the prison system upon conviction.

It is also no secret that the country's economy has stalled, and this has grave implications on the development of the country's legal system and the implementation of the rule of law. Although some years have been better than others, BiH's gross domestic product (GDP) growth has continued to decline. In 1996, with the rebuilding of the war-torn nation, its GDP grew by about 85 percent (due largely to the international community's presence). By 1997, GDP grew by about 40 percent, but by 2005, GDP growth had slowed to about 4 percent.[6] In 2008, the United Nations Development Program (UNDP) reported that unemployment in BiH was over 25 percent with about the same percentage of the country living in poverty (UNDP 2008). Domestic economic decline is exacerbated by declining amounts of international assistance going to the country. Between 1996 and 2007, for example, the international community flooded this country of about four million people with at least $14 billion.[7] However, assistance since the late 1990s has been declining precipitously; between 2003 and 2005, U.S. bilateral assistance exceeded $50 million annually (US Department of State 2005). The U.S. aid declined from $26 million in 2006 to $15 million in 2008 (USAID 2009).

The limited resources of the State Court and the WCC in particular undermine their credibility and effectiveness. Even under the best circumstances, the court is capable of trying a few war crimes cases each year while the country's other poorer courts will be required to try the majority of these war crime cases (Barria and Roper 2008). The establishment of a WCC with jurisdiction over criminal cases that included these offenses was a positive step, but still the State Court lacks the necessary funds to carry out its responsibilities. Donor conferences have provided much some funds for the Court and WCC, and the international community pledged an initial sum of €15.6 million in 2003 to set up the WCC (ICTY 2003b). Both the OHR and ICTY agreed this would be sufficient to meet the needs of the WCC for the first two years. Unfortunately, the international community's initial enthusiasm for BiH's new judicial system did not last long. At a second donors' conference in 2006, pledges dropped by more than half to €7.7 million; ICTY president Fausto Pocar expressed serious concern to the Security Council that the contributions fell "far short of what is required to ensure that these judicial systems are able to fulfill their essential function of entrenching rule of law in Bosnia and Herzegovina" (ICTY 2006). The implications of this drop-off in funding could have serious consequences. President Pocar even suggested the possibility that cases transferred to the State Court may need to be deferred back to the tribunal if there wasn't sufficient support from the international community. BiH's fragile judicial system runs the risk of failing before it has had the chance to succeed unless the international community is willing to commit the necessary support to maintain the court.

Other cultural obstacles have simultaneously hindered trials from realizing their full potential. Some point to the phenomenon of "judicial colonialism" and how international ignorance of the country's history of legal culture and the ICTY's primacy over domestic courts have together negatively impacted the country's legal development (Thakur 2005). Interviews with judges in BiH suggest that most believe that an emphasis on international justice has greatly impaired BiH's ability to develop its own judiciary (Fletcher and Weinstein 2004). In the process, the international community inadvertently ignored the country's common law system, steering the emerging judiciary toward embracing an adversarial model of criminal justice (Bohlander 2003, 80).

The involvement of international lawyers and consultants, many of whom are unfamiliar with the country's legal system have undermined courts' legitimacy and effectiveness (Bohlander 2003, 62). For example, the new criminal codes that were established in 2003 present difficulties for the State Court. Plea agreements and immunity are allowed under the new CPC but neither have any prior context in BiH's criminal proceedings. These tools are commonly used in other country to expedite proceedings or obtain vital information that will lead to the apprehension and prosecution of others. In BiH, however, individuals who are given the choice of a plea agreement or immunity may have committed serious crimes, exacerbating tension among ethnic groups who feel do not see these tools as appropriate in the local context (Human Rights Watch 2007). The result of this could be even less trust in the State Court and its handling of war crimes cases. Ultimately, this clash of legal cultures might reduce the legitimacy of the State Court. One victim, interviewed by Human Rights Watch, commented that although judicial efficiency is very important, plea bargaining and immunity are more acceptable in the context of minor crimes such as car accidents. He also noted that he would be very upset if the person responsible for his suffering during the war used bargaining tools to receive a reduced sentence (Human Rights Watch 2008). The State Court must find a way to strike a balance between efficiency and efficacy if it is to contribute to the rule of law.

Conclusions

To be sure, rebuilding BiH's justice system should remain a top priority, but it is clear that this is a daunting and costly exercise deeply embedded in the country's broader nation-building effort. As others have noted in their evaluation of transitional justice, there is neither a simple nor a quick fix for the complex problem of administering justice in post-conflict countries and the fate of domestic trials depends on many factors, both international and domestic (Fletcher et al. 2009, 165). There are few bright spots in Bosnia's development at present. However, the international community's ongoing commitment to BiH and the existence of credible institutions like the State Court and the WCC provide some reason to hope that one day domestic trials will, indeed, have a home court advantage.

Notes

1. Exceptions include the work of Bohlander (2003), Johnson (2005), and Mundis (2005).
2. McMahon has been travelling regularly to Bosnia since 2000, and in 2007, she conducted approximately a dozen open-ended interviews with international officials from the OHR, the UN, and the OSCE and with BiH officials dealing with justice issues.
3. PIC is a group of fifty-five countries charged with implementing the Dayton Agreement.
4. Although members of the Ministry of Civil Affairs, Ministry of Justice as well as the OHR agreed on a draft text of the law on a Court of BiH, the law did not pass through regular procedures by the Council of Ministers of BiH and the Parliamentary Assembly of BiH (Office of the High Representative 2000).
5. For more on the structure of BiH's consociational democracy and the use of quotas, see Bose (2002).
6. GDP growth rate for BiH comes from UN Economic Commission for Europe. Available at: www.w3.unece.org/pxweb/Dialog.
7. This includes assistance to the country after the war, not money spent during the war or after on securing the region. See the State Department's Bureau of European and Eurasian Affairs, September 2007.

References

Akhavan, Payam. 1998. "Justice in The Hague, Peace in the former Yugoslavia?" *Human Rights Quarterly* 20:737–816.

Barria, Lilian, and Steven D. Roper. 2008. "Judicial Capacity Building in Bosnia And Herzegovina: Understanding Legal Reform beyond the Completion Strategy of the ICTY." *Human Rights Review* 9:317–330.

Bass, Gary J. 2000. *Stay the Hand of Vengeance: The Politics of War Crimes Tribunals*. Princeton, NJ: Princeton University Press.

Bohlander, Michael. 2003. "Last Exit Bosnia: Transferring War Crimes Prosecution from the International Tribunal to Domestic Courts." *Criminal Law Forum* 14:59–99.

Bose, Sumantra. 2002. Bosnia after Dayton: Nationalist Partition and International Intervention. London: C. Hurst and Co.

Brahm, Eric. 2007. "Uncovering the Truth: Examining Truth Commission Success and Impact." *International Studies Perspectives* 8:15–35.

Chandler, David. 2000. *Bosnia: Faking Democracy after Dayton*. London: Pluto Press.

Council of Europe Venice Commission. 2000. "Law on the Court of Bosnia and Herzegovina." Available at: www.venice.coe.int/docs/2000/CDL(2000)106-e.asp.

Court of Bosnia and Herzegovina. 2005. "Indictments of Section 1 (2005): Stankovic, Radovan, Case No. X-KR-05/70." Available at: www.sudbih.gov.ba/?opcija=optuznice&godina=2005&odjel=1&jezik=e.

Court of Bosnia and Herzegovina. 2006. "Verdicts of Section 1 (2006): Stankovic, Radovan, Case No. X-KR-05/70." Available at: www.sudbih.gov.ba/?opcija=presude&godina=2006&odjel=1&jezik=e.

Court of Bosnia and Herzegovina. 2007. "Brochure of the Court of Bosnia and Herzegovina Brochure." Available at: www.sudbih.gov.ba/?jezik=e.

Donlon, Fidelma. 2008. "Rule of Law: From the International Criminal Tribunal for the Former Yugoslavia to the War Crimes Chamber of Bosnia and Herzegovina." In *Deconstructing the Reconstruction: Human Rights and Rule of Law in Postwar Bosnia and Herzegovina*, ed. Dina Francesca Haynes. Hampshire: Ashgate Publishing.

Drumbl, Mark A. 2007. *Atrocity, Punishment, and International Law*. New York: Cambridge University Press.

Elster, Jon. 2004. *Closing the Books: Transitional Justice in Historical Perspective*. New York: Cambridge University Press.

Fletcher, Laurel E., Harvey M. Weinstein, and Jamie Rowen. 2009. "Context, Timing and the Dynamics of Transitional Justice: A Historical Perspective." *Human Rights Quarterly* 31:163–330.

Goldstone, Richard. 1996. "Justice as a Tool for Peacemaking: Truth Commission and International Criminal Tribunals." *New York University Journal of International Law and Politics* 28:485–503.

Hagan, John. 2003. *Justice in the Balkans: Prosecuting War Crimes in The Hague Tribunal.* Chicago, IL: University of Chicago Press.

Hagan, John, and Sanja Kutnjak Ivkovic. 2006. "War Crimes, Democracy, and the Rule of Law in Belgrade, the Former Yugoslavia, and Beyond." *The Annals of the American Academy of Political and Social Science* 605:130–151.

Human Rights Watch. 2006. "Looking for Justice: The War Crimes Chamber in Bosnia and Herzegovina." Available at: www.hrw.org/en/reports/2006/07/07.

Human Rights Watch. 2007. "Narrowing the Impunity Gap." Available at: www.hrw.org/en/reports/2007/02/11/narrowing-impunity-gap-0.

Human Rights Watch. 2008. "Still Waiting: Bringing Justice for War Crimes, Crimes against Humanity, and Genocide in Bosnia and Herzegovina's Cantonal and District Courts." Available at: www.hrw.org/en/reports/2008/07/09/still-waiting.

International Criminal Tribunal for the Former Yugoslavia. 2003a. "Tenth Annual Report of the International Criminal Tribunal for the Prosecution of Persons Responsible for Serious Violations of International Humanitarian Law Committed in the Territory of the Former Yugoslavia since 1991." Available at: www.icty.org/sections/AbouttheICTY/Reports and Publications.

International Criminal Tribunal for the Former Yugoslavia. 2003b. "Donors Raise 15.6 Million Euros for War Crimes Chamber of BIH Court." Available at: www.icty.org/sid/8165.

International Criminal Tribunal for the Former Yugoslavia. 2006. "Assessment and Report of Judge Fausto Pocar, President of the International Criminal Tribunal for the Former Yugoslavia, Provided to the Security Council Pursuant to Paragraph 6 of Council Resolution 1534 (2004), U.N. Doc. S/2006/353." Available at: www.icty.org/sections/AbouttheICTY/ReportsandPublications.

International Criminal Tribunal for the Former Yugoslavia. 2009a. "Working with the Region." Available at: www.icty.org/sid/96.

International Criminal Tribunal for the Former Yugoslavia. 2009b. "The Cases." Available at: www.icty.org/action/cases/4.

International Criminal Tribunal for the Former Yugoslavia. 2009c. "Outreach." Available at: www.icty.org/sections/Outreach.

Kerr, Rachel. 2004. *The International Criminal Tribunal for the Former Yugoslavia: An Exercise in Law, Politics, and Diplomacy.* New York: Oxford University Press.

Kritz, Neil. 1995. *Transitional Justice: How Emerging Democracies Reckon with Former Regimes, Vol. 1 General Considerations.* Washington, D.C.: United States Institute of Peace Press.

McMahon, Patrice C., and David P. Forsythe. 2008. "The ICTY's Impact on Serbia: Judicial Romanticism meets Network Politics." *Human Rights Quarterly* 30:412–435.

McMahon, Patrice C., and Jon Western. 2009. "Bosnia: Unfinished and Still Vulnerable" *Foreign Affairs* (forthcoming September/October).

Meernik, James. 2005. "Justice and Peace? How the International Criminal Tribunal Affects Societal Peace in Bosnia." *Journal of Peace Research* 42:271–289.

Minow, Martha. 1998. *Between Vengeance and Forgiveness: Facing History after Genocide and Mass Violence.* Boston, MA: Beacon Press.

OHR. 1996. "Rome Agreement." Available at: www.ohr.int/ohr-dept/hr-rol/thedept/war-crime-tr/default.asp?content_id=6093.

OHR. 1998. "PIC Madrid Declaration." Available at: www.ohr.int/pic/default.asp?content_id=5190.

OHR. 2000. "Decision Establishing the BiH State Court." Available at: www.ohr.int/decisions/statemattersdec/default.asp?content_id=362.

OHR. 2003. "Decision Enacting the Criminal Code of Bosnia and Herzegovina." Available at: www.ohr.int/decisions/judicialrdec/default.asp?content_id=29095.

OHR. 2007. "Schwartz-Schilling: Stankovic Fiasco Highlights Need for State Prison." Available at: www.ohr.int/ohrdept/presso/pressr/default.asp?content_id=39891.

Peskin, Victor. 2008. *International Justice in Rwanda and the Balkans: Virtual Trials and the Struggle for State Cooperation*. New York: Cambridge University Press.

Roper, Steven D., and Lilian Barria. 2006. *Designing Criminal Tribunals: Sovereignty and International Concerns in the Protection of Human Rights*. Hampshire: Ashgate Publishing.

South East Europe Public Agenda Survey. 2002. *International Institute for Democracy and Electoral Assistance*. Available at: www.idea.int/europe_cis/balkans/.

Stover, Eric, and Harvey M. Weinstein, ed. 2004. *My Neighbor, My Enemy. Justice and Community in the Aftermath of Mass Atrocity*. Cambridge: Cambridge University Press.

Thakur, Ramesh. 2005. "Tyrants under the Gun." *The Japan Times*. November 10.

Thomas, Oskar N.T., James Ron, and Roland Paris. 2008. "The Effects of Transitional Justice Mechanisms: A Summary of Empirical Research Findings and Implications for Analysts and Practitioners." Working Paper. Centre for International Policy Studies, University of Ottawa.

United Nations. 2002. "Statement by the President of the Security Council, U.N. Doc. S/PRST/2002/21." Available at: www.un.org/Docs/sc/statements/2002/prst2002.htm.

United Nations. 2003. "Security Council Resolution 1503, U.N. Doc. S/RES/1503." Available at: www.un.org/Docs/sc/unsc_resolutions03.html.

United Nations. 2008. "Assessment and report of Judge Patrick Robinson, President of the International Tribunal for the Former Yugoslavia, provided to the Security Council pursuant to paragraph 6 of Council resolution 1534 (2004), U.N. Doc. S/2008/729." Available at: www.un.org/Docs/journal/asp/ws.asp?m=S/2008/729.

UNDP. 2008. "Poverty Reduction." Available at: www.undp.ba/index.aspx?PID=25&RID=26.

USAID. 2009. "Bosnia-Herzegovina Country Profile." Available at: www.usaid.gov/locations/europe_eurasia/countries/ba.

U.S. Department of the State. 2005. "United States Recaps Aid to Bosnia-Herzegovina for 1995." Available at: www.america.gov/st/washfile-english/2005/November/20051212172624xlrennef0.6925623.html.

Van Der Merwe, Hugo, Victoria Baxter, and Audrey R. Chapman, eds. 2009. *Assessing Transitional Justice*. Washington, D.C.: United States Institute of Peace Press.

PART IV

Sierra Leone

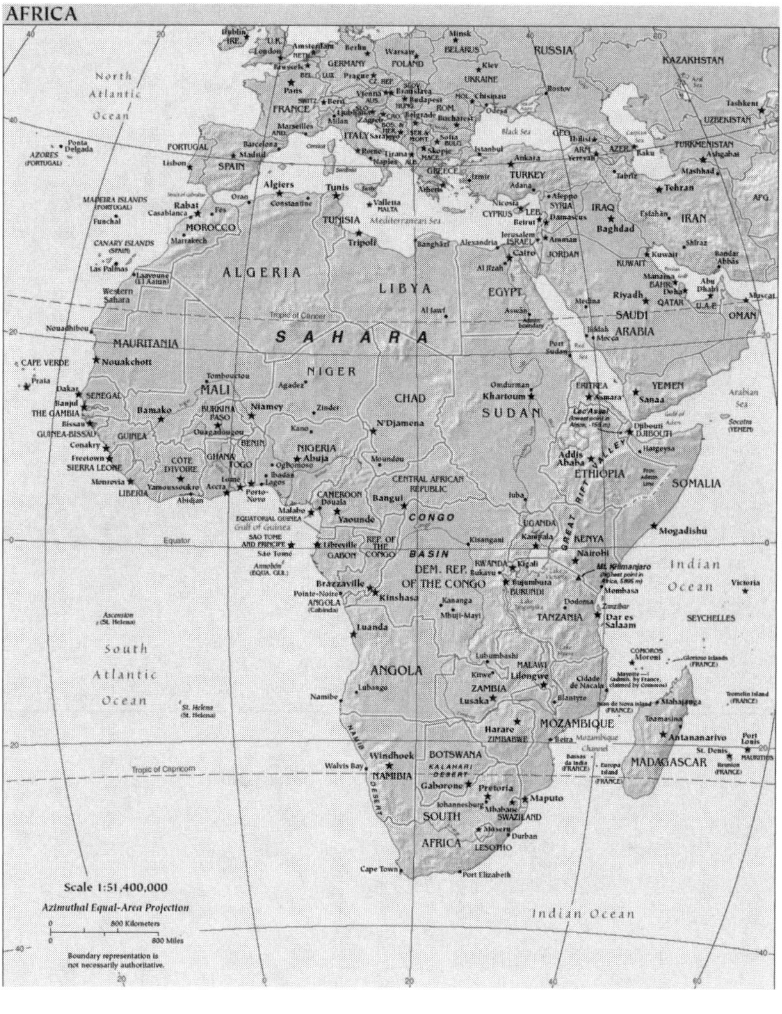

Map from the United States Central Intelligence Agency's World Factbook.

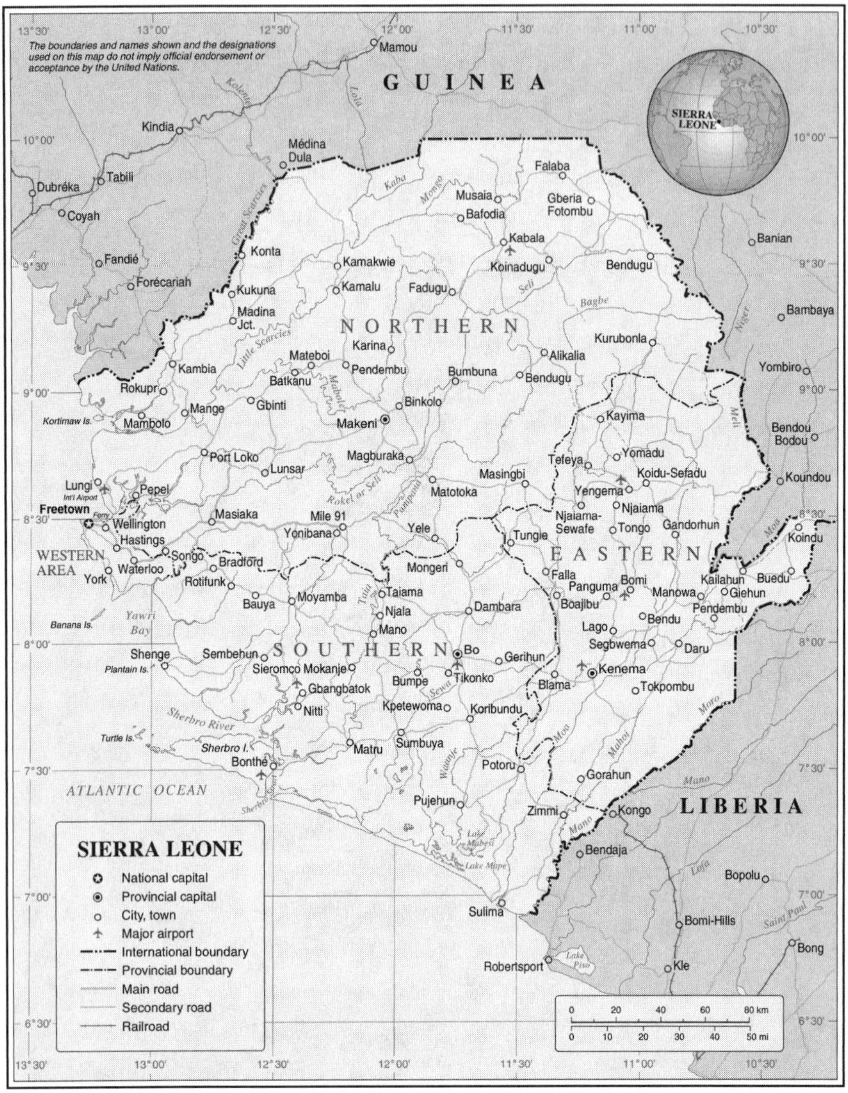

Map derived from the UNCS map.
http://www.un.org/Depts/Cartographic/map/profile/sierrale.pdf

CHAPTER 8

Genesis of the Sierra Leone Conflict and Its Human Rights Violations

ABU KARIMU MBOKA

Introduction

The conflicts in Sierra Leone have generated a great body of research in the last ten years. Many such scholarly endeavors focus on the roles played by diamonds, child soldiers, and international responses in the conflicts as well as the consequential gross human rights violations as preludes to understanding the conflict and its implications for Sierra Leone as a nation. The overwhelming conclusion, however, is that the conflict was a product of unfavorable internal factors: Sierra Leone's authorization of the Economic Community of West African States Monitoring Group (ECOMOG) to use its territory as a base for military interventions in Liberia and its alleged ties to the United Liberation Movement of Liberia for Democracy coupled with the country's deteriorating economic conditions, epidemic corruption, unregulated diamond trade, and longstanding history of patrimonial politics prompted the cross-border invasion by the Revolutionary United Front (RUF) in 1992 (Francis 1999; Zack-Williams 1999; Boas 2001; Zack-Williams 2001; Archibald and Richards 2002; Keen 2005).

The RUF was a rebel army that waged a decade-long civil war in Sierra Leone with the support of Liberia. Many of the worst atrocities during the civil war were committed by the RUF rebels. However, as this chapter demonstrates, RUF violence must be viewed in the broader context of post-colonial Sierra Leonean politics. Archibald and Richards (2002), for instance, point to the effect of poverty and injustice on youth and the lack of educational opportunities in Sierra Leone in the years leading to the RUF invasion as factors that instigated the war. Zack-Williams (1999) cites post-colonial development strategies and the decline of state apparatus and civil societies, disruption of local agricultural and economic institutions, and the glamorization of greener pastures outside the country, especially in the 1980s, as evidence of internal stimulation for the conflicts in the 1990s. He argues that the failing economic conditions created unstable socioeconomic and political circumstances that rendered the country ungovernable in the late 1980s and thus allowed the interventions of the RUF.

These debates and conclusions fail to explain, however, why the April 29, 1992 National Provisional Ruling Council (NPRC) military coup received overwhelming public support, especially given that the group of six young soldiers forming the council made their political debut with firm promises of crushing the RUF's rebellion. Similarly, the debate does not account for the outpouring of public outrage at the Armed Forces Revolutionary Council (AFRC) and its decision to absorb senior members of the RUF into its government. Indeed when the AFRC overthrew the government on May 25, 1997, it promised to curb corruption, end patrimonial politics, and immediately moved to end the conflict by appointing the RUF leader as the vice chairman. It is also hard to explain the internal context within which the popularity of the Civil Defense Forces (CDF) grew across all sections, especially in the southeastern parts of the country where the RUF concentrated its operations.

I argue that the RUF's attack on March 23, 1991 was orchestrated and launched as a result of changes taking place outside the borders of Sierra Leone, but that the country's colonial past and its economic and political conditions in the 1990s legitimized the uprising. However, the lack of discipline, goals, unified strategies, human resources, and logistics supports within RUF helped sustain and even aggravated the human rights violations that dominated the conflict. The question, therefore, is not so much about the basis of the war but rather what transformed pre-1990s aspirations for political change, as a prerequisite for political and economic development, into nine years of violence punctuated with outrageous and devastating human rights violations. In this context, this chapter talks about the conflicts with special focus on factors and strategies that enhanced the severity of the violence and the human rights violations. As a preface to the discussion of conditions that helped sustain the conflict for almost ten years, I start by examining aspects of the country's colonial policies, corruption, and diamond industry that explain its patrimonial and regional politics in the context of Southeast versus Northwest and protectorate against Crown colony. It is hoped that such an analysis will expose the complex dimensions of the political and socioeconomic conditions that dictated the roles played by different factions in the 1990s.

Pre-Independent Sierra Leone

The violent events that took place in Sierra Leone during the late 1980s and early 1990s were partly rooted in the country's pre-independent colonial relationships with the outside world. The relevant contact, which started forming in 1787 with the arrival of the first batch of freed African slaves in Freetown, quickly transformed the city from an international transit center for slavery to a refuge for transatlantic slave victims, especially after the British Chief Justice of the King Bench, Lord Mansfield, ruled that "a slave on setting foot in England, became free and could not be carried back into slavery"

(Cotay 1959, 210). As a result, formerly enslaved Africans from America, the West Indies, Jamaica, and Britain, and later those rescued from slave ships by British warships, continued to arrive in Freetown well beyond 1808, which is when Freetown became a British Crown colony.

The newly resettled freed Sierra Leoneans became known as Creoles. Logically, from the start, they were heavily involved in the day-to-day operations of the colonialists and quickly became one of the prominent ethnic and political groups in Freetown. The Creoles flourished in Freetown for over a century under an administrative system separate from the one used in outlying areas. Of course, this arrangement distanced the Crown colony from what became in 1896 the Sierra Leone British Protectorate. The Crown colony was ruled directly by a governor appointed by the British government, but the protectorate was only a territory protected against third party invasion. Sierra Leone has four regions, based on this colonial ethnicity grouping: Temne in the North, Mendes in the East and South, and Creoles in the West (Freetown). The Mendes and Temnes each accounted for about 30 percent of the population with the Creoles about 5 percent. This means that over 90 percent of the country's population lived in the protectorate.

In the eyes of the protectorates, the new settlers knew a lot about life in Freetown, the West Indies, Nova Scotia, Jamaica, and about their former slave masters, but beyond the fact that they were descendants of Africa and shared common local borders with the protectorate, the Creoles had very little in common with the rest of the population in the protectorate. In practical terms, the cultural, socioeconomic, political, and physical geographical distinctions between the Crown colony and protectorate made it rational to collapse the Creoles and the colonial administrators into one category and to also invent the concept of regional representation (via tribal chiefs) as opposed to the traditional territorial representation that existed prior to the formation of the Crown colony. Sierra Leone is not unique with regard to regional representation, but as a starting point for governance, identity politics was, and is, unhealthy for Sierra Leone. The policy is potentially flammable when it is influenced by the notion that government officials treat people favorably with whom they are ethnically affiliated and that therefore decisions made in Freetown were more likely to have been sympathetic to the needs of Creoles and colonists at the expense of the indigenous population. In the context of the 1990s, this situation represented the beginning of violent contentions in Sierra Leone as to remedies for the inequitable social outcomes and solutions as to who should govern that were based on physical characteristics or ethnic and regional affiliation rather than individual track records and positions on social matters. Obviously, this type of divisive policy is a recipe for violence, and pre-independent Sierra Leone was not an exception, as evidenced by a series of violent resistances like the 1889 response to the Crown colony's new hut or household tax on the protectorates.

The Hut Tax War between the protectorate and the Crown colony, during which many Creoles were murdered, was headed on the protectorate side by Bai Bureh (Dorjahn and Fyfe 1962). The Northern chief and his men refused to comply with the new tax policy arguing that it symbolized the Crown colony and Creoles' policies targeting the domination and exploitation of local residents. Though the Northern chief Bai Bureh was subsequently arrested and sent into exile in Ghana and most of his close comrades hanged to death by the Crown colony administrators in November 1889, the Hut Tax War provided the blueprint for a series of subsequent violent resistances like the riots in 1935, 1955, and 1956 in response to policy decisions made in the Crown colony that many thought grossly and negatively affected the collective interests of local inhabitants in the protectorate (Tangri 1976; Luke 1985; Edward 2005).

The Hut Tax War and each of the subsequent violent resistances that followed further alienated and portrayed the Crown colony as an oppressive political institution headed by people who did not represent the collective interests of the local populace. In the end, the two sides adopted opposing but at the same time somewhat complementary political approaches: The protectorate settled on "direct representation" as a solution to unfavorable representation while the Crown colony adopted the opposite doctrine of "indirect rule" as a means to govern the protectorate without direct confrontation.

Indirect rule emphasizes downward hierarchical structures of government based on administrative and geographical division of subjects into unique groups while direct representation relies on structures of government permitting opinions to flow upward (from the population to chiefs and then to the colonial government) but using the same administrative apparatus put in place by indirect rule. Therefore, under direct representation, confidence in the central government's operations is dictated by direct representatives, thus giving birth to the idea of regional and patrimonial politics. In this framework, politicians and civil servants act as intermediaries between the central government and the people. The heads of government in Freetown can therefore win local support by patronizing chiefs or direct representatives, and the masses can buy government services by bribing their direct representatives. These abuses explain the institutionalization of corruption.

At a systemic level, the division of Sierra Leoneans into protectorates and Crown and colony, and indirect and direct representation, rendered the central government invisible in the protectorates, and in the eyes of the Crown colony, it reduced residents in the protectorate to a number of paramount chiefs. These unfortunate relationships worked against the formation of a healthy political bond between 95 percent of the country's population and the capital. As a result, and unlike the images in Accra, Banjul, and Lagos or in Ghana, The Gambia, and Nigeria, where the capitals are seen as the headquarters of collective representation, Freetown emerged as representative of the Crown colony pledging loyalty to the colonialists. Even today, Freetown remains in the eyes of many as a political province that serves those who are directly represented in terms of province, district, chiefdoms, and thus ethnicity, since provincial and district borders were drawn long ago along ethnic lines.

Toward an Independent Sierra Leone

Under the indirect rule policy, the British colonial empire governed the Crown colony through its governor who in turn administered the protectorate through the district officers. The paramount chiefs reported to the district officers. These chiefs exercised direct jurisdiction over residents of their respective chiefdoms through section chiefs who oversaw town chiefs (Archibald and Richards 2002). Thus, Sierra Leone was administratively divided into provinces, districts, chiefdoms, sections, and towns, making it relatively easy for the Crown colony to collect taxes and enforce colonial policies. Obviously in this form of administration, local residents could not readily resist policies that were introduced by people within their immediate reach since the local leaders or indirect representatives of the Crown colony were made of family members, neighbors, landlords, and or members of their respective settlements acting on behalf of the different levels of the colonial administrative hierarchies. Indirect rule benefited all the different levels and parties in the administrative hierarchies. The chiefs were allowed to retain portions of the tax funds, and in turn, their cooperation soothed the Crown colony's fear of losing control over subjects in the protectorate, as tax revenues flowed into district headquarters and on to the Crown colony. The strategy also helped paramount chiefs establish themselves as direct representatives of their subjects. Similar outcomes were chronologically introduced throughout various hierarchies.

Systemically, the indirect rule policy justified bribery and corruption in general as a form of compensation for public service. The late President Saika Stevens once equated the concept with the right of a cow to graze around the object to which it is tied. In 1948 for example, out of a total of £134,302 tax revenue collected by 128 chiefdoms, only about £28,085 was spent on legitimate pubic projects while £83,870 was spent on "chiefdom administration" (Lange 2003). Under Stevens' "cow grazing" concept, since the chiefs' duties involved collecting taxes, they were rightfully expected to personally gain from the process, in other words, to eat from the tax bowls.

The chiefs could not be punished for failing to account for the £83,870 even if evidence showed that the funds were lavished on the chiefs personally because the success of the Crown colony depended on the cooperation of the chiefs, and local residents looked up to the same chiefs for protection against harsh government policies. The inevitable result was the emergence of a corrupt political system that relied on bribes and regional and patrimonial politics as its principal organs. Take for instance the Crown administration's authorization of paramount chiefs to keep portions of tax funds for local development. The policies directly infused public funds and services into the local traditional political system without a mechanism to provide oversight against corruption, favoritism, and inadequate leadership. A chief defined what constituted a public project and rendered judgment on the progress of such project. Such were the social and political environments into which Sierra Leone's diamonds, independence, and party policies were introduced.

History would have been different and the consequences of indirect rule in terms of factors that informed and sustained the violence in Sierra Leone would have been less severe if Freetown had not been carved out of the country as a separate territory, a Crown colony, for such a long period (Schneider 1962). Furthermore, an alternative Freetown would have introduced a civil service into the protectorate that was infused with a checks-and-balances system, which enforced accountability and performance, encouraged recognition and compensation, and fostered patriotic ties to Freetown or the central government as representative of all Sierra Leoneans irrespective of social status, ethnic backgrounds, political affiliations, and regional identity. Under such conditions patrimonial politics would not have developed to the current level because local chiefs would have had less reason to feel obligated to personally reward the section chiefs, and section chiefs would not have felt the need to reward the paramount chiefs and so forth. Diamonds would have earned their rightful place in the history of Sierra Leone as national resources for socioeconomic and political development.

Independent Sierra Leone

Politically, the Sierra Leone that emerged toward independence in the 1930s had a political system that emphasized indirect rule, was indifferent to direct representation, and viewed violent resistance as legitimate recourse for unresolved political differences between natives and the Crown colony. The socioeconomic systems of Sierra Leone endorsed financial patronization of civil servants, promoted corruption as a legitimate method of doing business with government, and transformed the diamond industry into a well-organized illicit mining syndicate. When diamonds were discovered in Sierra Leone in 1930, the Crown colony was still in many ways a foreign land, and many natives had no practical use for the precious stones. In fact at first, many natives could not understand why their white district officers willingly traded their goods for the diamonds (Mboka 2008). Things, however, changed when diamonds became a source of quick cash. Lebanese, Syrians, West African nationals, and native Sierra Leoneans flocked into designated diamond areas in the southeast of the country. Amid the chaos in 1933, the Crown colony granted exclusive mining and marketing rights to the British-based Sierra Leone Section Trust (De Beers) for ninety-nine years. A percentage of the royalties De Beers paid to the Crown colony went to respective local paramount chiefs for public projects. Not surprisingly, the colonial administrative structures that were in place to calm resistance and to enforce tax policies in the protectorates failed to control the kind of national and international characters that the illicit diamond mining and trade attracted. Unlike other colonial policies, which could not be challenged without support from chiefs or collective support to form a formidable resistance, the policy on mining allowed anyone to mine diamonds and trade them for cash without the assistance of direct or indirect representation. In an attempt to address this apparent weakness in the law, the Crown colony came up with a penal solution in 1936 by enacting the "Diamond Industry Protection Ordinance" (Cotay 1959).

The ordinance prohibited "strangers" from entering diamond-designated areas without specific government authorization. However, the ordinance's prohibition, which was intended to protect the exclusive monopoly rights granted to De Beers, failed and further weakened the Crown colony's control over many aspects of the diamond industry. First, the granting of exclusive rights to a company that represented the Crown colony reinforced the perception of Freetown as a non-native institution. Secondly, the allocation of portions of the diamond revenue to local governments, coupled with the regular cash inflow from illicit local mining proceeds and tax revenues into local government coffers without an efficient monitoring system, enhanced the institutionalization of corruption at all administrative levels.

Thirdly, the criminalization of the presence of natives in designated diamond territories forced the industry into an organized black market, operated by those who could mine and those who had the cash to pay for diamonds, since they could not afford or qualify for the expensive diamond mining dealer license. Fourthly, this kind of criminalization reinforced regional politics because it automatically banned northwestern nationals from entering diamond-designated lands in the southeastern part of the country. This meant the ordinance barred more than 80 percent of the country's population from benefiting from the lucrative diamond industry. In the end, these four factors increased the volume of illicit mining and trading, provided additional incentives for corruption, and provoked a series of clashes between natives and colonial security forces.

Indeed, it was a miscalculation on the part of the Crown colony to assume that local chiefs could enforce the prohibition of natives from entering their respective backyards and farming grounds in search of cash-generating diamonds. Even if such prohibition was enforceable, the law clearly conflicted with the natural conditions in the protectorate at the time. At the least, the Crown colony failed to take into account that the lands on which the diamonds were discovered served many other local purposes beyond mining and that the prohibition of access would generally constitute a deprivation of livelihood.

When Sierra Leone gained independence in 1961, it had to deal with the legacies of the Crown colony and protectorate, epidemic corruption, dysfunctional administrative systems, regional and contagiously patrimonial politics, a lack of national cohesiveness, and an uncontrolled diamond industry. Sadly, in the process of dealing with the problems of national unity and national economic prosperity, political development and stability became the first post-independence casualties. Failures became commonplace. Patrimonial and regional politics became the norm while politicians and civil servants latched onto corruption as a legitimate source of compensations while illicit diamonds fueled many of the country's problems.

Regional and Patrimonial Politics

The final preparation for an independent Sierra Leone started in 1953 when the first African cabinet was formed. Sir Milton Margai, a Southeasterner, headed the new cabinet and became the first prime minister in 1956. He led the country to independence on April 27, 1961. During this period, political parties were formed, including the Sierra Leone People's Party (SLPP) and All People's Congress (APC). Predictably, these parties were formed on regional and ethnic lines. The Mende-dominated Southeastern SLPP supported the people who lived in this region while the Temne-dominated APC supported those in the Northwest.

Sir Milton Margai headed the SLPP in the country's first general parliamentary election in May 1962 and won a landslide victory. Margai became the first elected prime minister and upon his death in 1964, his brother Albert Margai succeeded him as the country's second prime minister. By this time, allegations of the SLPP promoting corruption and practicing favoritism and patrimonial politics were mounting in the APC quarters. Some of the displeasures among APC stewards were triggered in part by the rapid improvements and political capital prompted by the discovery of diamonds in the Southeastern parts of the country. Anti-SLPP activists complained about an increased presence of SLPP supporters in civil and political offices because of political patronization and reciprocation of loyal Southeastern supports with appointments to key positions, especially in education and security forces.

The SLPP read many of these criticisms as direct products of regional politics, which at the time were hard to distinguish from tribal politics between the Mendes in the Southeastern part of the country and the Temne in the North. As a result, the SLPP made several attempts during its administration to suppress regional politics. For instance, after the death of Sir Milton Margai in 1964, the party unsuccessfully tried to introduce a one-party system (later in 1978, the APC managed to introduce a one-party state also in an attempt to create an atmosphere free of regional politics). These political developments transformed the 1967 general election into a regional fight for control of Freetown.

The results of the election indicated a very close fight to finish between SLPP and APC, but the governor-general ended speculations of who won by arbitrarily declaring Stevens, leader of the APC, the winner and the country's prime minister. The governor's decision sparked the first post-independence regional violence. Within hours, the Commander of the Armed Forces, Brigadier General David Lansana, ousted Stevens in a bloodless coup. Lansana, a Mende from the Southeastern part of the country, had been a strong supporter of Prime Minister Margai. It is important to note that during this period, tensions over political leadership were very high among the Temne-dominated North, the Creoles in Freetown, and the Mende-dominated Southeastern part of the country, which Lansana and Margai represented.

With Stevens under house arrest, a group of senior officers later took control of the government on March 23, 1968, arrested Lansana, suspended the constitution, and formed the National Reformation Council (NRC) headed by Brigadier General Andrew Juxon-Smith, a Creole with a Southeastern ancestry. Within a month of coming to power, the NRC was overthrown by the Anti-Corruption Revolutionary Movement (ACRM) under the command of Brigadier General John Amadu Bangura (a Northerner). When the ACRM reinstated Stevens as prime minister in 1968, he formed an all-APC cabinet. Sierra Leone subsequently became a republic in 1971, and Stevens became the republic's first president (Fisher 1969).

The new president took office in the midst of provincial disturbances and at the height of regional politics. The volatile political conditions triggered tough responses from Stevens, who had already lost the confidence of the country's security forces. With a state of emergency already in place, Stevens requested and received troops from neighboring Guinea. He stationed the troops in strategic locations throughout the country and retained them until 1973, after establishing the elite Internal Security Unit (ISU). The ISU members were feared for their brutality, and were highly trained in crushing uprisings. They were notoriously known for shooting at demonstrators. Thus, in popular speech ISU came to stand for "I Shoot U." Stevens later changed the name to Special Security Division (SSD) in an attempt to end such public sentiment.

In response to Stevens' authoritarian policies, the SLPP boycotted the 1973 general elections, alleging widespread intimidation and procedural obstruction, but the APC went ahead with the election and ended up winning 90 percent of the parliamentary seats it contested. In March 1976, Stevens was re-elected unopposed after an attempted coup in 1974. In the following year, Sierra Leone experienced some of the worst student-led political violence of its history, especially in the Southeast. When parliament approved a one-party state constitution in 1978, Stevens' APC-led government was already on record for running corrupt criminal justice institutions, dilapidated educational facilities, failed public projects, a bankrupt financial empire overwhelmed by inflation, destitute agricultural production lines, dysfunctional security agencies, structured regional and patrimonial politics, a disgruntled military force, and overburdened socioeconomic and political policies that nourished gross human rights violations. At the height of his notoriety for dictatorial and corrupt governance, Stevens announced his desire to relinquish power to Major General Joseph Saidu Momoh, a Northerner from the minority Limba tribe. Many political pundits speculated that Stevens' choice of Momoh was born out of his desire to neutralize regional politics. Whether neutralization was the policy or not, Momoh promised to eliminate corruption, improve the country's economy, and return the country to multiparty rule.

A one-party state referendum held on November 28, 1985 elected Momoh as the second president of Sierra Leone. He made reasonable progress on his campaign promises to curb corruption until the March 1987 coup attempt led by his Vice-President Francis Minah, a Southerner. Momoh had Minah and five other suspects executed in 1989, and thereafter his relationship with the Southeastern parts of the country was very poor. He fully embraced patrimonial and regional politics and surrounded himself with Northerners like APC Secretary General E. T. Kamara and Inspector General of Police Bamby Kamara (Zack-Williams 1999). Momoh gave many of his political cronies unregulated power to rewrite the laws of Sierra Leone as they wished. By the time Momoh returned the country to a multi-party system in 1991, he had already lost all the political traction that he had gained in the late 1980s. The anti-corruption crusade came to a complete halt; regional politics was in full swing, and a Libyan-backed civil war was raging in neighboring Liberia. Sierra Leone was by this time already a failed state with all the elements in place for what became the most horrific scene of human rights violations in the history of sub-Saharan Africa.

The External Connections: The Role of Liberian Politics in Sierra Leone

The RUF leader, Foday Sankoh, gained political attention in 1970 by accusing Stevens of widespread corruption including plundering the country's diamonds and other mineral resources. The allegations briefly landed Sankoh in prison, and upon his release, he fled the country and ended up in Libya, where he later became one of the many African dissidents who were undergoing Green Book radicalization. Muammar al-Gaddafi launched his "Green Book Revolution" in the 1970s, at first emphasizing Arab nationalism, liberation, and educational advancement. While the factors that led to the failure of his Pan-Arabian nationalist agendas are not the subject of this chapter, it is important to note that Gaddafi's strong opposition toward Western and American foreign influences was the linchpin of his Pan-African stance in the 1980s.

Gaddafi used colonial domination and exploitation in general, and more specifically British-American support for apartheid in South Africa, as his platform while playing key roles in the African Union and Pan-African debates. At the same time, he encouraged a mass influx of African nationals into Libya to take up unskilled jobs, learn Arabic, learn about Islam, and propagate his Green Book ideologies. Stateless sub-Saharan dissidents like Charles Taylor and Sankoh, many of whom were wanted by security forces in their respective countries of origin, saw Gaddafi's Green Book revolution as an opportunity to wage a war in hope of becoming presidents.

Sankoh was trained and radicalized in Libya along with Taylor who was head of the National Patriotic Front of Liberia (NPFL). It is widely reported that Sankoh was one of the soldiers under Taylor's command that attacked Liberia from bases in the Ivory Coast in late 1989. Taylor's initial strategy was to "emancipate" Liberia from so-called Western exploitation and then launch a coordinated attack against Sierra Leone to be followed by The Gambia, the Ivory Coast, and elsewhere in sub-Saharan Africa. At first, this plan seemed feasible until Taylor's revolution became an all-out violent ethnic conflict punctuated by rape, massacre, and displacement of various Liberian ethnic groups. The degradation of the revolution into a religious and ethnic war naturally created logistical and human resource nightmares for the NPFL and Taylor. Also by this time, the United Nations Security Council sanctions had already rendered Libya economically and politically impotent to render Taylor any support. With Gaddafi becoming sidelined in the regional politics, Taylor was deprived of Libyan logistical and financial support. Thus, the need arose to generate resources to help the NPFL capture the Liberian capital, Monrovia. These conditions stimulated illicit mining and the exploitation of child labor in the mines, a strategy that later gave rise to the premature invasion of Sierra Leone. The decision consequently paved the way for President Momoh's fall.

The Role of the RUF in Sierra Leone

At the time the RUF attacked Sierra Leone, the country's educational, financial, and security institutions were on life support, and with the increase in Liberian refugees and Sierra Leonean returnees taking their toll on the country's meager resources, Momoh publicly admitted that he had failed the country. Shortly thereafter, he was overthrown on April 29, 1992 and forced into exile in Guinea by the NPRC. This group of young disgruntled soldiers selected Captain Valentine Strasser as the council's chairperson on May 4, 1992. The new government promised to quickly and effectively crush and prosecute the RUF, eradicate corruption, return the country to multiparty system, and revitalize government institutions. The announcement was greeted with jubilant rallies all over Sierra Leone, with celebrations in expectation of what many thought was the end to three decades of dictatorship, corruption, poverty, gross human rights violations, and economic destitution. Many saw Strasser as the redeemer.

Within the first year, the NPRC arrested and executed over two dozen prominent APC politicians and made many enemies within and outside the Sierra Leone Army and other security agencies (Zack-Williams and Riley 1993). It appeared that each of the APC stewards executed by the NPRC left behind a group of soldiers and security elements bonded together by years of patrimonial and regional politics, and a strong desire to sabotage the NPRC's efforts by either forming into rebel groups or joining the RUF. The tainted Sierra Leone Army soon became unreliable as civilians started referring to its members as "sobels" (soldier-rebels). For instance, it is alleged that soldiers traded strategic secrets with rebels in exchange for payment or in an attempt to undermine the central government (Francis 1999). Alternatively, the NPRC contracted the service of foreign mercenaries like Executive Outcomes, Sandline International, and Gurkha Security. In the Southern part of the country, members of the CDF, almost exclusively consisting of Southeastern Mendes, created their own defense. The CDF or *Kamajors* organized themselves into a paramilitary organization as a response to the government's failure to protect against RUF brutality. The CDF received substantial regional support.

Indeed, the warm and welcoming sentiments the NPRC initially received quickly evaporated in the face of CDF propaganda (as well as due to the arbitrary exercise of power by NPRC security forces as well as extensive corruption). New anti-NPRC outcries mounted and rumors of Strasser showing signs of unwillingness to return the country to constitutional rule heated up. The NPRC's response came in the form of a crackdown on fundamental rights such as freedom of speech and press. Strasser's deputy chairman, Maada Bio, seized this opportunity and overthrew the NPRC in 1996. This move provoked overwhelming public support. Within six months, Bio reinstated the country's constitution and held general elections. The candidate for the SLPP, Ahmad Tejan Kabbah, won the election and became the country's third president. On May 25, 1997, the Armed Forces Revolutionary Council (AFRC) overthrew the newly elected government. Major General Johnny Paul Koroma, who at the time of the coup was in prison for an earlier attempted coup, was selected as the new head of state. Ten months later, the AFRC was chased out of power and President Kabbah was reinstated by ECOMOG forces.

Many internal and external factors hastened the downfall of the AFRC. For instance, the coup made it logistically difficult for the Nigerian-led ECOMOG to continue its operations in Liberia from bases in Sierra Leone, and also derailed the country's progress toward a healthy multi-party democracy. This means that the AFRC had to deal with resistance from members of the international community who had vested interests in the success of ECOMOG. However, the strongest resistance by many Sierra Leoneans within and outside the country was provoked by the regime's attempt to transform the conflict into a war between the government of Sierra Leone and the Southeastern part of the country, and secondly the appointment of the RUF leader Sankoh as the vice chairman. Certainly, it was perilous for the AFRC to use the Southeastern regional support for the CDF as a justification for the coup. The sudden and intense collaboration between the RUF and the AFRC also distorted any distinction between the AFRC and the RUF and further legitimized the concept of "sobels." From that point on, the AFRC lost not only the support of those who were victims of RUF operations but all those who were benefiting from CDF protection.

Failed Operational Strategies and the External Wars

The RUF's use of violence as a strategy to coerce chiefs and central government agents dismantled the century-old internal traditional cords that held local residents together. Indeed while the outcome of such strategies was different in Liberia, local settlements in Sierra Leone were, and are, governed by a number of traditional institutions held together by chiefs who are also the symbolic stewards of social institutions. When those pillars are dislocated, as the RUF succeeded in doing, the consequences lead to social unrest and violence. The British learned that lesson during the Hut Tax War which is why they succeeded, as far as British interests were concerned, to govern through indirect rule and managed to successfully dominate the protectorate without fragmenting traditional structures.

The use of foreign guerilla fighters, children and gross human rights violations in the name of Liberia and Taylor to dismantle traditional societies in Sierra Leone was a strategic blunder that laid the foundation for the rejections of the RUF and violent provocations in the Southeastern part of the country. Though the foreign fighters had prior knowledge fighting guerrilla warfare in Liberia, they lacked an understanding of what held Southeastern residents together and the role of regional and patrimonial politics in this region. Unlike in Liberia where ethnic difference made it possible for foreign nationals to easily fade into the population, in Sierra Leone, regional and patrimonial politics dictated political affiliation which is why throughout the conflict there was not a single event involving Mendes hunting Temnes or Creoles chasing down Mendes as was the case in Liberia.

One of the valuable tools Stevens effectively used to defuse regional politics was his ethnic and region-neutral approach. He distanced himself from ethnic politics so much that even today, many Sierra Leoneans do not know if Stevens was a Temne, Creole, Mende, or Limba since he forged ties with all four ethnic camps. The RUF not only disregarded the importance of such a lesson but did so through employing children and foreign nationals from mainly Benin, Burkina Faso, the Ivory Coast, The Gambia, Guinea, and Togo.

The sight of children under the influence of drugs, taking commands from foreign nationals and brandishing and firing AK-47s with grenades stuck to their waistbands and chests was bound to provoke resistance from provincial society. The fact that the RUF also disrupted illicit diamond mining activities suggests that from the onset, the RUF failed to understand the need to gain regional support. The decision to take over diamond mining fields meant a direct deprivation for many households of financial resources, a repeat of the events leading to the 1936 Diamond Industry Protection Ordinance. The more one examines the intricacy of Sierra Leone violence, especially in terms of the causes, strategies, parties, scope of gross human rights violations, underlying history and overall effects on Sierra Leone and the region, the clearer it becomes that without the contribution of external parties, gross human rights violations would have been minimal (Mboka 2008). The removal of Strasser from power by his deputy, the 1997 overthrow of Kabbah by the AFRC and the formation of the CDF and the RUF were by-products of external factors.

These internal conflicts were the effects of events in Libya and the civil war in Liberia (albeit sustained by internal patrimonial and regional politics, corruption, and the illicit diamond trade). The gravity of the human rights violations was informed by a series of ideological, cultural, social economic, and political blunders by the RUF in terms of timing, target, and strategies. Indeed if the war had been solely internally motivated, the NPRC would not have enjoyed overwhelming public support after promising to crush the RUF nor would the AFRC been rejected by the masses after the appointment of Sankoh as vice chairman. Furthermore, public reaction to foreign security agencies like Executive Outcomes, Sandline International, and Gurkha Security would have been less jubilant since those agencies were only in the country to prosecute the RUF.

Clearly the RUF's misreading of the histories and prevailing conditions at the time of their incursion, as seen by its targeting local chiefs and governments agents through foreign nationals, relying on child combatants, disrupting illicit diamond mining activities, and using violence as a means to effect change, set in motion the failure of the various parties to effect peaceful change in that country and dictated the consequential gravity of the gross human rights violations that followed. Such miscalculation blurred the lines between emancipation and exploitation, national development and destruction, and between the desire to effect positive change and the willingness to cause mayhem. Furthermore, the disregard for regional and patrimonial politics as well as the structure of direct representation that were in place at the time undermined national peace and security and coerced collective resistance toward RUF-led change. In short, had the RUF applied the correct strategies within the context of the country's history, it would have succeeded in a timely manner to take control of the country, and thus minimize the length of the conflict and the types of gross human rights violations that followed.

Conclusions

Undoubtedly, Sierra Leoneans are responsible for the mayhem they displayed in their country during the war, and there is no justification for the atrocious consequences of their actions. The concerns, therefore, at this juncture are the histories, and accounts of socioeconomic and political factors, that facilitated the kinds and length of violence in Sierra Leone. The obvious conclusions in this regard are that foreign or external domination, no matter how well-intended, can yield a variety of unpleasant outcomes with a wide range of socioeconomic and political implications. In the case of Sierra Leone, internal conditions associated with colonialism did not necessarily cause the violence, but aspects of unfavorable colonial policies helped sustain the conflicts. Also, the RUF's failure to operate within many pre- and post-independence cultural, socioeconomic, and political traditions prolonged the conflict and enhanced the severity of the human rights violations the country witnessed. The truth commission and the Special Court for Sierra Leone, to be discussed in Chapters 9 and 10, were established following the civil war to deal with this horrific legacy.

References

Archibald, S., and P. Richards. 2002. "Converts to Human Rights? Popular Debate about War and Justice in Rural Central Sierra Leone." *African* 72:339–367.

Boas, Morten. 2001. "Liberia and Sierra Leone—Dead Ringers? The Logic of Neopatrimonial Rule." *Third World Quarterly* 22:697–723.

Cotay, A. B. 1959. "Sierra Leone in the Post-War World." *African Affairs* 58:210–220.

Dorjahn, V. R., and Fyfe, Christopher. 1962. "Landlord and Stranger: Change in Tenancy Relations in Sierra Leone." *Journal of African History* 3:391–397.

Edward, David. 2005. "Sierra Leone." In *Encyclopedia of the Developing World*, ed. Thomas M. Leonard. New York: Routledge.

Fisher, Humphrey J. 1969. "Elections and Coups in Sierra Leone." *The Journal of Modern African Studies* 7:611–636.

Francis, David J. 1999. "Mercenary Intervention in Sierra Leone: Providing National Security or International Exploitation?" *Third World Quarterly* 20:319–338.

Keen, David 2005. "Liberalization and Conflict." *International Political Science Review* 26:73–89.

Lange, Matthew. 2003. "Structural Holes and Structural Synergies: A Comparative-Historical Analysis of State-Society Relations and Development in Colonial Sierra Leone and Mauritius." *International Journal of Comparative Sociology* 44:372–407.

Luke, David Fashole. 1985. "The Development of Modern Trade Unionism in Sierra Leone, Part I." *International Journal of African Historical Studies* 18:425–454.

Mboka, Abu Karimu. 2008. *The Politics of Chapter VII Interventions in Violent Conflicts: A Comparative Analysis of Bosnia, Iraq, Rwanda and Sierra Leone.* Saarbrucken, Germany: VDM Verlag Dr. Mueller.

Schneider, Kenneth. R. 1962. "Sierra Leone: Profile and Proposals." *African Today* 9:9–11.

Tangri, Roger. 1976. "Conflict and Violence in Contemporary Sierra Leone Chiefdoms." *Journal of Modern African Studies* 14:311–321.

Zack-Williams, Alfred. B. 2001. "Child Soldiers in the Civil War in Sierra Leone." *Review of African Political Economy* 87:73–82.

Zack-Williams, Alfred B. 1999. "Sierra Leone: The Political Economy of Civil War, 1991–98." *Third World Quarterly* 20:143–162.

Zack-Williams, Alfred. B., and S. Riley. 1993. "Sierra Leone: The Coup and Its Consequences." *Review of African Political Economy* 56:91–98.

CHAPTER 9

Addressing Impunity in Sierra Leone: The Truth and Reconciliation Commission

ZOE DUGAL

Introduction

The conflict described in Chapter 8 that devastated Sierra Leone from 1991 to 2002 was characterized by complex causes and the especially horrible nature of the violations committed against civilians. The end of hostilities left a country with its infrastructure in ruins, a destroyed economy, and a deeply traumatized population. Recognizing the need to move forward and reconstruct the country, Sierra Leoneans and the international community undertook a series of transitional initiatives, including a disarmament, demobilization, and reintegration process, the creation of the Special Court for Sierra Leone (SCSL), various reconciliation projects, and the establishment of the Truth and Reconciliation Commission (TRC) for Sierra Leone. In this chapter, I describe the objectives of the TRC, the history of its proceedings, and the context in which it operated. I provide an analysis of the impact the TRC has had on the people of Sierra Leone and a global effort at peace building in the country.

The Lome Peace Agreement and the Creation of the TRC

On July 7, 1999, parties to the conflict in Sierra Leone signed the Lome Peace Agreement. The agreement was the result of negotiations between the Revolutionary United Front (RUF) and the government to end the eight-year-old armed conflict. The United Nations (UN) acted as moral guarantor to the agreement, along with the Commonwealth, the Economic Community of West African States, and Togo. The negotiations started following a succession of events that included the January 1999 invasion of Freetown by a combined army of RUF and Armed Forces Revolutionary Council (AFRC) forces, and the subsequent push-back of the invasion forces by the Economic Community of West African States Monitoring Group.

The government, the RUF, and the AFRC were under tremendous pressure from the international community to negotiate a lasting settlement to the conflict. The invasion had significantly tarnished the image of the RUF and the AFRC when the international media portrayed the atrocities committed in Freetown. Growing dissatisfaction from several West African states that provided troops (especially Nigeria), and the realization that the war was unwinnable, forced the government to the negotiation table.

The Lome Peace Agreement included provisions for an immediate ceasefire, and the implementation of a general blanket amnesty and pardon for combatants who committed crimes between the start of the conflict in 1991 and the signing of the agreement. The provisions of the agreement were meant to foster national reconciliation and enable the RUF to transform itself into a party and its leaders to hold public office. Foday Sankoh, the RUF leader, was appointed vice president and given the chairmanship of the Board of the Commission for the Management of Strategic Resources, National Reconstruction and Development. The AFRC leader, Johnny Paul Koroma, was also granted a position in the government.

The international community, and especially the UN, was concerned by the amnesty provision. The level of brutality of the violations committed during the conflict seemed to call for some form of justice. The previous Abidjan Peace Accord of 1996 did include a similar amnesty clause but no provision for any mechanism to address impunity. The Abidjan process had been seen as offering too many concessions to the RUF, which was practically defeated on the ground and should have been pushed to surrender. Sankoh was even quoted saying that he wanted to sign the Abidjan Peace Accord to gain time for his troops to rearm and regain ground on the battlefield. In Lome, therefore, the government and the UN were concerned with finding a way to create a counter-balance to the amnesty provision and avoid the mistakes made in Abidjan. Civil society in Sierra Leone also applied great pressure on the government to address impunity. There was great shock at the amnesty clause and at seeing how the RUF was portrayed as a legitimate force fighting for the people while the atrocities they committed were well known all over Sierra Leone (Abraham 2004). The creation of a national Human Rights Commission and a TRC was then proposed at Lome, adopted by the government and the RUF and included in the agreement. The UN also added a note to the agreement stating that the amnesty and pardon clause could not apply to crimes against humanity, war crimes, and other violations of international humanitarian law. The abduction of UN peacekeepers by the RUF in May 2000 forced the government to rethink the amnesty and pardon clause and request the assistance of the Security Council to support the creation of a special tribunal to try members of the RUF, including Sankoh (Gberie 2005).

Truth commissions have been used in various parts of the world to address impunity after violent conflicts or the hosting of repressive political regimes. The idea is that establishing the truth and addressing impunity are necessary ingredients of reconciliation and sustainable peace. The relationship between truth-telling and peace-building is twofold. First, there is the idea that uncovering the truth prevents reoccurrence of conflict. UN Special Rapporteur Louis Joinet refers to the "inalienable right to truth," which he defines as a "collective right, drawing upon history to prevent violations from recurring" (*Question of the Impunity of Perpetrators of Human Rights Violations* 1997). Naming perpetrators and associating them with the violations they committed ensures public scrutiny of their future behavior. The inalienable right to truth comprises both the individual right to know what happened to dear ones and the societal right to know past events to prevent their re-occurrence.

Second, there is a general acceptance that uncovering the truth allows for the recognition of victims' suffering, which in turn fosters reconciliation. Many victims and perpetrators who appeared before a TRC express relief at having been offered a forum to tell their story. The amnesty and pardon clauses of the Lome Peace Agreement denied victims of the Sierra Leonean conflict the opportunity to seek legal redress (Stovel 2003). The truth-telling process undertaken by the TRC ensured that at least victims could be heard. This is not to say that truth telling is always reconciliatory or that each witness feels relieved by telling his story. Victims cannot count on an apology from their perpetrator, and likewise perpetrators cannot count on forgiveness from their victim. The choices to express remorse and to forgive are personal choices. Truth commissions, therefore, have to be cautious in what they promise to victims and humble in what they aim to achieve.

In his statement at the inauguration ceremony of the TRC in July 2002, President Ahmad Tejan Kabbah said that the commission should be seen "as an instrument of national reconciliation, and another means of strengthening the peace" and that the work of the TRC should be seen as a "therapeutic process." He further proceeded to invite "all parties, factions and individuals, all those who are committed to lasting peace in Sierra Leone, to cooperate with the TRC" recognizing that it might be "painful or even humiliating for some people to relate their experiences as perpetrators, victims or observers of abuses" but that it was their national duty. At the beginning of the TRC's operational work in October 2002, many politicians, journalists, and civil society leaders were adamant that Sierra Leoneans wanted to forget and move on and that no one would participate in the TRC process. Specifically, they told commission staff that no woman or girl would testify on sexual abuse. This proved to be a completely wrong assumption. The staff of the commission soon realized that there was a great urge among victims, witnesses, and even perpetrators to tell their stories and get recognition for their suffering. To the surprise of many observers, this also included victims of sexual abuse who testified in great numbers and presented great details about the horrendous violations committed against them. Thousands of Sierra Leoneans responded to President Kabbah's invitation and appeared before the TRC.

Structure and Jurisdiction of the TRC

An act of parliament created the TRC on November 22, 2000, long after the expiration of the ninety-day timeframe required by the Lome Peace Agreement. This delay was due to the resumption of hostilities in May 2000. Further delays occurred, and the TRC was only inaugurated in July 2002. The mandate of the TRC was ambitious. It was to "create an impartial historical record of violations and abuses of human rights and international humanitarian law related to the armed conflict in Sierra Leone" and to address impunity for crimes perpetrated during the conflict, to address the causes of the conflict with a view to prevent re-occurrence, to address the needs of victims, and to promote reconciliation (*Witness to Truth: Report of the Sierra Leone Truth and Reconciliation Commission* 2004a, 24). The commission was also asked to pay special attention to the experiences of children and victims of sexual abuse. While the historical record was meant to cover only the period from the start of the conflict in 1991 to the signing of the Lome Peace Agreement in 1999, the fact that the commission was asked to address the causes of the conflict allowed it to explore historical, political, and social events long before 1991. The commission was given an eighteen-month mandate to complete its activities, with the option to request an additional six-month extension.

The first six months were supposed to be used by the commission to conduct a public relations exercise, including reaching out to civil society and organizing a sensitization campaign to explain the TRC process. While some work was done during this preparatory phase, results fell short of what was expected, and this led to difficulties once the commission started planning its operational phase. Moreover, a funding crisis at the end of the preparatory phase and the failure of the Commission Secretariat to efficiently undertake a recruitment process to staff the commission led to further delays. The recruitment process for statement takers and secretariat staff extended into November 2002 and February 2003, respectively, putting additional timeframe pressure on the operational phase of the commission. Therefore, a six-month extension was requested by the commission and granted by the government in the summer of 2003, resulting in a deadline of March 2004 for the commission to complete its activities, including the writing of the final report.

The commission was composed of seven commissioners, three of whom were international dignitaries (from Canada, The Gambia, and South Africa) and four Sierra Leonean nationals. The national commissioners each came from one of the four provinces (East, North, South, and West) in order to ensure geographical and ethnic representation, and were chosen through a consultative process including civil society organizations. The UN High Commissioner for Human Rights appointed the three international commissioners (Parlevliet 2000). The commission hired a mixture of international and national researchers, investigators, and administrative and financial staff. All statement takers and regional field coordinators appointed were Sierra Leonean nationals so as to ensure their fluency in local languages, awareness of local customs, and knowledge of the local terrain helps in effectively recording the statements of the victim, witness, or the perpetrator.

The commission was not meant to function as a court of law and did not have arrest or prosecution powers. It was granted subpoena powers to ensure that all witnesses deemed necessary by the commission could be called to testify, *in camera* or in public and that the commission would have access to all information available to write its findings. Witnesses were allowed to request confidentiality. This meant that the commission would publish no information leading to the identification of the witness. It did not mean, however, that this information was not recorded. The credibility of the commission's findings rested on keeping detailed records of sources and this was done systematically. The commission published, in its final report, the names of witnesses who chose not to request confidentiality. Confidential statements and hearing recordings were attributed to a number, which allows tracing of the archived materials.

The commission used its subpoena powers on several occasions to compel perpetrators and witnesses to testify; however, recognizing its mandate to address the needs of victims, the commission never issued a subpoena to victims. The TRC issued a subpoena to a few witnesses who were reluctant to testify, including Valentine Strasser, former head of state under the National Provisional Ruling Council (NPRC) regime. Strasser refused to respond, and the TRC had to request the help of law enforcement agencies to execute the subpoena. Contrary to the South African TRC, the Sierra Leone TRC did not have an amnesty committee since the amnesty was granted at Lome and could not be made dependent on any disclosure of information. Witnesses were asked to sign an oath declaring that they would tell the truth to the commission. Information was cross-referenced from several sources and witnesses were called again if the commission found that they had not disclosed all relevant information.

Relationship with the Special Court for Sierra Leone

As discussed in the next chapter, the SCSL was established in March 2002, following a request from the Sierra Leonese government to the UN. There is no mention of the TRC in the statute of the SCSL and therefore no legal guidelines specifying the nature of the relationship between the two institutions. The UN secretary-general acknowledged the complementary nature of the two institutions in a report to the Security Council. Harwell and Le Billon argue that truth commissions can do what trials cannot by uncovering "institutional and structural injustices at the root of abuses and violence" (2009, 300). In Sierra Leone, the TRC was to focus on the needs of victims and on uncovering the causes of the conflict while the SCSL was to focus on individual perpetrator responsibility. The attorney general of Sierra Leone and the SCSL task force, in a paper jointly published in 2002, recognized the complementary role of the two institutions in the fight against impunity in Sierra Leone and emphasized the need for cooperation.[1]

On the other hand, the paper goes on to outline that while both institutions are working toward the same goal, the TRC is a national institution (created under national law by an act of parliament) and SCSL has an international status, giving it primacy over any national law or national institutions of Sierra Leone.[2] This statement gave rise to the idea that the SCSL was above the TRC in its jurisdiction and paved the way for some subsequent misconceptions regarding the relationship between the two institutions. Indeed, the obligations of the government and its institutions to cooperate with the SCSL could not have included the TRC, as it was established as a body fully independent from the government, by an act of parliament that could only be revoked by the parliament (*Witness to Truth: Report of the Sierra Leone Truth and Reconciliation Commission* 2004c, 380).

Recognizing the important role of the TRC in addressing impunity and attempting national reconciliation, the first prosecutor of the Special Court, David Crane, declared in a public statement in September 2002 that he would not use confidential information collected by the TRC as evidence and would not use subpoena powers granted to the court to acquire any material belonging to the TRC. The prosecutor's decision was probably also based on the fact that the non-legal nature of the TRC proceedings would render most evidence collected not allowable in a court of law. While the prosecutor was faithful to his word, there were no legal guarantees whatsoever to protect TRC witnesses from being called by the SCSL. As Evenson (2004) argues, guidelines and a legally binding document should have been developed to shape the relationship between the two institutions and address cases of conflicts.

In practice, the work of the two institutions proceeded concurrently with few difficulties at first, although there was no formal cooperation and tremendous confusion existed in the minds of the population regarding the roles of the two institutions.[3] Mostly due to the fact that the creation of the TRC was delayed, the start of the operational phase coincided with the beginning of the Special Court's investigations. This caused huge challenges to TRC staff who had to explain to a mostly illiterate population the difference between the two institutions and the guarantees that perpetrators' testimonies would not be handed to the SCSL and would not be used to prosecute them. As Sawyer and Kelsall's (2007) survey demonstrates, the local population was still confused about the role and mandate of the two institutions (this after the end of the TRC's activities and well into the trials of the SCSL). It took several months and the first wave of indictments by the SCSL in March 2003 for the rank-and-file of the various armed groups to realize that the SCSL would only prosecute a small number of top commanders.

Major challenges arose when the TRC attempted to interview SCSL detainees, starting with Samuel Hinga Norman (former minister of internal security) in September 2003. Norman wrote to the TRC in August requesting to appear before it. His letter was followed by similar requests from two other detainees of the SCSL, Augustine Gbao and Issa Sesay, both former RUF commanders. The TRC was informed that no mechanism was in place to allow access to the detainees. They were allowed outside communication and could have written their testimonies for submission to the TRC; however, what they were seeking was to be allowed to appear before the commission in person and answer questions. They believed that they had the right, as Sierra Leoneans, to testify before the commission. Moreover, because they were all named in other witnesses' accounts, they should have been given the right to respond and to provide their side of the story.

The SCSL prosecutor objected to the hearings. The prosecutor's arguments were that the testimonies would endanger the integrity of the proceedings before the Special Court and that Hinga Norman would make inflammatory statements in public, which could cause social disturbances. Among other issues, it was expected that Hinga Norman might express his opinion that President Kabbah should also be indicted by the SCSL if the prosecutor was to follow the chain of command to its end (Dougherty 2004).

The TRC, in collaboration with the detainees' defense teams, presented arguments to the Special Court judges. After two months of representations, Judge Robertson finally ruled against public hearings and granted the detainees the right to testify in writing or meet with the TRC commissioners. This decision came very close to the end of the TRC's operational phase and for this reason and others, none of the detainees testified. The TRC was, however, able to access several RUF detainees in the Freetown Central Prison and record their testimonies. This provided the TRC with invaluable information on many aspects of the RUF's involvement in the conflict.

History of the TRC's Work

Statement Taking

The operational phase of the TRC started in November 2002. Information gathering took several forms.[4] The commission started its operational phase with statement taking. Previous work had been done by civil society in support of the TRC. For example, Campaign for Good Governance had collected around 1,000 statements in a first testimony-gathering project. Manifesto 99 had also done some work in mapping out existing traditional reconciliation and conflict resolution mechanism, which the TRC used in the design of its reconciliation strategy.

The first step of the statement-taking exercise was to design a statement form to be used for the written recording of oral testimonies given by victims, witnesses, and perpetrators. The commission's statement takers were asked to categorize the person they were interviewing according to the nature of the story told. They were allowed to fill more than one section of the statement form if they considered the person interviewed to belong to more than one category. Indeed, the conflict in Sierra Leone is characterized by the fact that many perpetrators were also victims (a prominent example is the case of child soldiers).

The commission hired seventy-five statement takers, all Sierra Leonean nationals, to be deployed at the countryside with the mandate to collect the written statements. The fact that the public outreach phase of the commission had not gone according to initial plans placed the burden of explaining the mandate and purpose of the TRC on statement takers, who were already working under extreme time constraints and logistical pressures. The mandate of the TRC had to be explained in simple terms to illiterate villagers in remote areas who were not at all familiar with any legal process. The statement takers were provided with a short training session before they started their fieldwork.[5] They were then deployed for three weeks, after which, they were recalled to the TRC head office in Freetown, and the statement forms they gathered were evaluated for quality. One major issue identified during the evaluation was the lack of details in the actual narratives, and the lack of clarity in the identification of the armed factions involved. This was crucial information if the TRC was to use the statements for research and investigation purposes. Statement takers were thus briefed on the need to record more details from witnesses without asking leading questions. For instance, statement takers were encouraged to use probing questions such as the language spoken by the perpetrators. Many witnesses relating stories from the beginning of the conflict answered that the perpetrators spoke "Liberian English," which helped the Commission establish the pattern of Taylor's NPFL-led initial invasion.

The statement form contained some guidance for statement takers on how to approach witnesses: A short summary of the TRC mandate, a section on what it meant to make a statement to the TRC, a brief explanation of the concept of confidentiality, and a section on the need to tell the truth, followed by a declaration form to be signed or thumb-impressed (for the illiterate) by the witness. The policy of the TRC was to take statements on a one-on-one basis, where possible; however if the witness requested that a family member be present, this was usually granted. Statement takers were also encouraged to seek other witnesses to a reported incident, for instance in the same village, which allowed the commission to get detailed accounts of specific local incidents.

The Lome Peace Agreement, in its preamble, recognized the special suffering of children during the conflict, both as victims of human rights violations and as forcibly recruited combatants by all armed forces. This was also inserted in the legislation mandating the creation of the TRC, asking the commission to give "special attention to...the experiences of children within the armed conflict." As Cohn (2001) points out, no truth commission had previously received the mandate to expose abuses perpetrated on and by children. In order to fulfill this mandate, the TRC entered into an agreement with the Child Protection Agencies' network coordinated by the United Nations Children's Fund (UNICEF). The agreement included referral of child witnesses to the TRC for both statement taking and *in camera* hearings. The agreement also included some provisions for counseling before and after the testimonies. This arrangement worked with mixed results, and in several instances, the commission interviewed children who had not been refereed by a child protection agency.

The statement-taking phase of the TRC lasted for a total of four months, during which close to 9,000 statements were collected. These also included some statements collected from Sierra Leonean refugees and expatriates in Guinea, Ghana, Nigeria, the United States, and Britain. The short timeframe of the TRC prevented this period from being extended further. Despite the high number of statements collected, many Sierra Leoneans who wanted to talk to the TRC were not able to do so. The statements collected were all coded and input into a database that served researchers and investigators of the commission to categorize violations, count them, and establish patterns by crossing variables. For example, the database made it possible for the commission to determine that diamond dealers had been specifically targeted by the RUF and the AFRC. This was done through the crossing of three variables, namely the word "diamond" recorded in the narrative of the statement, a category of violation such as abduction or murder, and the location where the violation took place. The database also allowed the commission to link statements reporting the same events and to corroborate the information using multiple witnesses.

Hearings

The second part of the commission's operational phase consisted of five months of public and *in camera* hearings. There were two types of hearings: Individual hearings and thematic/event hearings. Individual hearings were conducted in all of the twelve district capitals and thematic hearings were conducted in Freetown. As Dougherty notes (2004), the district hearings brought the commission closer to the people, which greatly increased local ownership. During the individual hearings, victims, witnesses, and perpetrators appeared before the TRC commissioners and were asked to tell their stories. If the hearing was public, the community filled the hall and listened to the testimony; if the hearing was *in camera*, only the commissioners were present to hear the testimony. *In camera* hearings were granted to children, victims of sexual abuse, and certain perpetrators. When the perpetrator could convince the commission that his life would be put at risk by public testimony, the commission granted an *in camera* hearing. The commission recognized that public hearings ensured transparency of the truth-telling process, but considered the evidence provided by some perpetrators to be of high enough value to grant such a favor.

It was a surprise to the commission that many victims of sexual abuse and rape insisted on testifying in a public hearing, arguing that they wanted their communities to hear about their experiences, the stigma that they still faced, and the identity of their perpetrators. The commission granted these requests for public hearings, but children were not given the choice and were allowed to only appear during *in camera* hearings. The commission allowed, where and when possible, perpetrators named by a victim in a public hearing the right to respond in public to the allegations made against them. In many circumstances, this was impossible due to the failure of the commission to trace the named perpetrators. A main characteristic of the conflict in Sierra Leone is the high level of population displacement. This made the localization of many perpetrators difficult at best and sometimes impossible with the resources and time the commission had at its disposal. The commission used thematic and event-specific hearings to listen to experts, civil society groups, political parties, UN agencies, and others on a specific theme related to the conflict, including the experiences of women and girls, issues of corruption and governance, the AFRC coup of 1997, the January 1999 invasion of Freetown, and several other themes. Radio UNAMSIL and SLBS radio's broadcast and telecast of the selected moments of the hearings also took place.

The hearing phase of the commission concluded on August 6, 2003 with the appearance of President Kabbah in a public hearing in Freetown. The hearing was broadcast live on national television and many radio stations. It lasted for more than three hours and was a disappointment to the commission staff and the population in general. After having read a lengthy statement that lasted two hours, President Kabbah was questioned by TRC staff and politely asked to offer an apology on behalf of the state to the people of Sierra Leone. The apology, in the eyes of the commission staff, was meant to address wrongs done by the state throughout the conflict, including the failure to effectively protect the civilian population. However, President Kabbah did not understand it in that way and proceeded to explain that he had done nothing wrong and had committed no crime; therefore, he did not see the need for an apology. It is unfortunate that he did not see the social importance in the gesture by offering his sympathy to the countless victims of the conflict. In contrast, the leaders of the All People's Congress (APC), President Ernest Bai Koroma, and RUF party leaders apologized on more than one occasion for the mistakes committed by their institutions.

Research and Investigation

Concurrently to the statement-taking and hearings phases, the commission conducted research and investigation. Researchers were each assigned a theme, in accordance with the mandate of the commission as spelled out in its legislation. These themes included the following: The antecedents and causes of the conflict, history of the conflict, nature of the violations committed, the role of diamonds, and other mineral resources in the conflict, experiences of women and children, and the role of external actors. These themes became chapters of the TRC's final report. The commission also identified incidents to be investigated as "window cases" based on criteria of geographical balance, impact of the incident on the conflict, particular dynamics or behavior, and the range of victims or perpetrators involved. Thirteen window cases were selected.[6]

The Final Report

After months of research, investigation, and testimony gathering, the commission had in its possession a wealth of information on the conflict. This information was evaluated, cross-referenced, and put in context using primary (testimonies and submissions to the TRC) and secondary (publications and reports) sources. When in doubt, the commission included the information in its report, indicating the doubt and calling for more research on the fact or event reported. At the beginning of the commission's work, the general perception in the international community was that conflict in Sierra Leone was resource-driven and that the war had been caused by the desire to gain access to diamonds. This idea was part of a larger vision of the conflict as started by Liberia's NPFL. Prosecutor Crane also shared this view that his investigations would start on this assumption.[7]

The commission investigated this topic thoroughly and concluded that this view of the conflict was simplistic and tended to overshadow more complex and fundamental causes and dynamics. The commission's conclusion on the role of diamonds and other mineral resources was "that the exploitation of diamonds did not cause the conflict in Sierra Leone, but [that] different fighting factions did target diamond areas for purposes of supporting their war efforts," thus making diamonds and other mineral resources a fueling factor in the conflict (*Witness to Truth: Report of the Sierra Leone Truth and Reconciliation Commission* 2004b, 107). On the causes of the conflict, the commission found that:

> [T]he conflict and the post-independence period preceding represent the most shameful years of Sierra Leone's history. These periods reflect

> an extraordinary failure of leadership on the part of all those involved in government, public life and civil society. The Commission finds that the central cause of the war was endemic greed, corruption and nepotism that deprived the nation of its dignity and reduced most people to a state of poverty. The Commission holds the political elite of successive regimes in the post-independence period responsible for creating the conditions for conflict. (*Witness to Truth: Report of the Sierra Leone Truth and Reconciliation Commission* 2004b, 27)

These conditions included successive governments' abuse of states of emergency, unlawful use of the safe custody provision to imprison political opponents, and the complete closing of the political space to the peaceful expression of social grievances. Popular frustrations could no longer be expressed and addressed in the public space, and various sections of the society started to radicalize (*Witness to Truth: Report of the Sierra Leone Truth and Reconciliation Commission* 2004c, 82). In particular, the youth were alienated and turned to violent action as a way to bring about change in the country. At the same time, high corruption and nepotism had rendered the state apparatus and the security sector incompetent to respond to the threat of violent action.

TRC Recommendations

As per its mandate, the TRC was asked to formulate recommendations to address the root causes of the conflict, the needs of victims, and to prevent reoccurrence of violent conflict. In formulating these recommendations, the commission kept in mind the situation in Sierra Leone and the very limited resources of the government. Moreover in an effort to remain pragmatic, the commission divided its recommendations into the following three categories: "Imperative recommendations" (to be implemented in priority, immediately or as soon as possible), "work towards recommendations" (to be considered by the government and given a time frame for implementation), and "seriously consider recommendations" (to be evaluated and considered by the government, no time frame attached) (*Witness to Truth: Report of the Sierra Leone Truth and Reconciliation Commission* 2004b, 120).

All recommendations were based on the TRC's findings and linked to them. The commission paid special attention, when designing the recommendations and the reparations program, to stick to the facts it had uncovered and address causes of the war, impunity, and violations of human rights, with a view to create a climate of reconstruction and rehabilitation. The imperative recommendations were developed under the following categories or themes as follows: (i) Recommendations on good governance and fighting corruption addressing the root cause of the conflict; (ii) recommendations on protection of human rights and establishment of the rule of law proposing changes in the constitution and the legal system to address impunity, human dignity, and corruption; (iii) recommendations on security forces addressing past abuses by the security apparatus and re-establishing the state monopoly over the use of force; (iv) recommendations on mineral resources addressing diamond smuggling, conflicts of interest in the mining sector, and at increasing the legitimate revenues the state can derive from diamond exploitation, and (v) recommendations on women, youth, and children, with a view of providing reparations for wrongs committed during the conflict.

These recommendations included a number of legal and constitution reforms to address the status of women and children, such as criminalizing sexual exploitation of children and abolishing customary law provisions that discriminate against women's rights.[8] They also include some measures to implement information and sensitization campaigns to reduce stigma affecting victims of sexual abuse and ensure a better place for women in society. According to the TRC legislation, the government was required to "faithfully and timely implement" the recommendations of the commission. However, since the commission had finished its work when the final report was presented to the government, there was no institution officially mandated to ensure proper follow-up.

Publication of the Final Report

The TRC's final report was only published and handed to the government on October 5, 2004, two years after the start of the commission's operational phase. Along with the four volumes of the complete final report, the commission published a children's version (in collaboration with UNICEF) and a video relating the major findings and recommendations (produced by Witness, a U.S.-based non-governmental organization). The TRC report along with all submissions and other annexes is also available on the TRC website. The National Vision for Sierra Leone, an initiative of the TRC, asked Sierra Leoneans to illustrate their vision for the future of the country in works of arts. The commission received hundreds of contributions, including paintings, sculptures, essays, poems, songs, and plays. During the final phase of the commission and for several years after, TRC staff organized several exhibits of the contributions in Freetown, in the countryside, and abroad. Some of the artwork is currently displayed in the offices of the Human Rights Commission of Sierra Leone.

The commission recommended that all non-confidential statements, submissions, and public hearing transcripts be immediately made available to the public for further research. However, after the conclusion of the work of the commission, the government adopted a different approach. The archives of the TRC were entrusted to the University of Sierra Leone at Fourah Bay College. The statement forms, video and audiotapes, documents, and pictures were placed in boxes. The procedure to access them is currently as follows: Non-Sierra Leoneans have to contact the government archivists, fill a form, and ask for permission before they are authorized to consult the archives. Sierra Leonean nationals are not allowed to consult the archives for a period of twenty-five years following the publication of the TRC report. The only Sierra Leoneans excepted from this policy are former TRC commissioners, the government archivist, and assistant. The government's explanation for this policy is that there is still too much trauma in the country and the archives could be disruptive. However, this decision contravenes the right to know the truth and undermines the reconciliatory effect that the TRC report was meant to achieve. The Human Rights Commission of Sierra Leone has recently undertaken a process to revise accessibility of the TRC archives. The aim is to provide public access to non-confidential TRC material, including the database.

Conclusion: After the TRC

In its final report, the TRC indicated "that many of the causes of the conflict that prompted thousands of young people to join the war have still not been adequately addressed. High among these factors are elitist politics, rampant corruption, nepotism and bad governance in general. They are potential causes of conflict, if they remain un-addressed" (*Witness to Truth: Report of the Sierra Leone Truth and Reconciliation Commission* 2004b, 29). The government's response came in the form of a white paper released on June 27, 2005, almost a year after the publication of the commission's final report. Usually, a green paper is issued first, inviting reactions from the public. After considering suggestions and comments, the government then issues a white paper stating its final position. However, this white paper was drafted and published without prior consultations with civil society and had an overly defensive tone, trying to defend the government's actions rather than considering the commission's recommendations in a constructive manner. Moreover, large sections of the recommendations chapter were completely ignored by the white paper (Ojielo 2009).

Since the parliamentary and presidential elections of August 2007, the new APC government and president have devoted more attention to the TRC recommendations. Numerous efforts and initiatives have also been undertaken by civil society in Sierra Leone to force the government's attention on the TRC recommendations. The Sierra Leone Human Rights Commission has also take upon itself the following-up on the TRC recommendations and putting pressure on the government for implementation of the TRC's recommendations.

Notes

1. For more information see, "Briefing Paper on the Relationship between the Special Court and the Truth and Reconciliation Commission" (2002), 4.
2. *Ibid*, 5.
3. Another important aspect is the discrepancy between the two institutions' resources: The SCSL's annual budget for the first two years was set at $50 million per year while the overall budget of the TRC's operational phase was only $6.5 million. This created numerous logistical constraints for the TRC that are beyond the scope of this chapter.
4. The TRC also undertook a series of reconciliation activities. Since I was working on the truth seeking side of the commission, I choose not to describe the reconciliation activities in this chapter.
5. The training included sessions on the mandate and role of the TRC, human rights violations and sexual abuse, techniques of statement taking, and a session on how to deal with traumatized witnesses and victims. The TRC also designed a manual for statement takers that explored these

issues in more details and could be used in the field to answer questions about substance and procedures.

6. For the complete list and description of window cases, see *Witness to Truth: Report of the Sierra Leone Truth and Reconciliation Commission*, 2004a, 148–151.
7. David Crane (Prosecutor for the SCSL), interview with the author, September 2002, Ottawa, Canada.
8. Two sets of laws govern Sierra Leone: Constitutional law, which is the law of the land, and customary law applied in traditional, rural settings. Under customary law, women have no right to property and self-determination directly but only through male family representatives, such as their father or husband. Customary law is applied by traditional authorities such as paramount chiefs.

References

Abraham, Arthur. 2004. "The Elusive Quest for Peace: From Abidjan to Lome." In *Between Democracy and Terror*, ed. Ibrahim Abdullah. Council for the Development of Social Research in Africa.

"Briefing Paper on the Relationship between the Special Court and the Truth and Reconciliation Commission." 2002. Office of the Attorney General and Minister of Justice and Special Court Task Force, Planning Mission Briefing Series.

Cohn, Ilene. 2001. "The Protection of Children and the Quest for Truth and Justice in Sierra Leone." *Journal of International Affairs* 55:1–34.

Dougherty, Beth K. 2004. "Searching for Answers: Sierra Leone's Truth and Reconciliation Commission." *African Studies Quarterly* 8:39–56.

Evenson, Elizabeth. 2004. "Truth and Justice in Sierra Leone: Coordination between Commission and Court." *Columbia Law Review* 104:730–767.

Gberie, Lansana. 2005. *A Dirty War in West Africa: The RUF and the Destruction of Sierra Leone*. Bloomington, IN: Indiana University Press.

Harwell, Emily, and Philippe Le Billon. 2009. "Natural Connections: Linking Transitional Justice and Development through a Focus on Natural Resources." In *Transitional Justice and Development: Making Connections*, ed. Pablo De Greiff, and Roger Duthie. New York: International Center for Transitional Justice and Social Science Research Council.

Ojielo, Ozonnia. 2009. "Beyond the TRC: Governance in Sierra Leone." In *Rescuing a Fragile State*, ed. Lansana Gberie. Waterloo: Wilfrid Laurier University Press.

Parlevliet, Michelle. 2000. "Truth Commissions in Africa: The Non-case of Namibia and the Emerging Case of Sierra Leone." *International Law Forum* 2:98–111.

Question of the Impunity of Perpetrators of Human Rights Violations. 1997. UN Doc. E/CN.4/Sub.2/1997/20.

Sawyer, Edward, and Tim Kelsall. 2007. "Truth versus Justice? Popular Views on the Truth and Reconciliation Commission and the Special Court for Sierra Leone." *The Online Journal of Peace and Conflict Resolution* 7:36–68.

Stovel, Laura. 2003. "When the Enemy Comes Home: Restoring Justice after Mass Atrocities." Paper presented at Restorative Justice Conference, Vancouver, British Columbia.

Witness to Truth: Report of the Sierra Leone Truth and Reconciliation Commission. 2004a. Volume 1.

Witness to Truth: Report of the Sierra Leone Truth and Reconciliation Commission. 2004b. Volume 2.

Witness to Truth: Report of the Sierra Leone Truth and Reconciliation Commission. 2004c. Volume 3.

CHAPTER 10

Mixed Justice, Mixed Legacy: The Special Court for Sierra Leone

ELLEN EMILIE STENSRUD

Introduction: The Dilemmas of Local Justice

Can a criminal court possibly be a legitimate answer to the needs of a post-conflict society? This chapter presents some of the issues at stake during the negotiations over the Special Court for Sierra Leone (SCSL), and discusses how the specific features of the court have affected its legitimacy on the ground. The legitimacy challenges of the SCSL are seen in light of its dual role as both a backward-looking and forward-looking mechanism. As a criminal court, its main task is to punish past crimes, but it is also expected to have an effect on Sierra Leonean society.

The SCSL is an example of a relatively new development in international criminal justice, the so-called "mixed" or "hybrid" tribunal. It is located in Sierra Leone and consists of a mix of international and Sierra Leonean personnel. The jurisdiction of the SCSL is limited to "persons who bear the greatest responsibility" for crimes committed during the civil war (Statute of the Special Court for Sierra Leone 2002). It was established on January 16, 2002 by an agreement between the government of Sierra Leone and the United Nations (UN).[1] The funding of the court is based on voluntary contributions.

The mixed composition of judges and jurisdiction, its location in the capital of the affected country, its tight budget, and short timeframe distinguish the SCSL from the International Criminal Tribunal for the former Yugoslavia (ICTY) discussed in Chapter 6. These features, if fulfilled in a positive way, could contribute to the legitimacy of the court, by ensuring quick and cost-effective justice in proximity to the affected population. At the same time, these features have created challenges for the court. First, its location in Freetown and involvement of Sierra Leonean personnel generated local expectations of effects from the court, which have been difficult to meet. Second, the tight budget and limited jurisdiction make the mandate of the court narrow compared to the widespread atrocities during the war. The narrow version of accountability of the Special Court has prompted some commentators to apply the term "shoestring" justice to it (Cockayne 2005b; McDonald 2007).

War, Amnesty, and Legal Response

As discussed in Chapter 8, the civil war in Sierra Leone lasted from 1991 until 2002. In March 1991, the Revolutionary United Front (RUF) started their rebellion against the Sierra Leonean government. Discontent over corruption and mismanagement of the country by the elite was a major drive behind the RUF rebellion (Boas 2000, 561). Although the RUF initially claimed that the goals of its rebellion were to end corruption and install democracy (Boas 2000, 564), the war that followed turned brutal and was characterized by severe human rights abuses. A peace agreement was concluded in Abidjan on November 30, 1996 but soon was abandoned. In May 1997, the Armed Forces Revolutionary Council (AFRC) launched a *coup d'etat*, and the continued warfare was characterized by serious violations of international humanitarian law. These violations culminated in January 1999 when the RUF and the AFRC together took control of the capital Freetown. On July 7, 1999, a new peace agreement was signed between the government of Sierra Leone and the RUF in Lome, Togo. The agreement provided "absolute and free pardon" for all combatants in the war (Lome Peace Agreement 1999). The amnesty was disputed by civil society actors and the UN but was important for the conclusion of a peace agreement.

The Lome Amnesty and its Aftermath

The pardon and amnesty for all combatants was granted in the Lome agreement to "consolidate the peace and promote the cause of national reconciliation" (Lome Peace Agreement 1999). The "peace versus justice" dilemma was obvious at the Lome negotiations. The government's military capacity was weak, but since many enemies of the government had already been imprisoned or executed for their role in the war, the threat of prosecutions was perceived as real. An agreement would have been impossible without an amnesty (Hayner 2007, 6). Hayner has interviewed central actors from the negotiations, and writes that "everyone seemed to accept, virtually without discussion, that a proactive criminal justice approach was outside the bounds of reality" (Hayner 2007, 12). Also, the toll of the war on the population made peace more urgent than justice. Since all parties had committed atrocities during the war, it was perhaps also in the interest of the government to provide an amnesty in the agreement (Hayner 2007, 7,17). Instead of a justice mechanism, a Truth and Reconciliation Commission discussed in Chapter 9 was established (Lome Peace Agreement 1999). Many civil society actors expressed their opposition to the blanket amnesty. Also, the human rights community had suggested that there should be established a truth, justice, and reconciliation commission, but in the agreement, the word "justice" was left out (O'Flaherty 2005, 9-10).

In the last minutes of the negotiations at Lome, the UN representative added a disclaimer to the agreement, noting that the amnesty should not apply to the international crimes of genocide, crimes against humanity, war crimes, and other serious violations of international humanitarian law (UN S/2000/915). The other delegates were unaware of the decision by the UN representative, and RUF leader Foday Sankoh had actually signed the agreement before the disclaimer was added in handwriting to one of the copies of the agreement (Hayner 2007, 5–6).

As amnesty was granted in the Lome Peace Agreement, it looked like the war criminals in Sierra Leone would get away with impunity. But the prospects for justice changed in May 2000 when the peace process collapsed. Renewed fighting, including hostage-taking of 500 UN personnel, led to calls for prosecutions of the war criminals (Human Rights Watch 2000). The amnesty provision had obviously failed to ensure the peace, and the Sierra Leonean government renewed its interest in prosecuting Sankoh and other RUF leaders. Sierra Leonean president Ahmad Tejan Kabbah preferred an international justice mechanism due to the weakness of the Sierra Leonean judiciary and judicial problems of national prosecutions for the kidnapping of the UN peacekeepers (Hayner 2007, 25).

Could prosecutions cover the time preceding the signing of the Lome agreement despite the agreement's explicit amnesty for acts before that date? The position held by the UN special representative of the secretary-general for Sierra Leone, that the amnesty should not apply to the most serious international crimes, was accepted by the Sierra Leonean government. In other words, both parties to the negotiations over the court agreed that the temporal jurisdiction of the court could go back beyond July 7, 1999, the date of the Lome agreement, potentially back to 1991 when the civil war began (UN S/2000/915). However, the legal status of the disclaimer by the UN is unclear. Although the disclaimer might have been important in the arguments for the establishment of a court, its legality is contested (Hayner 2007, 26).

Negotiations, Jurisdiction, and Judgments

In a letter dated June 12, 2000, President Kabbah requested UN assistance to establish a court. He argued that since the peace agreement was broken, and UN peacekeeping personnel had been taken hostage, individual accountability was necessary to ensure peace (UN S/2000/786). On August 14, 2000, the UN Security Council resolution 1315 requested "the Secretary-General to negotiate an agreement with the Government of Sierra Leone to create an independent special court" (UN S/RES/1315). In response to the Security Council resolution, the UN secretary-general presented a report on October 4, 2000, which included the draft statute of the Special Court.

The Special Court was established by an agreement between the government of Sierra Leone and the UN. The secretary-general appointed the majority of the judges while the Sierra Leonean government appointed a minority (Statute of the Special Court for Sierra Leone 2002). The court's jurisdiction covers "serious violations of international humanitarian law and Sierra Leonean law," including crimes against humanity, violations of article 3 common to the Geneva Convention, and other serious violations of international humanitarian law, including attacks on UN peacekeepers and the enlistment and use of child combatants (Statute of the Special Court for Sierra Leone 2002).

The court's prosecutor does not have the power to ask the Security Council to intervene to investigate, prosecute, or surrender persons of a third State. While the secretary-general wanted the Special Court's prosecutor to have such powers (UN S/2001/40), the Security Council argued against it (UN S/2001/95). Another limit to the court's scope is its temporal jurisdiction. Despite the position held by both the UN and the Sierra Leonean government that the temporal jurisdiction could go back to the beginning of the war in 1991, the start date of the court's temporal jurisdiction was set to November 30, 1996 with the objective of not overburdening the prosecutor. This date marked a shift in the conflict since the Abidjan Peace Agreement was concluded on that day but was soon breached by the warring parties (UN S/2000/915). In addition to the lack of power to seek the Security Council's intervention, and the limited temporal jurisdiction, two issues have in particular affected the court's ability to deliver justice. These are the funding mechanism of the court and the limits to its personal jurisdiction, over which the secretary-general and the Security Council disagreed.

Financial Mechanism

The UN secretary-general suggested that the Special Court should be financed through assessed contributions arguing that: "[a] financial mechanism based entirely on voluntary contributions will not provide the assured and continuous source of funding which would be required...The risks associated with the establishment of an operation of this kind with insufficient funds, or without long-term assurances of continuous availability of funds, are very high" (UN S/2000/915). The Security Council, on the other hand, maintained that the court should be financed through voluntary contributions (UN S/2000/1234). This is in contrast to the tribunals for the former Yugoslavia and Rwanda, which had taken a heavy toll on the UN budget. The secretary-general remained skeptical of the suggestion by the Security Council to base the court on voluntary contributions, but he nevertheless negotiated agreement to establish the Special Court on this basis (UN S/2001/40).

The amount of voluntary contributions available required a scaling-down of the operations of the court (UN S/2001/693). However, there were still shortfalls in the pledged contributions. The worries expressed by the secretary-general relating to the funding mechanism proved to be well-grounded. In a report on the Special Court, Cassese writes that "financing of the court...has been an ongoing problem" and that the court's "lack of financial stability has been a noteworthy weakness"

(Cassese 2006, 11). A problem has been that the registrar and the prosecutor have spent time and resources to raise money for the court, and the financial insecurity has affected the possibilities of planning and recruitment (Cassese 2006, 11).

The Court's Personal Jurisdiction: Those Who Bear the Greatest Responsibility

The secretary-general recommended that the court should prosecute those "most responsible" for the crimes whereas the Security Council recommended that court should prosecute those "who bear the greatest responsibility" (UN S/2000/915; UN S/2000/1234). This is a question of the scope of the court's personal jurisdiction. The Security Council wanted a narrower prosecution than envisaged by the secretary-general's suggestion (International Center for Transitional Justice 2006, 15).

The final agreement to establish the court gives it jurisdiction over "persons who bear the greatest responsibility." The prosecutor of the Special court has interpreted the already limited mandate narrowly (War Crimes Studies Center 2005, 6). Thirteen indictments have been issued. Three of the accused have died either before or during the trial, and one remains at large. Importantly, though, the prosecutor issued indictments against representatives from all three parties to the war. The mandate of the court is *not* restricted to prosecute President Kabbah's enemies in the war, namely the "Revolutionary United Front (RUF) and their accomplices" as suggested by Kabbah in the letter requesting assistance to establish the court (UN S/2000/786). The United States and Britain influenced the negotiations to ensure that the court's jurisdiction was not restricted to any particular group such as the RUF (Moghalu 2008, 107). Although many would agree that the RUF indeed played the most brutal part in the war, and many see the Civil Defense Forces (CDF) as liberators, prosecution of only the RUF would certainly be seen as one-sided justice.

Interestingly, the sentences in the Trial Chamber of the two CDF members on trial were only six and eight years, for war crimes and crimes against humanity, including acts against a civilian population, murder, inhumane acts, and cruel treatment. The Trial Chamber considered that the two CDF members had based their participation on a sense of civic duty to restore democracy in Sierra Leone. These were considered as mitigating factors and influenced the length of the sentences. The Appeals Chamber overturned this decision by the Trial Chamber, and sentenced the two CDF members to fifteen and twenty years, respectively. From the AFRC, three members have been sentenced—two for fifty years and one for forty-five years. All three were convicted of counts of war crimes, crimes against humanity, and other serious violations of international criminal law. The crimes include acts of terrorism, collective punishments, extermination, murder, rape, enslavement, pillage, and the conscripting and enlisting of child soldiers. At the time of this writing, three members of the RUF have been sentenced and are awaiting a judgment from the Appeals Chamber.

The Trial of Charles Taylor

Former Liberian president Charles Taylor has been charged with crimes against humanity, war crimes, and other serious violations of international humanitarian law. The indictment was politically controversial, as it was issued during peace talks in which Taylor participated. The talks collapsed when the indictment was made public in June 2003. Moreover, it raised issues of the court's mandate to prosecute heads of state. The Special Court has concluded that since it is an international criminal court, heads of state are not immune from prosecution (International Center for Transitional Justice 2006, 18). On March 29, 2006, Taylor, then in exile in Nigeria, was captured. He was transferred to the SCSL and later to The Hague for his trial, and was detained in the building of the International Criminal Court. Especially since RUF leader Sankoh had died and another high-level RUF member, Sam Boqkarie, was killed in Liberia, the arrest and trial of Taylor was important in order to fulfill the mandate of trying individuals with "the greatest responsibility" for the crimes. Although experts might disagree as to whether it would have been more appropriate to prosecute him for crimes committed in Liberia, he is certainly the most high-ranking and well-known of the indicted at the Special Court. In Sierra Leone, the capture of Taylor seemed to be widely appreciated.[2] At the same time, civil society actors interviewed by this author criticized the transfer of Taylor, and many did not believe in the argument that his trial had to be held in The Hague because of regional security issues.[3]

Responses to Mass Atrocities: Forward-Looking and Backward-Looking

Compared to other war crimes tribunals, the SCSL is characterized by its narrow mandate and hybrid composition. These characteristics represent both challenges and opportunities for the court's legitimacy. The potential of this model is that it might provide justice efficiently and in proximity to the affected population. The challenges arise from the discrepancy between the narrow mandate and the scale of atrocities committed, and the expectations of local effects that are generated when the court is located in the affected country.

By many accounts, "transitional justice" mechanisms are supposed to facilitate the transition to a more peaceful, reconciled, and democratic future by addressing crimes of the past. In this way, transitional justice is both forward-looking and backward-looking (Teitel 2000, 6). Transitional justice mechanisms cannot simply be judged by to their ability to fulfill their backward-looking role, the punishment of past crimes. They must also be judged by their ability to fulfill their forward-looking role: Their effect on the society in which they operate. This is particularly the case with mixed courts. Compared to purely international tribunals, the role in the conflict-ridden society is clearer when the court is located in the affected country.

During the negotiations for the court, issues at stake were the financial and the political strength of the court and the scope of the jurisdiction, which relate to its backward-looking role. However, expectations of a forward-looking role of the Special Court are reflected in the documents that led to its establishment. According to President Kabbah, "it is only by bringing the RUF leadership and their collaborators to justice in the way now requested that peace and national reconciliation and the strengthening of democracy will be assured in Sierra Leone" (UN S/2000/786). In Security Council Resolution 1315, the Council argues that justice and accountability in Sierra Leone "would end impunity and would contribute to the process of national reconciliation and to the restoration and maintenance of peace" (S/RES 1315 2000). Moreover, the resolution emphasizes the importance or rebuilding the Sierra Leonean justice system (UN S/RES/1315/2000).

How have these issues affected the legitimacy of the Special Court? Regarding the backward-looking role of the court, the primary question is whether the court's mandate corresponds with people's views on fairness. Of particular concern is the discrepancy between the narrow jurisdiction of the court, and the massive scale of crimes committed. Regarding the forward-looking role of the court, the question is if expectations of effects on Sierra Leonean society are fulfilled. Expectations relating to its forward-looking role are perhaps even more important than the question of the legitimacy of the court as a retributive, or backward-looking institution. When the international community locates such an expensive postconflict mechanism in the affected country, expectations that it will generate change locally will certainly be high.

Is the Court's Mandate Justifiable?

The mandate, jurisdiction, and results of trials must be justifiable, or perceived as fair, in order to be legitimate on the ground. In this perspective, legitimacy depends on how people believe the trial *ought to be* (Beetham 1991, 3). Cockayne argues that the war crimes trial prosecutions must present its narrative of the crimes in a way that the local community can identify with (Cockayne 2005a, 465). If not, the trial will fail to transform the values of the society—a transformation that is needed for a true transition to take place. Similarly, Higonnet argues that to affect the culture of accountability and rule of law, the court must be accepted by "the bulk of the concerned population" (Higonnet 2005, 10). This chapter does not raise the issue of whether the criminal trial as such is an appropriate mechanism in the Sierra Leonean context. The focus here is on the mandate of the court, and the challenges the mandate has created for the Special Court's legitimacy. There is obviously a huge discrepancy between the crimes committed during the decade-long civil war and the limited mandate vested with the court and its prosecution of the war crimes.

The Court's Narrow Jurisdiction: An Acceptable Compromise?

The narrow jurisdiction of the Special Court, confined to persons "who bear the greatest responsibility" inevitably raises issues of legitimacy: Is the court really handling impunity? (War Crimes Studies Center 2005, 6). The prosecutor has focused on these issues at high levels of the command structure while critics have argued that this approach does not sufficiently take into consideration the fluidity, complexity, and nuances of these organizations. Moreover, many of those who might have been prosecuted with a broader mandate have been insider witnesses to the court. The dilemma was pointed out by the first prosecutor as "dancing with the devil." The prosecutor argued that the narrow mandate is a political compromise; a higher number of prosecutions would be politically impossible and destabilizing, and it would not be possible to complete the trials within an acceptable time frame (War Crimes Studies Center 2005, 6–7). The limited jurisdiction illustrates that there might be a trade-off between different criteria for legitimacy. While the court is expected to mark a clear break with impunity, it must deliver justice within reasonable time and with a limited budget.

Contrary to much of the criticism of the Special Court's narrow prosecution, Shaw argues that the concept of prosecuting only those with "greatest responsibility" was widely appreciated in Sierra Leone because it corresponds with local practices of reintegrating large number of perpetrators by "forgiving and forgetting" (2005, 11). A wider prosecution could have conflicted with these traditional practices. Although the limited personal jurisdiction of the court has been the source of much criticism, many interest group representatives in Freetown have seemed to accept this compromise. In interviews with this author, few raised this as a particularly problematic issue. Rather, the narrow jurisdiction was often accepted as the only possible solution or a necessary trade-off.[4]

The question of the narrow jurisdiction might be more of a problem to ordinary Sierra Leoneans than to civil society actors in Freetown who might be more likely to understand and accept the concept of "greatest responsibility." This perspective seemed to be shared by many civil society representatives in Freetown: They themselves accepted the narrow jurisdiction of the court as a necessary compromise but argued that it was a problem for the court because it was not accepted or understood by ordinary people.[5]

This view is supported by observations done by the Outreach Section at the Special Court, which has documented the opinions of Sierra Leoneans on the court.[6] Patrick Fatoma from the Outreach Section says that people's perceptions of the Special Court have changed over time. Initially, people were skeptical of the court, fearing that it would bring new unrest. Over time, this attitude changed, and people wanted more offenders to be prosecuted. He emphasized the need to prosecute larger numbers of offenders in order to bring closure.[7]

One cannot expect victims of the war to see the discrepancy between the Special Court's mandate and the atrocities of the war as fair and just. But it may be seen as an acceptable trade-off. The narrow jurisdiction does not reflect the massive scale of abuses during the civil war. This certainly creates legitimacy challenges for the court, but many interest group representatives have accepted the jurisdiction as a necessary compromise. Their acceptance of the concept of "greatest responsibility" may influence the court's legitimacy positively, as they explain the jurisdiction to their grass-root members.

The Impartiality of the Court

The Special Court's mandate and the prosecutor's focus have not been limited to the RUF and their accomplices. The prosecutors decided to indict representatives of all sides involved in the conflict. This is of principal importance for the legitimacy of the court. It has ensured the image of the court as impartial, but may at the same time be a challenge to its legitimacy since all parties may not be seen as equally responsible for the war and the crimes committed. The case against the CDF is the most problematic. The vast majority of atrocities were committed by RUF and AFRC. CDF members are seen by many, particularly in the Southeast of the country, as heroes and liberators (War Crimes Studies Center 2005, 9). CDF's Sam Hinga Norman, who was charged but died before his case was finished, is seen as an important person in securing President Kabbah's return to power.

The decision to include CDF members in the trial is clearly in accordance with international principles of accountability. The political role of the warring parties should not influence prosecutorial decisions. But the inclusion of CDF has been "widely contested and has generated substantial criticism of the court within Sierra Leone" (War Crimes Studies Center 2005, 10). The views on the approach by the prosecution will depend on people's political sympathies, which are often determined by regional divides. Many argue that the court is dividing and that CDF and Norman should not have been tried because Norman is seen as a hero.[8]

Expectations of the Effects of the Special Court

Issues relating to the court's backward-looking role are important when discussing its legitimacy, since it is, as a criminal trial, essentially a backward-looking institution. However, the ability of the court to contribute positively to the society affected by the crimes against humanity must also be addressed when discussing its legitimacy challenges. In fact, for many civil society actors interviewed by this author, the forward-looking role of the court was of primary importance. In his report on rule of law and transitional justice, the UN secretary-general writes that efforts in dispensing justice must support domestic reform, build national capacity, and "fill the rule of law vacuum" in postconflict societies (UN S/2004/616). The benefits of localizing tribunals in the affected countries include enhanced "national capacity-building contribution," which can "ensure a lasting legacy in the countries concerned" (UN S/2004/616). In line with the views expressed by the secretary-general, among civil society actors interviewed by this author, the expectations related to the forward-looking role of the Special Court often related to the potential legacy on the Sierra Leonean judiciary. Another issue of concern was the contrast between the costs of the court and the needs of victims.

The Costs of Justice and the Needs of Victims

Roht-Arriaza argues that reparations may be the "most tangible and visible expression of both acknowledgement and change" and may be important for reconciliation and social construction (2004, 136). The SCSL has no mandate to award reparations or compensations to victims for crimes addressed at the court. For many, especially representatives of victim's groups, it is problematic that the court does not provide for reparations for individual victims.[9] Some non-governmental organization representatives raised this issue as being particularly difficult, given the fact that a lot of resources have been spent on reintegration programs for ex-combatants. Generally, civil society actors seemed to share the concern that the court is doing too little for the victims, particularly by not providing economic compensation.[10]

The lack of reparation for victims must be seen in light of the costs of the Special Court in a Sierra Leonean perspective. Fritz and Smith write that is often expressed that the money spent on the court should instead be spent on other more pressing needs in Sierra Leone (Fritz and Smith 2001-2002, 427). The high costs of the Special Court, by Sierra Leonean standards, create legitimacy challenges for it, since the contrast between the resources spent on a few defendants and the living conditions for most of the victims and even ordinary Sierra Leoneans is so stark. At the same time, the court would not have lived up to its international obligations if it had not spent resources on defense personnel and proper detainment conditions. This dilemma is bound to arise when international or internationalized justice efforts are employed in extremely poor societies.

The Legacy of the Court

The fifth annual report of the Special Court published in 2008 states that it is committed to making a contribution to the rule of law in the country. The legacy is supposed to be generated both through the symbolism of the court and activities aimed at strengthening the Sierra Leonean justice system. The potential legacy of the court is emphasized by some of the literature in the field. Fritz and Smith argue that the SCSL is likely to "inject new life into Sierra Leone's domestic legal system" (Fritz and Smith 2001–2002, 406). Sieff and Vinjamuri argue that the court's administration, by both foreigners and Sierra Leoneans, should "encourage a diffusion of legal expertise to the West African nation" and that this should "help the court to contribute to the consolidation of peace and the establishment of the rule of law within the country" (2002, 110). Pham writes that the court contributes to the rebuilding of the national judicial system by its "presence, visibility, and accessibility" (2006, 108).

However in 2006, a report from monitors of the court argued that the potential of it to affect the justice system in Sierra Leone is extremely limited due to "financial and political constraints" and that "the United Nations has made no real effort to integrate the work of the Special Court into a wider justice reform project in Sierra Leone" (War Crimes Studies Center 2006, 22). This problem is also pointed out by Higonnet, who argues that the combination of international and national staff will not automatically lead to capacity-building (2005, 13). Bangura argues that there have been expectations that the Special Court would contribute to the national judiciary through the diffusion of legal knowledge, but that the Special Court has been institutionally separated from the national judiciary and only a few local lawyers and judges have been included. Thus the Special Court has not contributed to developing Sierra Leonean law (Bangura 2005, 56). These critical viewpoints were echoed by many civil society actors in Sierra Leone.

There were, however, other views as to how and whether the Special Court would affect the Sierra Leonean judiciary and rule of law. Many saw the training of national lawyers at the court and the diffusion of knowledge to the national judiciary as the most important potential legacy of the court. Others were disappointed that this potential has not been fulfilled. The representative of the Sierra Leonean Bar Association argued that the main concern with the court was that too few Sierra Leoneans were among its staff.[11] He argued that the court should have included more Sierra Leoneans to generate experience. Other civil society representatives also shared the view that the court has hired too few Sierra Leoneans, and that this has lowered its potential impact on the national judicial system.[12] Some argued that the idea of Sierra Leonean lawyers working side-by-side with international lawyers is a good one, but the effects, in terms of training and capacity-building, have been too weak.[13] The lack of interaction between Sierra Leonean and international staff at the court was also raised.[14]

Others saw the deterrent effect of the trials as the most important contribution of the Special Court.[15] A similar view was that the prosecution of high-ranking leaders will set a standard for the Sierra Leonean judiciary and human rights in the country.[16] Sierra Leonean lawyers at the court believe in the importance of the capacity-building that they receive by working at it, according to the War Crimes Studies Center (2006, 24). But for the capacity-building of individual lawyers to have a broader effect on the Sierra Leonean judiciary, the national judiciary and the government must be receptive to change and judicial reform. The question of legacy cannot simply be accomplished by the court hiring a few more Sierra Leoneans in senior positions. The representatives at the local Amnesty International office in Sierra Leone argued that the Special Court does not work as a model court because it is not used as one by the national courts.[17]

The legacy in terms of effects on the national judiciary also depends on the willingness of individual Sierra Leonean lawyers to take up an agenda for reform. It has been reported that initiatives to introduce human rights into domestic cases have been met with skepticism (War Crimes Studies Center 2006, 24–25). Also, the Sierra Leonean lawyers at the Special Court will not necessarily bring their experience and knowledge back to the national judiciary, since many come from the Sierra Leonean diaspora, and others will probably pursue careers at other international tribunals (War Crimes Studies Center 2006, 26). Although the question of legacy was very important for civil society actors, this is not necessarily the case for the population in general. A report from the SCSL Outreach Section on questions asked by the public during outreach meetings shows that very few of the questions (2 percent) related to legacy issues.[18]

Conclusions: The Special Court for Whom?

The SCSL has been characterized by its restricted mandate, limited budget, and mixed nature. The aim of SCSL by incorporating these features was to "avoid the pitfalls" of the ICTY and the International Criminal Tribunal for Rwanda (Cassese 2006, 65). However, it can be argued that this attempt on "right-sizing" justice resulted in a court that lacked the necessary muscle, both economically and politically, to achieve its goals (Dougherty 2004, 324–328). It has also been counterproductive to the aims of creating quick and cost-efficient justice. The tight budget and voluntary funding has created delays in the court's operations and added costs related to fund-raising (Cassese 2006, 11 and 65–66). More importantly, its limited mandate has created a huge discrepancy between the scale of crimes and the scope of prosecutions. However, while many interest group representatives see the narrow jurisdiction as problematic, many also accept it as a necessary compromise.

It is not only the number of people prosecuted that has affected its legitimacy on the ground. Its mixed nature has generated expectations of legacy effects of the court. Despite the mixed characteristics of the Special Court, both in terms of jurisdiction and personnel, the court is in many ways an international mechanism. The judges have ruled that the Special Court is an international court (International Center for Transitional Justice 2006, 17). While the statute gives the Special Court a mandate to prosecute certain crimes under Sierra Leonean law, the charges have only included crimes under international law (War Crimes Studies Center 2005, 7). The dominance of international personnel in senior positions has contributed to the strong international character of the court. The transfer to The Hague of the trial of Charles Taylor, the "biggest fish" among the defendants, further reduces the Sierra Leonean components of the court. The international character of the court has reduced its potential in terms of generating effects locally. Expectations of local learning effects from the trial have not been met.

The challenge faced by the SCSL in achieving legitimacy on the ground should not be read as an argument to abandon the hybrid court model. It was the almost unanimous view among civil society actors interviewed by this author that prosecution of war crimes would not have been credible, or even possible, without the participation of the UN.[19] Also, there was great appreciation of the fact that the court was located in Sierra Leone—a view that is also reflected in much of the criticism of the transfer of the Taylor trial to The Hague.[20] Importantly, evidence indicates that Sierra Leoneans in general support the idea that perpetrators from the war are put on trial.[21] The question is not whether the mixed tribunal model as such is legitimate in the Sierra Leonean context. Rather, the question is whether its possibilities have been properly utilized, and whether the expectations raised by the mixed model have been met.[22]

Notes

1. Agreement between the UN and the government of Sierra Leone was signed on January 16, 2002.
2. Before the capture of Taylor, the Outreach Section at the Special Court reported that in public meetings about the court, there were more questions about Taylor than any other indictee. Special Court for Sierra Leone 2003–2005, 28. A survey of 1,717 respondents showed that 89 percent were aware of the trial of Taylor (BBC World Service Trust and Search for Common Ground 2008, 21).
3. Muhammed Suma (SLCMP), interview with author, November 22, 2006, Freetown; Nancy Sesay (Timap for Justice), interview with author, November 24, 2006, Freetown; Edward B. Koroma (National Accountability Group), interview with author, December 5, 2006, Freetown. Some, however, accepted the security argument. Philip Lansana from the Coalition of Civil Society and Human Rights Activists explained that in his home village close to the Liberian border, people were happy that Charles Taylor is not tried in Sierra Leone. Interview with author, December 4, 2006, Freetown.
4. Nancy Sesay (Timap for Justice), interview with author, November 24, 2006, Freetown; John Caulker (Forum of Conscience), interview with author, December 5, 2006, Freetown.
5. For example, Jabati Mambu (Amputees and War Wounded Association) supported the limited jurisdiction, although himself a victim of the war. But he argued that many of the victims "in provinces" want more to be punished and want the death penalty. Interview with author, December 4, 2006, Freetown. Philip Lansana (Coalition of Civil Society and Human Rights Activists) argued that in the districts, people asked questions about grass root perpetrators. Interview with author, December 4, 2006, Freetown. Sulaiman Jabati (Coalition for Justice and Accountability) thought the limited jurisdiction was the greatest problem of the court, but personally did not think the court's prosecution should be wider because of the costs. Interview with author, December 1, 2006, Freetown.
6. This documentation does not provide a representative overview of Sierra Leonean opinions, but it still provides information about issues important to Sierra Leoneans. The information gathered by the Outreach Section is an important addition to the information and viewpoints presented by civil society representatives.
7. Patrick Fatoma (SCSL Outreach Section), interview with author, December 2006, Freetown.
8. Emmannuel Abduiai (Society for Democratic Initiative) expressed this view. Interview with author, November 26, 2006, Freetown.
9. Jabati Mambu (Amputees and War Wounded Association), interview with author, December 4, 2006, Freetown.
10. Emmannuel Abduiai (Society for Democratic Initiative), interview with author, November 23, 2006, Freetown; Philip Lansana (Coalition of Civil Society and Human Rights Activists), interview with author. December 4, 2006, Freetown; Nancy Sesay (Timap for Justice), interview with author, November 24, 2006, Freetown.
11. Emmanuel Roberts (Sierra Leone Bar Association), interview with author, November 29, 2006, Freetown.
12. Sulaiman Jabati (Coalition for Justice and Accountability), interview with author, December 1, 2006, Freetown.
13. Emmannuel Abduiai (Society for Democratic Initiative), interview with author, November 23, 2006, Freetown; Philip Lansana (Coalition of Civil Society and Human Rights Activists), interview with author. December 4, 2006, Freetown; John Coulker (Forum of Conscience), interview with author. December 5, 2006, Freetown.
14. Alfred Carew (National Forum for Human Rights), interview with author, December 1, 2006, Freetown.
15. Mohammed S. Turay (Network Movement for Justice and Accountability), interview with author, December 6, 2006, Freetown.
16. This view was held by Nancy Sesay (Timap for Justice), interview with author, November 24, 2006, Freetown.
17. Brima A. Sheriff and Rodney Lowe (Amnesty International, Sierra Leone), interview with author, November 29, 2006, Freetown.
18. Special Court for Sierra Leone 2003–2005, 27 and 47.

19. For example, Emmanuel Roberts (Sierra Leone Bar Association) argued that the UN gives the process credibility and neutrality. Interview with author, November 29, 2006, Freetown. Muhammed Suma (SLCMP) argued that there would never have been a tribunal without the UN. Interview with author, November 22, 2006, Freetown. Philip Lansana (Coalition of Civil Society and Human Rights Activists) believed a purely Sierra Leonean court would have been corrupt and manipulated. Interview with author, December 4, 2006, Freetown.
20. Some explained the importance of having the court in Sierra Leone by referring to the importance for victims in seeing the perpetrators. Philip Lansana (Coalition of Civil Society and Human Rights Activists), interview with author, December 4, 2006, Freetown. Edward B. Koroma (National Accountability Group) argued that it is important that the offenders are tried in front of Sierra Leoneans. Interview with author, December 5, 2006, Freetown.
21. A survey of 1,717 respondents reports that 88 percent of respondents believed that those involved in wrongdoing should be put on trial (BBC World Service Trust and Search for Common Ground August 2008, 17–18). Ninety-six percent of the respondents were aware of the court, but of those, only 7 percent said they know a lot about the court. Of those who are aware of the court (both those who know a lot and a little), 86 percent are positive toward the court. The overall trust in the court among respondents is high: Seventy-six percent either agree (55 percent) or strongly agree (21 percent) that the Special Court can be trusted in bringing justice. One should be careful, however, in relying too much on these numbers, since many of those whose attitudes are measured know little of the court.
22. The International Center for Transitional Justice (2006, 3) concludes that the court's problems stem from the implementation, rather than the model itself.

References

Bangura, Zainab. 2005. "Sierra Leone: Ordinary Courts and the Special Court." *Open Society*. Available at: www.justiceinitiative.org/db/resource2/fs/?file_id=15283&rand=0.529036733975.

BBC World Service Trust and Search for Common Ground. 2008. "Building a Better Tomorrow. A Survey of Knowledge and Attitudes toward Transitional Justice in Sierra Leone."

Beetham, David. 1991. *The Legitimation of Power*. Atlantic Heights, NJ: Humanities Press International.

Boas, Morten. 2000. "Borgerkrigen i Sierra Leone." *Internasjonal politikk* 58:559–582.

Cassese, Antonio. 2006. *Report on the Special Court for Sierra Leone Submitted by the Independent Expert Antonio Cassese*. December 12.

Cockayne, James. 2005a. "Hybrids or Mongrels? Internationalized War Crimes Trials as Unsuccessful Degradation Ceremonies." *Journal of Human Rights* 4:455–473.

Cockayne, James. 2005b. "The Fraying Shoestring: Rethinking Hybrid War Crimes Tribunals." *Fordham International Law Journal* 28:616–680.

Dougherty, Beth K. 2004. "Right-Sizing International Criminal Justice: The Hybrid Experiment at the Special Court for Sierra Leone." *International Affairs* 80:311–328.

Fritz, Nicole, and Alison Smith. 2001–2002. "Current Apathy for Coming Anarchy: Building the Special Court for Sierra Leone." *Fordham International Law Journal* 25:391–430.

Hayner, Priscilla. 2007. "Negotiating Peace in Sierra Leone: Confronting the Justice Challenge." The Center for Humanitarian Dialogue.

Higonnet, Ethel. 2005. "Restructuring Hybrid Courts: Local Empowerment and National Criminal Justice Reform." *Yale Law School Student Scholarship Series* Paper 6.

Human Rights Watch. 2000. *Sierra Leone: Priorities for the International Community*. June 20. Available at: www.hrw.org/en/news/2000/06/20/sierra-leone-priorities-international-community.

International Center for Transitional Justice. 2006. "The Special Court for Sierra Leone under Scrutiny." Available at: www.ictj.org/static/Prosecutions/Sierra.study.pdf.

Lome Peace Agreement. 1999. Available at: www.sc-sl.org.

McDonald, Arvil. 2007. "Sierra Leone's shoestring Special Court." *IRRC 84*:121–143.

Moghalu, Kingsley Chiedu. 2008. *Global Justice. The Politics of War Crimes Trials*. Stanford, CA: Stanford University Press.

O'Flaherty, Michael G. 2005. "Human Rights in Negotiating Peace Agreements: Sierra Leone." International Council on Human Rights Policy. Available at: www.ichrp.org/files/papers/60/128_-_Sierra_Leone_Human_Rights_in_Negotiating_Peace_Agreements_O_Flaherty__Michael__2005.pdf.

Pham, J. Peter. 2006. "A Viable Model for International Criminal Justice: The Special Court for Sierra Leone." *New York International Law Review* 19:37–109.

Roht-Arriaza, Naomi. 2004. "Reparations in the Aftermath of Repression and Mass Violence." In *My Neighbor, My Enemy. Justice and Community in the Aftermath of Mass Atrocity*, ed. Eric Stover and Harvey M. Weinstein. Cambridge: Cambridge University Press.

Shaw, Rosalind. 2005. "Rethinking Truth and Reconciliation Commissions. Lessons from Sierra Leone." *United States Institute of Peace*. Special Report 130.

Sieff, Michelle, and Leslie Vinjamuri. 2002. "Prosecuting War Criminals: The Case for Decentralization." *Conflict, Security and Development* 2:103–113.

Statute of the Special Court for Sierra Leone. 2002. Available at: www.sc-sl.org.

Teitel, Ruti G. 2000. *Transitional Justice*. Oxford: Oxford University Press.

UN S/2004/616. 2004. "The Rule of Law and Transitional Justice in Conflict and Post-Conflict Societies." Report of the Secretary-General, August 23.

UN S/2001/693. 2001. "Letter Dated 12 July 2001 from the Secretary-General Addressed to the President of the Security Council."

UN S/2001/40. 2001. "Letter Dated 12 January 2001 from the Secretary-General Addressed to the President of the Security Council."

UN S/2000/1234. 2000. "Letter Dated 22 December 2000 from the President of the Security Council Addressed to the Secretary-General."

UN S/2000/915. 2000. "Report of the Secretary-General on the Establishment of a Special Court for Sierra Leone."

UN S/RES/1315. 2000. "UN Security Council Resolution 1315."

UN S/2000/786. 2000. "Letter Dated 9 August 2000 from the Permanent Representative of Sierra Leone to the United Nations Addressed to the President of the Security Council."

War Crimes Studies Center. 2006. *Second Interim Report on the Special Court for Sierra Leone*. Berkeley, CA: University of California.

War Crimes Studies Center. 2005. *Interim Report on the Special Court for Sierra Leone*. Berkeley, CA: University of California.

PART V

East Timor

Map from the United States Central Intelligence Agency's World Factbook.

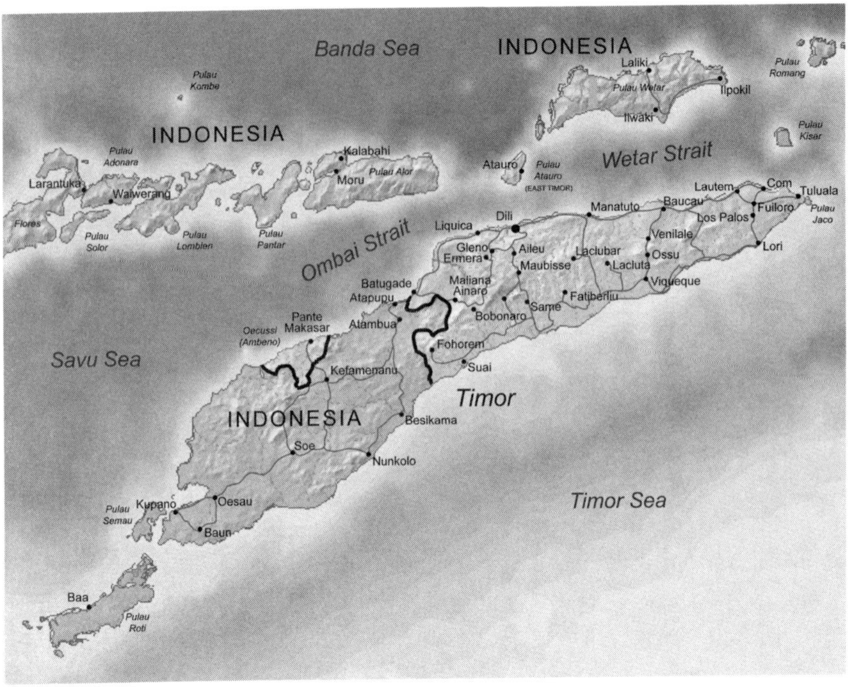
Banda Sea
INDONESIA
Laliki
Pulau Wetar
Ilpokil
Ilwaki
Pulau Romang
Pulau Kisar
Pulau Kombe
INDONESIA
Pulau Adonara
Kalabahi
Moru
Pulau Alor
Atauro
Pulau Atauro
(EAST TIMOR)
Wetar Strait
Larantuka
Waiwerang
Flores
Pulau Solor
Pulau Lomblen
Pulau Pantar
Ombai Strait
Liquica
Dili
Manatuto
Baucau
Lautem
Com
Tuluala
Fuiloro
Pulau Jaco
Los Palos
Venilale
Lori
Gleno
Ermera
Aileu
Maubisse
Laclubar
Laclutа
Ossu
Viqueque
Batugade
Atapupu
Maliana
Ainaro
Same
Fatiberliu
Bobonaro
Pante Makasar
Oecussi (Ambeno)
Atambua
Savu Sea
Fohorem
Suai
Kefamenanu
Timor
INDONESIA
Besikama
Soe
Nunkolo
Pulau Semau
Kupang
Oesau
Baun
Timor Sea
Baa
Pulau Roti

CHAPTER 11

East Timor and the Struggle for Independence

Clinton Fernandes

Introduction

The nation of East Timor occupies the Eastern half of the island of Timor as well as the enclave of Oecussi-Ambeno (located in West Timor) and the small islands of Atauro and Jaco. At just under 15,000 square kilometers, it is about the size of Northern Ireland or the state of Connecticut in the United States. It was invaded by Indonesia in 1975 and was occupied until 1999. This chapter provides an overview of the twenty-four-year conflict between East Timor and Indonesia. It begins by examining the historical background of the conflict, showing how Portugal's colonial presence in the area influenced the political situation prior to the Indonesian invasion. It then describes the internal political conflict during the process of decolonization from Portugal, when Indonesia manipulated the situation through covert operations with the aim of eventual annexation. It shows how Indonesia stepped up its military incursions, captured several towns in the border regions, and then invaded the territory. It then examines the twenty-four-year occupation of East Timor by Indonesia and East Timor's struggle for independence.

The chapter outlines the reinforcement of a nationalist consciousness in a new generation of East Timorese youth, the "Indonesianization" of the struggle through participation in the Indonesian pro-democracy movement, and the "internationalization" of the struggle in order to exert international diplomatic pressure on the Indonesian authorities. It describes the ballot for independence, the campaign of state-sponsored terror that accompanied it, and the final, tumultuous period followed by the liberation of the country. It is through the struggle for independence that East Timorese now confront a legacy of human rights violations that need to be addressed.

Background

Human settlement continued to occur in East Timor for thousands of years. Portuguese involvement in the island nation commenced in the 1500s although as late as the mid-nineteenth century, its presence was limited to a few tiny settlements on the Northern coast. The Portuguese exploited rivalries between various groups in East Timor, ensuring that indigenous political alliances remained weak and the sense of national identity remained undeveloped. For much of the twentieth century, Portugal itself was under the rule of the Salazar dictatorship. Strikes, lockouts, and political parties were banned in Portugal by the Salazar rule. It used censorship, propaganda, and political imprisonment to "neutralize" the society, while according special privileges to the church in the areas of law and education. Portuguese rule inside East Timor reflected this relationship between the church and the state.

On April 25, 1974, the Portuguese armed forces, radicalized by the experience of fighting liberation movements in Portugal's African colonies, overthrew the Caetano dictatorship that succeeded Salazar and set in motion a decolonization process in East Timor. Political organizations that had developed in East Timor under Portuguese rule were able to come out into the open although they continued to avoid using the word "party," choosing instead the words "union," "association," or "front." On May 11, 1974, the Uniao Democratica Timorense (UDT) or Timorese Democratic Union was the first party to be formed. It was followed on May 20 by the Associacao Social Democratica Timorense (ASDT) or Timorese Social Democratic Association, which became Frente Revolucionaria do Timor-Leste Independente (Fretilin) or Revolutionary Front for an Independent East Timor in September 1974. The third organization was the Associacao para Integracao de Timor na Indonesia (APODETI) or the Association for the Integration of Timor into Indonesia. It later changed its name to the electorally acceptable Associacao Popular Democratica Timorense (also shortened to APODETI) or the Timorese Popular Democratic Association. It gained very little support in East Timor, however.

Fretilin and UDT established themselves as the two leading parties. Both argued for an independent East Timor, with the former promoting rapid independence while the latter advocated gradual independence. Fretilin also sought to pursue land reform, administrative reform, popular education, and the development of small industries based on primary products like coffee. Although no elections had been held, Fretilin asserted that it was the East Timorese peoples' "sole legitimate representative" (Commission for Reception, Truth and Reconciliation Final Report 2005). Such rhetoric increased its differences with UDT, which was dominated by conservative land-owning families and therefore opposed to Fretilin's land reform program. The political inexperience of all the leaders, which was the result of years of living under Portuguese authoritarianism, was seen in their verbal and sometimes physical attacks on one another in the political contest that followed. Their political inexperience was manipulated by neighboring Indonesia, whose intelligence services had been carrying out covert operations inside East Timor with the aim of eventual annexation.

A Campaign of Destabilization

A decade before, during 1965–1966, Indonesia had come under the rule of General Suharto, a pro-Western, right-wing dictator who led what would be called the "New Order" regime. His regime was based on economic development, political exclusion, and popular disenfranchisement. Suharto had come to power in a bloodbath that saw the destruction of two large parties, the Indonesian Communist Party and the Indonesian Nationalist Party. The estimated number of people killed range from 500,000 to 2 million. The regime banned political organizations including trade unions, cultural organizations, and farmers' federations. The whole of Indonesian society was forcibly depoliticized and subjugated to a highly authoritarian political system devoted to the prevention of any challenge to elite interests.

The Indonesian New Order regime was hostile to the prospect of an independent East Timor that sought to pursue land reform, public education, and democratic processes because it would have been a successful example of a democratic alternative in the middle of the Indonesian archipelago. This situation would be intolerable because it would allow the Indonesian public to see an alternative to the New Order in their geographic midst. Regional policymakers understood the Indonesian regime's concern. Michael Curtin, Head of the Indonesia Section at Australia's Department of Foreign Affairs, and previously with the Australian Mission to the United Nations (UN), acknowledged this frankly when he wrote:

> If an independent and politically radicalized East Timor were to make a go of it, with political and economic help not to Indonesia's liking, it would certainly become something for discontented Indonesians to look to (Way 2000).

Indonesia used anticommunist pretexts to justify its opposition to an independent East Timor. It claimed (falsely) that communists from China were attempting to enter East Timor, that East Timor would give the Soviet Union a naval base that would enable the latter to divide Indonesian waters into two zones, that Vietnam might send troops to East Timor, and other (equally false) cold war–inspired claims. The real issue was that the existence of a democratic alternative to the New Order dictatorship might have inspired other Indonesians to take to democracy.[1]

Indonesia stepped up its intelligence gathering efforts in East Timor soon after April 1974. Through its consulate in the East Timorese capital of Dili, it convinced a number of local politicians to support integration with Indonesia. The consulate enabled an Apodeti representative, Tomas Goncalves, to visit Indonesia's military chief, General Maradean Panggabean, in Jakarta in September 1974. Soon after, Indonesian special forces began training Apodeti personnel in West Timor as part of a destabilization campaign known as Operation Komodo. This operation also involved inflammatory radio broadcasts alleging that Portugal was about to withdraw and that Vietnamese and Chinese communists were involved in East Timor. Similar stories were planted in the Indonesian and foreign media. By early 1975, however, Indonesian strategists realized that they could not acquire the territory through these methods. They therefore began to plan for a military takeover.

The Internal Political Conflict

In January 1975, Fretilin and UDT united in what would be a short-lived political coalition. Both parties agreed that East Timor should become independent, and that they would form a transitional government led by members from both parties. However, their mutual suspicion proved to be too strong, and their political inexperience meant that they had no mechanisms to deal with their differences. In particular, the UDT was threatened by Fretilin's overwhelming popular support. The two parties continued to attack each other verbally and tensions rose in the districts. These tensions were exploited by Indonesia, which sought to undermine potential East Timorese unity by playing off one side against the other. The coalition between the UDT and Fretilin collapsed after four months.

In early August 1975, key UDT figures met Indonesian intelligence chief General Ali Murtopo in Jakarta. They launched a coup against Fretilin on their return. In this so-called "armed movement" of August 11, UDT captured some key installations and detained hundreds of Fretilin leaders and supporters. Fretilin withdrew to the hills of Aileu, south of Dili, beginning its fight back on August 20.[2] The Portuguese administration left Dili on August 26 for the island of Atauro and would never return. Some members of the police and some military units supported UDT but most supported Fretilin, which defeated UDT by early September. Fretilin established an administration, distributed food, and continued to recognize Portuguese sovereignty. It ensured that the Portuguese flag flew in the capital and prevented the use of the governor's office there. The Portuguese administration ignored Fretilin's requests to return.

The Indonesian Military Operations

Meanwhile, Indonesia had stepped up its military incursions into the territory in October 1975 in a campaign known as Operation Flamboyan. It captured several towns on the East Timorese side of the border. Faced with Indonesian destabilization, propaganda, and military incursions, Fretilin declared independence on November 28, 1975. The next day representatives of UDT and three other small groupings issued the so-called "Balibo Declaration," which was a proclamation requesting the Indonesian government to annex East Timor. Although called the Balibo Declaration, witnesses to its signing later testified that it was drafted in Jakarta and signed in a Bali hotel under coercive circumstances.

Indonesia invaded East Timor on December 7, 1975. Fretilin made a fighting withdrawal to the interior along with its military wing, the Armed Forces for the National Liberation of East Timor (Falintil). Indonesia would occupy East Timor for the next twenty-four years. It installed a "provisional government" ten days after the full-scale invasion but the character and extent of human rights violations shocked many East Timorese who had supported the invasion, including those who now found themselves in the provisional government.

In mid-1976, Fretilin regrouped and held a national conference in the eastern interior. It established a series of *zonas libertadas* (liberated zones) within which were located *bases de apoio* (resistance bases). Falintil troops, militia companies, and civil defense units protected civilians within these bases; in turn, the civilians provided logistical support to the fighters. However, the Indonesian military was able to press its attacks thanks to the use of U.S.-supplied OV-10 Bronco, Sky hawk A-4, and F-5 aircraft. Military operations that targeted the civilian population caused widespread famine in East Timor from late 1977 to 1979.

The Indonesian military exerted control over domestic relief operations and banned international relief agencies and international media from entering East Timor. Nearly half the population (approximately 300,000 people) was forcibly displaced into Indonesian-controlled centers between 1978 and 1979. Civilians who surrendered were interrogated, and sexual slavery was institutionally tolerated and supported by the Indonesian military. Women who were not held in military bases were summoned for sexual abuse by soldiers. According to a detailed and credible investigation, "women's names were on a list or file held by the military, which required them to make themselves available sexually for military personnel. These lists or files were handed down from one battalion to another" (Commission for Reception, Truth and Reconciliation Final Report 2005, 51). The last of the resistance bases fell in early 1979, and the Indonesian military declared that East Timor was pacified on March 26, 1979. The territory was then shut off from the outside world for the next decade.

Fighting Back

Only three Fretilin Central Committee members survived Indonesia's military campaign. One of them was Xanana Gusmao, who conducted a National Reorganization Conference in March 1981 at Maubai in Lacluta. The political and military structure of the resistance was reorganized under the overall command of a Revolutionary Council of National Resistance (CRRN). The CRRN was to be a forum for all pro-independence elements. There was opposition from some staunchly socialist members of Fretilin, but Fretilin's Central Committee officially emphasized the need for national unity (rather than ideological purity), and committed itself to the greater good of national liberation.

A secret meeting in 1982 between Gusmao and the Catholic Church's Apostolic Administrator of East Timor, Monsignor Martinho da Costa Lopes, showed that the church did not see the resistance as a communist organization, which had been the claim of the Indonesian government, but as a nationalist one. In 1983, the Church in East Timor adopted Tetum, the most widely spoken indigenous language, as the official language of the liturgy. This decision further emphasized East Timor's cultural differences from Indonesia because the Indonesian Catholic Church used Indonesian as its liturgical language.

Even though Indonesia controlled East Timorese territory, the Portuguese government remained the administering power of East Timor under international law. At the 1982 UN General Assembly session, a resolution referring the matter to the "good offices" of the UN secretary-general succeeded by only four votes, but this slim diplomatic victory kept East Timor's right to self-determination on the UN agenda for the next twenty-four years. In diplomatic terms, the East Timorese resistance ensured it gained a hearing on the right to self-determination at the annual meetings of the UN Commission on Human Rights in Geneva and the UN Special Committee on Decolonization in New York. It also worked with global civil society in support of its campaign.

A New Generation Joins the Struggle

In the mid-1980s, secret communications were opened between Catholic youth and Gusmao, with the former asking questions about resistance strategy and the latter advising the youth to persist in their identity as East Timorese and to continue the struggle. East Timorese students established several clandestine cells and then went on to form the East Timorese Catholic Youth Organization (*Organizacao de Juventude Catolica de Timor-Leste*). In addition during this time, a few thousand East Timorese worked or studied in Indonesia. Many students started clandestine cells in Indonesian cities such as Bandung, Semarang, Solo, Jakarta, Malang, and Denpasar under the banner of RENETIL (*Resistencia Nacional dos Estudantes de Timor-Leste*) or National Resistance of East Timorese Students. RENETIL's formation preserved a nationalist consciousness in these East Timorese students, who might otherwise have succumbed to Indonesia's cultural and political influence. It "Indonesianized" the struggle by participating in the Indonesian pro-democracy movement and forging links with Indonesian human rights activists. It "internationalized" the struggle by receiving human rights reports from inside East Timor and distributing them to Indonesian and international human rights organizations. It worked with the clandestine front inside East Timor to coordinate the visits of foreign diplomats and activists to the territory. This would lead to significant victories in the 1990s.

Towards the end of 1988, however, the Resistance was once again modified with the aim of creating a unified, nation-wide structure. This modification was known as the Structural Readjustment of the Resistance, whereby the Revolutionary Council of National Resistance was replaced by the National Council for Maubere Resistance (CNRM). This too would be a forum for all pro-independence elements, with the additional change that Falintil would be the army of CNRM and not part of Fretilin. Accordingly, although Gusmao retained his position as commander in chief of Falintil, he resigned from Fretilin and assumed the presidency of CNRM. Although national unity grew during the occupation, the creation of CNRM caused serious tensions between the Fretilin leadership and Gusmao, tensions that remain very much alive even today. CNRM would later became the CNRT (National Council of Timorese Resistance).

The Visit of the Pope

Pope John Paul II visited East Timor on October 12, 1989. The visit carried some risk to the Indonesian authorities, but it offered a potentially huge diplomatic payoff: a successful visit would be the first step in winning international recognition without having to carry out a vote on self-determination. The Indonesian military took direct control of the organization of the Pope's visit. For their part, the East Timorese understood what was at stake, writing to the Pope to warn against anything that might be construed as a formal act of recognition. The East Timorese clergy insisted that the Pope say Mass in Tetum, not Bahasa Indonesian. The Vatican envoy preparing the Pope's visit, Father Tucci, suggested a compromise of Latin, with a few sentences in Tetum and arranged for a short meeting between the Pope and a group of local priests during the visit. While these details were being worked out, the Vatican continued to downplay the political significance of the visit. While affirming that it did not recognize the Indonesian annexation, the Vatican said that its position of non-interference would not change for as long as East Timor remained on the UN list of non-autonomous territories.

When the Pope arrived at Dili's Comoro Airport, he disappointed many East Timorese by not kissing the ground, his traditional action on reaching a new country. The Papal Mass was held at Taci-Tolu, a plain seventeen kilometers west of Dili. The Pope spoke in English and, far from condemning the brutal occupation, called on the East Timorese to reconcile themselves with the Indonesians. A demonstration broke out at the front of the congregation as the Mass was coming to a close. The inevitable police crackdown followed. Bishop Carlos Belo, the successor to Monsignor da Costa Lopes, sheltered forty demonstrators at his residence but they were subsequently removed from there by the security forces, arrested, and sentenced to prison.

The Santa Cruz Massacre

A parliamentary delegation from Portugal was supposed to visit East Timor in October 1991. This visit had been under negotiation for seven years. When the Indonesian government objected to the inclusion of some individuals, Portugal refused to accept Indonesia's veto and cancelled the visit entirely. Young members of the clandestine resistance had spent months preparing for the visit, possibly exposing themselves to capture by the Indonesian intelligence services. The cancellation resulted in a volatile atmosphere as all the pent-up frustration was suddenly deprived of an outlet. On October 28, 1991, within a day of the cancellation, soldiers attacked a crowd of twenty young East Timorese, who had taken shelter in the Motael Church in Dili, in order to evict them from the church. A clandestine activist named Sebastiao Gomes Rangel was killed along with another man, and about twenty-five others were arrested.

On November 12, 1991, fourteen days after the death of Sebastiao Gomes, mourners gathered in his memory at Motael Church. After an hour-long Mass beginning in the early morning, a procession left the Church and headed toward the Santa Cruz Cemetery on a winding, four-kilometer route. Also arriving at the Santa Cruz Cemetery from Taibessi (at the base of the southern foothills of Dili) were troops from the Indonesian military (including the riot-control police, which were part of the military at the time). These troops perpetrated violence what has come to be known as the Santa Cruz Massacre. According to an eyewitness:

> Suddenly a few shots rang out, continued by an explosive volley of automatic rifle fire that persisted for two to three minutes. It sounded like the whole 15 in the front row had their fingers pressed firmly on the trigger. They were firing directly into the crowd. (Anderson 1991)

Civilians were shot in the back as they tried to escape the shooting. Soldiers kicked and stabbed the wounded and other survivors inside the cemetery. More wounded civilians were killed in the neighboring villages, on the way to the hospital and in the hospital itself. Unknown to the Indonesian authorities, British journalist Max Stahl had captured the massacre on film, which he buried in the cemetery. He was searched on his way out of Dili but some of the key tapes were smuggled out to Jakarta and then to the Netherlands by a Dutch reporter, Saskia Kouwenberg. British photographer Steve Cox, who was severely beaten, had taken graphic photos, which were also smuggled out. Amy Goodman and Allan Nairn, two reporters from the United States, were also present. Their camera was smashed and both were badly beaten but they survived and became the United States's best-known campaigners for East Timorese self-determination. When Stahl's film was broadcast a few days later, there was an international outcry. Portugal held a national day of mourning a week after the massacre, outraged by the film and deeply moved by the sight of dying East Timorese saying their final prayers in Portuguese. Indonesian groups supporting self-determination for East Timor were also formed in a number of cities across Java.

Conditions Worsen Inside East Timor

Although the Santa Cruz massacre is today recognized as a turning point in the independence struggle, it did not seem that way to East Timorese at the time. For them, conditions inside the territory had worsened. Major intelligence and military operations in the aftermath of the massacre had resulted in the penetration of the clandestine network and the capture of key resistance leaders. Indeed, the supreme commander of the resistance, Gusmao, was captured on November 20, 1992. This serious setback not only demoralized the resistance but also emboldened the Indonesian military. Previously, Indonesian diplomats had achieved ascendancy over their military counterparts, fueling pressures for a reduced military presence in East Timor and a negotiated settlement to the conflict. But these new successes had strengthened the position of the military, which was able to argue that it was resolving the problem through decisive action. Elite elements in Indonesia began to take the view that a more hard-line approach was yielding dividends and that this was the best approach to pursue.

In the early 1990s the Indonesian occupying forces appeared to have the upper hand. But a spectacular example of strategic nonviolent action at the Asia Pacific Economic Cooperation (APEC) summit in Jakarta in 1994 stole the regime's thunder, regained the initiative, and gave renewed confidence to Indonesian pro-democracy activists and East Timorese campaigners. With the international media present at the APEC summit, twenty-nine East Timorese students jumped the fence into the U.S. Embassy in Jakarta on November 12, the anniversary of the Santa Cruz massacre, and demanded a meeting with visiting U.S. president Bill Clinton. Although they did not meet him, they made world headlines for days at the height of what was supposed to be a showcase event for the Suharto regime. They later obtained political asylum in Portugal.[3]

Protests inside East Timor continued, particularly when foreign journalists and activists on tourist visas visited the territory. According to one foreign visitor, the clandestine resistance activists would let foreigners know "that at such and such a time in such a place there would be a demonstration. It got to the point where they would almost demand the presence of TV cameras, without which it made little sense to run such risks" (Nogueira 1994). The Indonesian authorities were frustrated by the protests and negative international publicity. In order to maintain the pressure on the population while somehow avoiding international criticism, they resorted to a strategy of plausible denial, commencing covert operations by training and deploying militia groups.[4] In January and February 1995, Dili began to be terrorized by gangs of masked, black-clad men, known locally as "ninjas" who bashed and intimidated people between sunset and sunrise. Credible reports indicated that the gangs had been trained in Kupang (West Timor) under the supervision of Indonesia's special forces (Wagstaff 1995b).

The existence of the gangs could not be disputed, not even by the vice-governor of East Timor, Brigadier Johannes Haribowo (Associated Press 1995). Local youths organized themselves into self-defense squads to fight back against the ninja gangs. They soon captured two ninjas during an attack in Dili, beating them and taking them to the local police. The entire neighborhoods were then mobilized into self-defense groups, with nightly patrols and early-warning networks (Wagstaff 1995a). Many more ninjas were captured, beaten, and handed over to the police. The ninja strategy sometimes had embarrassing consequences for the occupying forces; on one occasion, a special forces commander was forced to fly to East Timor to obtain the release of his subordinate, Martinho Fernandes, who had been captured by Air Force personnel at their housing complex in Dili while operating as a ninja leader (CNRM Report 1995).

The ninjas disappeared following other embarrassing episodes but the concept was revived a few months later when they were reorganized into a paramilitary group called Young Guards Upholding Integration (*Garda Muda Penegak Integrasi* or Gadapaksi) on July 17, 1995, which is the anniversary of Indonesia's annexation of East Timor (*Jakarta Post* 1995). Gadapaksi targeted the clandestine resistance and enjoyed strong links to Indonesia's special forces. Its members were also involved in petty criminal activities such as smuggling, gambling, and protection rackets. The clandestine resistance responded by infiltrating Gadapaksi, so much so that its leader Marcal de Almeida complained that it was "full of spies" (Commission for Reception, Truth and Reconciliation Final Report 2005). The Indonesian authorities intensified covert operations against the clandestine resistance. They captured the leader of the clandestine front, Pedro Nunes (better known as "Sabalae"), along with his driver, Remigio Tilman, on June 30, 1995. Neither was ever seen again.

The Tide Turns

From 1996 onwards, several events combined to deal a severe blow to Indonesian rule. On January 29, 1996, three women entered the British Aerospace Military Base at Warton armed with household hammers. They smashed the radar nose and control panel of a Hawk ground attack aircraft, which was part of an order of twenty-four aircrafts destined for Indonesia. They called their act a Ploughshares Action, which was inspired by the biblical injunction "to beat swords into ploughshares." A British activist named Chris Cole had performed a Ploughshares action on British Aerospace three years earlier. The three women, borough counselor Joanna Wilson, gardener Lotta Kronli, and nurse Andrea Needham, were charged with illegal entry and criminal damage. The fourth member of the group was environmental campaigner Angie Zelter, who had supported them and publicly announced her intention to carry out another Ploughshares Action. Zelter was arrested the next year while on her way to a public meeting. International solidarity activists organized blockades, sit-ins, teach-ins, and other vigils at the trial, generating enormous negative publicity for the Indonesian occupation. Sensationally, the four activists were acquitted after the jury accepted their defense—they claimed they had acted lawfully because they were using "reasonable force" to prevent the much greater crime of genocide.

The negative publicity for Indonesia grew even more pronounced in 1996 with the awarding of the Nobel Peace Prize to Bishop Belo and the pre-eminent East Timorese independence campaigner Jose Ramos-Horta. Belo visited the United States after the award was announced by the Nobel Committee. He met many influential members of Congress and spoke to large numbers of people. The Nobel Prize meant that U.S. president Clinton could no longer avoid meeting Belo, the first Roman Catholic bishop ever to win the Nobel Peace Prize, even though he still refused to meet Jose Ramos-Horta.

As the Asian financial crisis began in 1997, the first cracks in President Suharto's *facade* of invincibility were becoming visible. Suharto traveled to Vancouver, Canada, in November 1997 for the APEC Economic Leaders' Meeting (AELM). Canadian activists had been busy mobilizing public opinion in the months leading up to the AELM. Public talks, leafleting, and other awareness-raising actions were carried out with growing intensity. A team of thirteen exiled East Timorese and several Indonesians crisscrossed the country, calling on the Canadian government to "bar Suharto or put him behind bars." Despite Suharto's wish to prevent any "affront to his dignity," the conference publicity was hijacked by issues completely unrelated to trade when a strong police response resulted in "the lasting image of the summit, seared in Canada's collective memory... of a Canadian Broadcasting Corporation television cameraman being pepper-sprayed by an irate-looking police officer" (Milewski 2000).

By this time, Indonesia was facing a currency crisis that severely devalued the rupiah. Weeks of indecision went by as Suharto and his advisors considered the terms offered by the International Monetary Fund in exchange for assistance in arresting the plunge. Finally, Suharto closed sixteen insolvent banks and announced a series of austerity measures. This only accelerated the fall of the rupiah as financial panic ensued and demonstrations erupted across the country. As intense pressure built on Suharto at this time, the Indonesian military abducted and killed several Indonesian political activists. Protesting students at Jakarta's Trisakti University were shot by soldiers and more than 1,100 people were killed in Jakarta alone. Chinese women and children were made the target of a systematic campaign of murder and rape. Suharto finally resigned in May 1998, and B.J. Habibie replaced him as president of Indonesia.

Countdown to Independence

The people of East Timor and their supporters overseas sensed the opportunity provided by the leadership change in Indonesia. Students at the University of East Timor organized free speech forums nearly every day during the first two weeks in June 1998. They discussed the reform process and demanded the release of political prisoners. Protests in Dili were accompanied by protests in the Indonesian heartland of Java, where thousands of university students of East Timorese descent picketed the offices of the Indonesian Ministry of Foreign Affairs. The military leadership, already unsettled by these mass mobilizations, was further stunned by a helicopter crash near Dili that killed most of its high-ranking officers in the military command responsible for East Timor.

While these events were taking place, the economic situation in Indonesia was plunging to new lows. In the second quarter of 1998, real GDP was sixteen percent below the same period in 1997. The Indonesian rupiah had lost more than four times its value relative to the U.S. dollar, imported goods had become prohibitively expensive, and inflation was sky-rocketing. The price of food was soaring and domestic unrest was threatening to get out of control. To compound all this, oil prices, a key source of government revenues, were stagnating at $10 to $12 per barrel. In the midst of all this, international activism on East Timor continued and the situation was becoming a serious problem for President Habibie.

Besieged from all sides, Habibie moved to take some more steam out of the issue by announcing that 1,000 combat troops would be withdrawn from the East Timorese territory, with a promise of more such withdrawals. Soon after, however, an Australian activist named Andrew McNaughtan smuggled a large number of Indonesian army personnel records out of East Timor. The records, showing that Indonesia's claims of withdrawal and demilitarization in East Timor were lies, came at a crucial moment, and ratcheted up the pressure on Habibie and on the Australian government, which had always provided vital diplomatic cover for the Indonesian occupation. Sensing that the independence of East Timor was once again a live issue, Australian Prime Minister John Howard moved to assist the Indonesian government. He wrote to Habibie suggesting that Indonesia could adopt the formula of "a substantial period of autonomy" followed by "an act of self-determination by the East Timorese at some future time."[5] Howard was attempting to take the heat out of the independence issue by proposing that it be deferred for a substantial period.

An electronic copy of Howard's letter was transmitted by cable to Australia's ambassador in Jakarta. The ambassador presented the cable to President Habibie who rejected Howard's suggestion but knew that he (Habibie) was bearing the diplomatic burden of the original decision to invade East Timor although, he had played no part in it. When the original arrived later via diplomatic bag, Habibie scribbled his thoughts on it and sent copies to five ministers: "If the question of East Timor becomes a burden to the struggle and image of the Indonesian people and if, after twenty-two years, the East Timorese people cannot feel united with the Indonesian people... it would be reasonable and wise if... East Timor can be honorably separated from the unitary nation of the Republic of Indonesia" (Greenlees and Garran 2002).

Habibie discussed the idea of a rapid process of separation of East Timor via a referendum with members of his cabinet and his close advisers. Most cabinet members were of the view that Indonesia would win any referendum. Much later, Foreign Minister Ali Alatas would recall that most members of cabinet "were then very convinced we would win the referendum. Everything was painted with optimism" (*Tempo* 2000). Alatas and Information Minister Yunus Yosfiah announced on January 27, 1999 that the East Timorese would be given the choice of staying within Indonesia or obtaining independence. In order to ensure that the ballot delivered a result in favor of autonomy, the Indonesian military (Tentara Nasional Indonesia [TNI]) began to intensify operations under the guise of proxy forces, known as "militias."

On April 6, 1999, a number of militia went to Liquica village accompanied by army and police. They surrounded a church where villagers were sheltering and threw tear gas inside it. When the villagers ran out, the militia rushed toward them, attacking women and children with fists, sticks, rifle butts, stones, arrows, and machetes. More than fifty people died and seven were injured during this attack. Afterwards, the militia forced the local people to hoist the Indonesian national flag. Eleven days after the Liquica massacre, militia groups in Dili attacked the houses of prominent independence supporters and the local newspaper office. At that very moment, the Irish foreign minister David Andrews was in Dili on a scheduled visit. Andrews was accompanied by Tom Hyland of the East Timor Ireland Solidarity Campaign, which had been instrumental in building support for East Timor at the European Union. Andrews ended his visit immediately and returned to

Jakarta, where he raised the alarm about the mass murders. Hyland also raised the alarm, which rapidly escalated the international pressure on Indonesia.

While witnessing the use of military-backed terror, the UN-sponsored talks between Portugal and Indonesia to discuss the modalities of the independence ballot for East Timor. In particular, the talks sought to address crucial issues including the disarmament of the militia, a reduction in the number of Indonesian military personnel, and the presence of international monitors. On May 5, 1999, Portugal and Indonesia signed a formal agreement at the UN headquarters in New York. The May 5 Agreement, as it came to be known, provided for an autonomy proposal to be put to the East Timorese people. If they accepted this proposal, the East Timor issue would be considered solved once and for all and East Timor would enjoy autonomous status within Indonesia. If they rejected it, authority would be transferred to the UN, allowing East Timor to begin its passage to independence. Crucially for what would follow, Indonesia would have complete responsibility for maintaining security during the balloting. The UN Assistance Mission in East Timor (UNAMET) began arriving in late May. Its electoral teams would be supported by 300 unarmed international civilian police and fifty military liaison officers.

UNAMET was accompanied by an influx of observers from international civil society and the international media. Their activities showed the international community that the Indonesian military was the main source of repression and violence. The unprecedented foreign presence began to steadily uncover evidence that the Indonesian military was recruiting, arming, training, and organizing the militias. UNAMET accredited 600 journalists, nearly 2,300 observers, 500 international observers, as well as about 1,700 East Timorese and Indonesian non-governmental observers and a range of other civil society groups (Commission for Reception, Truth and Reconciliation Final Report 2005).

On August 30, 1999, there was a huge voter turnout. The results were announced on Saturday, September 4, 1999. Despite the climate of fear and intimidation, the one-sided pre-ballot election campaign, the presence of dubious voters from West Timor and the fact that many voters did not believe their votes were secret, 78 percent of registered voters opted for independence from Indonesia. Once the ballot results were announced, the Indonesian authorities moved rapidly to reverse it by creating new demographic facts on the ground. They evacuated foreign observers to Australia with the cooperation of Australia's Department of Foreign Affairs and Trade. They drove East Timorese across the border to West Timor. Despite the dramatic scenes of human suffering and violent imagery, the execution of the terror campaign was carefully controlled; the Indonesian military was attempting to remove all foreigners from East Timor so that it could execute its plan without the impediment of outside attention. The campaign would work in the following sequence of steps: First, the militia proxies would contain and remove foreign observers. Second, with foreigners unable to report, the militia would attack the local population and use transport and logistics assets to move them across the border. Third, Falintil would be drawn into a conventional war. Fourth, the TNI would announce that it was forced to intervene between the "factions" and then freed from restraints, it would attack and destroy Falintil in conventional warfare. Finally, the authorities would create new facts on the ground, ensuring that the results of the ballot were irreversibly overturned.

Foreigners were treated very differently to native East Timorese. They were intimidated and corralled into confined areas where they could not provide eyewitness reports to the outside world, but they were largely unharmed. Ian Martin, the head of UNAMET, ordered the evacuation of UN staff, journalists, and observers from the besieged compound on September 8. This evacuation would have resulted in the rape or murder of the 1,500 refugees sheltering there. Outraged, the international staff collectively refused to be evacuated until all the refugees had first been taken to safety.[6] As a consequence, the refugees were airlifted to Darwin, Australia. The international staff left the compound only when this evacuation was guaranteed. In contrast to foreign observers, East Timorese were attacked and forced out of their homes. They were rounded up and taken via land and sea transport to West Timor and elsewhere. Approximately 70 percent of the buildings in East Timor were destroyed. Vital infrastructure was crippled, leaving Dili and major towns without running water, electricity, or telephones. Approximately 250,000 people are thought to have been driven across the border.

The military plan envisioned that the terror campaign would provoke Falintil into a desperate retaliation, thereby drawing it into something approaching conventional warfare, where the TNI clearly had the advantage. Although Falintil's operational commander Taur Matan Ruak was under intense pressure to retaliate, Gusmao implored him by satellite telephone to stay in the cantonments. Ruak obeyed. The TNI strategy failed because it came under overwhelming international pressure, particularly from the United States, which advised the Indonesian military at the highest level that the time had come for it to withdraw. Admiral Dennis Blair, Commander of the U.S. forces in the Pacific, informed Indonesia's defense minister and military chief, General Wiranto, that the United States was suspending its military ties with Indonesia. U.S. defense secretary William Cohen warned that there would be serious economic consequences. State Department spokesperson James Rubin warned Indonesia publicly that its relations with the international community, including the United States, were at risk. The Chairman of the Joint Chiefs of Staff General Hugh Shelton applied further pressure on General Wiranto. Finally, U.S. ambassador to the UN Richard Holbrooke warned Indonesia at the Security Council that it faced the point of no return in international relations. Indonesia's resistance ended within hours. On September 12, 1999, Habibie emerged from a special cabinet meeting, stood alongside Wiranto, and announced that his government had decided to allow a UN force into East Timor. Wiranto's presence beside Habibie sent a clear signal that the TNI had agreed to support the decision.

Conclusions

Thus came about the independence of East Timor. Years later, Ramos-Horta's chief of staff, Juan Federer, wrote that "despite the efforts of their leaders to portray it otherwise, and the often-heroic performance of the resisting population, the East Timor armed resistance did not defeat the occupier and was an almost depleted force in the end" (2004). Indonesia's departure was the result of a complex international diplomatic and political campaign "in which the military resistance activity was a mere token component." Therefore, "unlike in decolonization cases where the resistance movements generally became the legitimate and uncontested recipients of sovereignty, the East Timor resistance was not the obvious recipient of sovereignty" (Federer 2004).

An international force led by Australia, for years the staunchest defender of the occupation, began peace enforcement operations in East Timor on September 20, 1999. The country's independence was celebrated on May 20, 2002. In their struggle for independence, the East Timorese people suffered one of the largest death tolls relative to total population since the Holocaust. For those men and women who survived, but especially the women, the crimes were immense: rape, torture, enslavement, arbitrary arrests, destruction of property, and forcible relocation. There is no statute of limitations on these crimes against humanity.

Notes

1. In fact, in the late 1980s, Indonesians interested in alternative education, health, and cooperatives had their interest sparked in East Timor when they learned that Fretilin had similar interests in 1975. These Indonesians became the core of the pro-democracy movement against the Suharto regime, and supported the cause of East Timor after the Santa Cruz massacre of 1991.
2. Today this date is celebrated as the anniversary of the formation of the Armed Forces for the National Liberation of East Timor (Falintil).
3. East Timorese students conducted a number of similar actions at other embassies in the 1990s.
4. This argument has been made with great force and sophistication by Kammen (2001).
5. Howard cited the "Matignon Accords" signed between France and constituencies in New Caledonia. These accords had effectively deferred a decision on New Caledonia's final status for more than a decade.
6. See Martinkus (2002).

References

Anderson, Russell. 1991. Submission to Australia's Joint Parliamentary Committee on Foreign Affairs, Defence and Trade (December 2).

Associated Press. 1995. "Death squads operating in Timor." February 4.

Commission for Reception, Truth and Reconciliation Final Report. 2005.

CNRM Report. 1995.

Federer, J. 2004. *The UN in East Timor.* Darwin: Charles Darwin University Press.

Greenlees, D., and R. Garran. 2002. *Deliverance: The Inside Story of East Timor's Fight for Freedom.* Sydney: Allen and Unwin.

Jakarta Post. 1995. "RI sets up Guard to Defend Integration." March 25.

Kammen, Douglas. 2001. "The Trouble With Normal: The Indonesian Military, Paramilitaries and the Final Solution in East Timor." In *Violence and the State in Suharto's Indonesia*, ed. B. Anderson. Ithaca, NY: Cornell University Press.

Martinkus, J. 2002. *A Dirty Little War: An Eyewitness of East Timor's Descent into Hell 1997–2000.* Sydney: Random House.

Milewski, T. 2000. "Forces of Journalism." In *Pepper in Our Eyes: The APEC Affair*, ed. Pue W. Wesley. Vancouver: University of British Columbia Press.

Nogueira, Paolo. 1994. "The Repression Will be Resumed in Just a Few Moments." *Expresso*. December 10.
Tempo. 2000. "Santa Cruz Incident a Turning Point in Our Diplomacy." September 18–24.
Wagstaff, Jeremy. 1995a. "East Timorese Fight Back against Terror Gangs." Reuters. February 13.
Wagstaff, Jeremy. 1995b. "East Timorese Complain of New Terror Wave." Reuters. February 10.
Way, Wendy, ed. 2000. *Australia and the Indonesian Incorporation of Portuguese Timor, 1974–76*. Melbourne: University of Melbourne Press.

CHAPTER 12

Promoting Human Rights through Hybrid Courts: The Serious Crimes Process in East Timor

JAMES DESHAW RAE

Introduction

This chapter evaluates the conduct of the hybrid tribunal model used to address crimes against humanity and massive human rights violations in East Timor following its historic act of self-determination in 1999 (as discussed in Chapter 11). As a new experiment, the court faced serious obstacles to fulfill its mandate and ultimately its efforts to promote accountability for human rights violations were stymied. Yet understanding the barriers to the full attainment of such goals may be instructive as the hybrid model grows in usage. This case study first examines the bargaining among East Timor, Indonesia, and the international community that led to the creation of a hybrid tribunal. Next, it describes the structure and jurisdiction of the court and its relationship to other concurrent transitional justice mechanisms. Third, the chapter traces the evolution of the court and the sometimes insurmountable hurdles placed in its path from its origins in 2000 to its closure in 2005 and its temporary resurrection in 2008. Finally, the chapter offers some concluding reflections on the legacy of the trial process.

Unfamiliar Terrain: Negotiations over the Creation of the Hybrid Court

Hybrid or "mixed" tribunals have arisen in response to the shortcomings of the *ad hoc* international tribunals, balancing international and domestic jurists, prosecutors, and public defenders embedded within a domestic court system and allowing the dual use of international law alongside a national constitution and domestic legal concepts. As also discussed in Chapter 10, hybrid tribunals seek accountability for violations of international human rights standards while building local courts and instructing domestic actors in effective and efficient judicial practices. With reduced travel expenses and the hiring of more domestic personnel, hybrid tribunals are presumed to be more affordable than the costly *ad hoc* international tribunals and more likely to promote lasting domestic improvements to the rule of law through the tutelage of international advisers and court staff. Whereas the International Criminal Tribunals for Yugoslavia (ICTY) and Rwanda (ICTR) were independently mandated by the United Nations (UN) Security Council, the Special Panels for Serious Crimes (SPSC) in East Timor were created within a unique peace-building operation in which the UN held full sovereignty over the former Indonesian territory. The United Nations Transitional Authority for East Timor (UNTAET) was authorized in October 1999 and assumed the responsibility to govern East Timor the following month. While the decision to formulate transitional justice occurred later after the UNTAET operation began to function, the UN would continue to support the hybrid process after East Timor gained its independence and UNTAET's mandate expired in 2002 with the creation of three follow-on missions: The United Nations Mission in East Timor (UNMISET), the United Nations Office in Timor-Leste, and finally the UN Integrated Mission in Timor-Leste (UNMIT).

Trilateral Bargaining: East Timor, Indonesia, and the UN

The UN, and Secretary-General Kofi Annan specifically, demonstrated a clear conviction favoring some form of accountability following the horrible militia violence that occurred after East Timor's 1999 vote for independence from Indonesia and initiated an investigation into potential transitional justice options. In September 1999, the UN Commission on Human Rights called on the secretary-general to establish an international commission of inquiry in cooperation with the Indonesian National Commission on Human Rights to gather and compile information on possible human rights violations and acts that may have constituted breaches of international humanitarian law committed in East Timor since January 1999. The commission saw a pattern of serious violations of fundamental human rights and humanitarian law and urged the secretary-general to establish an independent international body to conduct further investigations, identify the persons responsible for those violations (including those with command responsibilities), ensure reparations for the violations from those responsible, prosecute those guilty of serious human rights violations, and consider the issues of truth and reconciliation. The commission further suggested that the UN establish an international human rights tribunal consisting of judges appointed by the UN, preferably with the participation of members from East Timor and Indonesia. The tribunal would sit in Indonesia, East Timor, and any other relevant territory to receive complaints and to try and sentence those accused by the independent investigation body of serious violations of fundamental human rights and international humanitarian law regardless of the nationality of the individual or where that person was when the violations were committed. Not only were international actors in support of an international tribunal to address this latest chapter of violence authored by Indonesian officials, but prominent Timorese civil society organizations strongly advocated such a process. This coalition composed of victims' families and civil society groups, the National Alliance for an International Tribunal, provided a consistent indigenous voice in favor of trials.

Of course, as a primary target of any investigatory process, Indonesia was very reluctant to support any mechanism that probed too closely into its political and military hierarchy. In responding to the mooted idea of an international tribunal, Indonesian foreign minister Alwi Shihab outlined the government's criticisms: Indonesian sovereignty would be violated (since the crimes occurred on Indonesian territory), national judicial mechanisms were functioning and capable of dispensing justice, Indonesian laws were the only laws applicable, national remedies had yet to be exhausted, the degree, and extent of the alleged violations of human rights did not justify the establishment of an international human rights tribunal, and the process itself would only create obstacles to friendly relations between East Timor and Indonesia and reconciliation between their peoples.[1] While key states recognized that Indonesia bore responsibility for the campaign of militia violence and displacement that ransacked the territory of East Timor, justice and accountability were not the only values of interest to the international community. Indonesia is a geostrategic linchpin in relations throughout Southeast Asia and the broader Asia Pacific region. Not only do much of the world's resources pass through the straits and passages of the Indonesian archipelago on their way from the Middle East to China, Japan, and elsewhere, but Indonesia itself is an important supplier of minerals, natural gas, and petroleum as well.[2]

With these dynamics at play, the UN decided to forego an international tribunal and allow Indonesia to conduct its own independent accountability process while simultaneously conducting trials in East Timor. In respecting the sovereignty of Indonesia and the ability of its courts to be conducted effectively, the UN pressured Jakarta to conduct domestic trials to hold top Indonesian leaders accountable for the atrocities in East Timor associated with the 1999 referendum. The international community warned that if Indonesia failed to demonstrate that justice was delivered, an international tribunal might be created in response. Despite its 1998 democratization process, the Indonesian judiciary was still not considered able to capably uphold adequate standards of fairness and impartiality in its dispensation of justice. Furthermore, the judicial system in East Timor was not fully functioning, was hampered by the withdrawal of Indonesian civil servants, and would have been incapable of handling the entire justice process as it was in the throes of reconstruction. Therefore, the Timorese share of the prosecutions was assisted by international support and a new experiment in a hybrid court was undertaken.

As the decision to have two separate prosecutorial apparatuses was being formulated in early 2000, local non-governmental organizations (NGOs) and judicial personnel reported that no real consultation occurred prior to the establishment of the hybrid Special Panels (Reiger and Wierda 2006). In fact, the National Alliance for an International Tribunal continued to call for international trials throughout the Special Panels' proceedings. The new Timorese government itself, composed of victims of the Indonesian oppression to be sure, was generally ambivalent about the creation of the hybrid court. Where once Timorese exile leaders had supported the idea of war crimes trials during Indonesia's occupation, good relations with its powerful neighbor quickly became a greater priority than prosecutions. The Timorese leadership in the interim National Council was content to move forward on the two parallel tracks outlined by the UN while they prepared for eventual self-governance in 2002. The decision to overlook local and international NGOs and press for the establishment of parallel prosecutions in each locale was a useful compromise by the UN Security Council and other states, including interested Asian nations protective of state sovereignty. With an initial settlement of the issue, the operational plans for each court were quickly established.

Time, Place, and Manner: Structure and Jurisdiction of the Hybrid Court

Defining the jurisdiction, the subject matter, temporal range, and physical location of the court caused controversies. On March 6, 2000, UNTAET Regulation 2000/11 on the organization of courts in East Timor established a hybrid court, the Serious Crimes Unit (SCU). Ultimately, the tribunal was organized into three sections: First, the judges formed the Special Panels for Serious Crimes; second, the prosecutors operated within a Serious Crimes Unit, and third, public defenders were nominally under the authority of East Timor's Ministry of Justice. According to UNTAET Regulation 2000/15, the SPSC judicial panels were composed of two international judges and one Timorese judge, who had universal jurisdiction if the serious criminal offense had been committed within the territory of East Timor and either the defendant or the victim was an East Timorese citizen. Formally, all judges answered to East Timor's Supreme Court of Justice of the Court of Appeals, which comprised two Timorese judges and one international judge. This Court of Appeal served a dual function as the appellate court for the hybrid Special Panels as well as the top domestic tribunal. The Public Prosecution Service was within the Office of the General Prosecutor (OGP) and was divided into two departments, one for ordinary crimes and the other for serious crimes, each led by a deputy general prosecutor. Although a Timorese was appointed to act as prosecutor-general, the real decision-maker in the serious crimes process was the deputy prosecutor-general. Five different deputy prosecutors-general served in this leadership role over the life of the court; each of the deputy prosecutors-general was a UN-employed international civil servant.

The entire staff appointed to the SCU was international except for the interpreters. Since the SCU and the Ordinary Crimes Unit (OCU) were not located together, the two groups had very little contact with each other. While the serious crimes process was based in the capital city of Dili, four newly formed district courts presided over ordinary crimes. With a UN staff, the deputy prosecutor-general for serious crimes was given exclusive authority to investigate and prosecute serious crimes. The hybrid court prosecuted cases of individual incidents of violence and other notorious atrocities that were grouped together under a single indictment. For instance, widespread massacres committed by numerous perpetrators such as the attacks on the churches at Liquica and Suai were prosecuted under a single comprehensive indictment that incorporated as many as a dozen persons together. Public defenders were officially under the authority of East Timor's Ministry of Justice. Originally inexperienced Timorese advocates defended cases, but very quickly international lawyers were hired to conduct the defense.

Meanwhile, Indonesian Law No. 26/2000 of November 23, 2000 established an *ad hoc* Human Rights Court as a special chamber within the existing legal system and created its own National Commission of Inquiry on Human Rights Violations in East Timor to identify alleged perpetrators. The division of labor in the two separate courts was that predominantly Indonesian senior military and civilian officials would be tried in the Jakarta court while mostly Timorese senior and mid-level militia members would be tried in Dili. By the time the courts began conducting their hearings, a further division of labor was devised when East Timor's National Council formed a truth and reconciliation commission on June 20, 2001 (formally established by UNTAET Regulation 2001/10 on July 13, 2001) charged with three duties: To establish the facts of events in the conflict between April 25, 1974 and October 25, 1999, to help achieve community reconciliation and reintegration of people who committed minor acts of violence, and to report on how to prevent future human rights violations. The introduction of this new venue further delineated responsibilities, inasmuch as "serious crimes" would be addressed by the hybrid court while junior level militia members who had committed only "lesser crimes" would be processed through the reconciliation component of the Commission for Truth, Reconciliation, and Reception (known by its Portuguese acronym CAVR).[3]

A loose coordination between Timor's hybrid court and truth and reconciliation commission was also formulated, though actual coordination was limited to a narrow aspect of each mechanism. Individual petitions for a reconciliation hearing were first vetted with the SCU, which determined the severity of the crime; if the prosecutor's office deemed a crime serious, it could indict the perpetrator. Between October 2002 and February 2004, the court received 1,541 statements from the CAVR; in eighty-five cases, the SCU stopped individuals from entering into "community reconciliation agreements" (CRA) due to suspected participation in serious crimes. Of these, eighteen were indicted, and five were later returned to the reconciliation program.[4] If the charge was determined to be less serious, the CAVR took over the process; thirty-two cases were adjourned as they were later deemed to be serious offenses or the deponent was refused by the community. East Timorese who experienced "lesser crimes" (*e.g.*, kickings, beatings, and the destruction of homes and personal property) may not have believed "lesser" to be the appropriate terminology, yet a definite distinction separated these abuses from massive atrocities such as disappearance, forced deportation, murder, torture, and other crimes against humanity. At the end of the reconciliation process, the fate of the perpetrator was in the victim's hands. If victims forgave the offender, who then observed the community reconciliation agreement, the offender was no longer subject to criminal legal proceedings; however, if victims did not accept the result of the reconciliation process, they maintained their right to take criminal action through the courts. The greatest weakness of this lack of coordination was the inequity of the outcome, which caused significant resentment. The least responsible culprits, such as Timorese who partook in lesser crimes, participated in the reconciliation process while few of those who committed serious crimes, and none of the major perpetrators faced accountability at all due to Jakarta's obstruction.

The limited time period also elicited debate, as it ignored the most extreme violence that occurred during the first several years after Indonesia's 1975 invasion, when over 100,000 Timorese perished in massive killings and famine related to forced deportations. Compared to other atrocities committed in East Timor during Indonesia's twenty-four-year occupation, the violence associated with Indonesia's withdrawal was relatively minor but still caused enormous international uproar since foreign observers were on the ground to witness the carnage. In September 1999 during Operation Clean Sweep, rampaging Indonesian-sponsored militia and the Indonesian military ransacked the province, burning, looting, and pillaging as approximately 300,000 refugees fled or were forcibly deported across East Timor's Western frontier into Indonesia while perhaps 100,000 to 200,000 others were internally displaced in the mountains. The carnage cost over 1,000 lives and resulted in millions of dollars worth of economic damage. Timor's own constitution, drafted with the guidance of international advisers, identified the creation of national and international courts to judge crimes against humanity for the wider 1974–1999 period. Ultimately, the prosecutorial mandate of the UN-sponsored hybrid tribunal was specifically limited to genocide, war crimes, crimes against humanity, murder, sexual offenses, and torture committed between January 1 and October 25, 1999. The parallel trials in Indonesia also narrowed the scope of the time period and subject matter. Indonesia's own internal review was mandated to investigate the degree of involvement by the state apparatus and/or other national and international agencies in gross violations of human rights in East Timor since January 1999, including genocide, massacre, torture, forced displacement, crimes against women and children, and systematic destruction of property as preliminary evidence for the imminent investigation and prosecution. Changes were made as the report was formulated into law: The beginning date of the mandate was moved from January to April and only murder and persecution were listed as crimes.

Trials and Errors: The Proceedings of the Hybrid Court

Starting from Scratch and Selecting Priority Cases

The initial opportunity in October 1999 to arrest suspected perpetrators was quickly lost since no transitional justice process was immediately included as part of the post-referendum humanitarian intervention nor in the initial peace-building operation. Not until March 2000 was a hybrid court conceptualized and trials began only haphazardly in late 2000; they would operate with increasing efficiency until May 2005 when the court was closed. Although in a very limited fashion, a small group of Australian military police and UN civilian police began investigations in December 1999, which were soon expanded by the UN Human Rights Unit. However, hiring the wide variety of both domestic and international court staff would inhibit a timely start to the trials and sufficient resources were never truly forthcoming. Inadequate support for East Timor's hybrid tribunal directly affected the justice process; investigations could not be effectively conducted, the quality of court personnel was substandard and victims, witnesses, and perpetrators were harmed by poor transportation services or bad prison conditions. The budget of the SCU was enormous in relation to the ordinary crimes component; however, its funds were miniscule when compared with the ICTY and ICTR. For the period 2003–2005, the total operating cost of the SCU and Special Panels was $14.4 million or around 5 percent of the overall assessed contribution to UNMISET, which amounted to approximately $300 million; the majority of costs were incurred by the salaries of international staff (Reiger and Wierda 2006).

In November 2000, the UN Security Council decided that "UNTAET [was] facing significant difficulties in bringing to justice those responsible for the serious violations of human rights that occurred in East Timor in 1999" (United Nations 2000, 2). Accordingly, the UN commissioned Australian diplomat James Dunn to document the 1999 human rights violations. His report of February 2001 recommended an international tribunal only if those responsible in Indonesia were not brought to justice by some other means (Dunn 2001). With that impetus, the SCU's first indictments for domestic crimes were issued in December 2000, a year after the outbreak of violence. Trials began in January 2001, though it would take almost a year before charges of domestic crimes were reformulated as crimes against humanity. Due to time and resource limitations, the court decided to focus on ten "priority" cases.

In 2000, among the nearly 1,400 murders that had been identified, the SCU selected ten priority cases to pursue more vigorously: The Liquica Church massacre of April 6, 1999; the murders in Dili District on April 17, 1999 (including the Manuel Carrascalao house case); the Kailako killings of April 1999 and the Maliana Police Station Killings of September 2–8, 1999; the Los Palos case of April 21 to September 25, 1999; the Lolotoe case of May 2 to September 16, 1999; the Suai Church massacre of September 6, 1999; the attack on Bishop Belo's compound and the Dili Diocese of September 6, 1999; the Passabe and Makaleb massacres of September–October 1999; cases of deportations, persecution, killing of UN Advance Mission in East Timor (UNAMET) staff and atrocities carried out by army Battalion 745 from April–September 1999, and sexual violence cases carried out in various districts from March to September 1999. In 2001, twelve trials that included twenty-one defendants were held. On December 11, 2001, the Los Palos case resulted in ten convictions for crimes against humanity that occurred at a church in the Lautem district on September 25, 1999 after the arrival of the Australian-led

International Force East Timor. On that same date, the Lolotoe case found *Kaer Metin Merah Putih* militia commanders Joao Franca da Silva, Jose Cardoso Ferreira, and village chief Sabino Gouveia Loite guilty of crimes against humanity. In the final judgment on the last trial before the Special Panels for Serious Crimes in 2005, *Laksaur* (Flying Eagle) militia members Sisto Barros and Cesar Mendonca were sentenced to nine-year prison terms for committing crimes against humanity in the Suai region in October 1999. In between, the accountability process would face the primary obstacle of Indonesian noncompliance, for despite the Timor-based hybrid court's universal jurisdiction, it was unable to successfully extradite Indonesian perpetrators.

Legal Brinkmanship: Extradition and the Wiranto Indictment

Though innovative and with broad powers of indictment, East Timor's SCU was hamstrung by the failure to establish a meaningful process of accountability in Indonesia, where the principal culprits resided beyond the reach of international justice. In fact, the SCU was unable to extradite or arrest the accused even when warrants and in some cases Interpol red notices were issued. The SCU needed Indonesian cooperation, which was gained only by international pressure, to have suspects returned to Timor for questioning and/or prosecution. Meanwhile, the United States remained apprised of the matter and for a time halted weapons sales and lethal defense articles to pressure Indonesia to extradite those indicted by the SCU, conduct a public audit of the Indonesian military's funds and prosecute army human rights violators, and punish those found guilty. The SCU list of indictments and the legal process itself created diplomatic tensions with Indonesia, which refused to hand over notable figures.

The Wiranto case proved to be the breaking point in the relationship between the Timorese political leadership and the hybrid court as both bodies disassociated themselves from the Wiranto arrest warrant. On February 24, 2003 the prosecutor's office of the SCU indicted former Indonesian minister of defense and commander of the Armed Forces General Wiranto for crimes against humanity, as well as six senior army members and the former governor of East Timor. In turn, Indonesia blamed the UN for what it saw as a politically motivated case. In response, UNMISET issued a statement declaring that the indictment was issued through East Timor's prosecution service and *not* by the UN. With a sense of abandonment, the Timorese government's already limited support for the justice process evaporated as it publicly declared that the indictment was the work of the UN and not of East Timor and quickly tried to revise the indictment. The Special Panels refused to reconsider the indictment, and an arrest warrant for General Wiranto was issued on May 10, 2004. The Timorese leadership pressured the SCU's Timorese prosecutor general to alter the charges, who then denounced the "international staff" and unsuccessfully tried to withdraw the Wiranto indictment before deciding not to submit the warrant to Interpol.

Jakarta's Obstruction

At the same time that the hybrid court in East Timor was preparing its work, Indonesia incessantly stalled in its efforts to formulate domestic trials for war criminals. In its January 2001 final report, Indonesia's National Commission of Inquiry concluded that the Indonesian government was implicated in funding, arming, and supporting militias in East Timor and that the Indonesian military had carried out operations with these militias. The commission named thirty-three individual perpetrators, including several high-ranking military officials and more than 100 others were recommended for review. Thirteen criminal cases were outlined in the report. However, Indonesia's court investigated only four cases in three specific districts of East Timor from April to September 1999: The attacks on the churches in Liquica and Suai and the homes of Manuel Carrascalao and Bishop Belo. Dragging its feet, Indonesia failed even to select its judges to the special human rights court until January 14, 2002. Indonesia ignored almost half of those named by the investigative commission, including the general in-charge, Wiranto. The Indonesian trials failed to ascribe command responsibility to those in civilian and military leadership positions in the Indonesian government. Initially, all eighteen prominent suspects were tried and all but six were acquitted; those found guilty at the time were given short sentences of three to ten years but remained free, pending appeal. In the end, all defendants were acquitted on appeal. At the conclusion of the Indonesia Human Rights Court trials in August 2003, both the UN and United States publicly stated that the outcome of the trials was unacceptable.

The international community once again re-evaluated transitional justice for East Timor and would spend several years pondering a solution. In July 2002, the UN had commissioned a report to document the 1999 human rights violations, this time from Canadian academic Geoffrey Robinson, who in July 2003 recommended the establishment of an international tribunal (Robinson 2006). Secretary-General Kofi Annan and six prominent international NGOs, including Amnesty International, Human Rights Watch, the Coalition for International Justice, and the Open Society Justice Initiative then suggested a commission of experts to evaluate justice efforts. Kofi Annan appointed a three-member UN Commission of Experts in February 2005 and they conducted an investigation in Indonesia and East Timor to determine the merits of holding an international tribunal. On May 26, 2005, the commission recommended an *ad hoc* international tribunal if Indonesia did not take action to secure accountability within six months, finding that the Jakarta trials were "manifestly inadequate." In the end, the secretary-general's follow-up report acknowledged that the Indoensian process could not be relied upon and appealed for renewed serious crimes investigations in East Timor (though not prosecutions) and the establishment of a solidarity fund to promote justice and community restoration programs (United Nations 2006).

Meanwhile, following the schism over the Wiranto indictment, the now independent Timorese government moved to promote more harmonious relations with Indonesia while sacrificing demands for accountability. President

Xanana Gusmao met Indonesian president Megawati Sukarnoputri in Bali to adopt a reconciliatory approach, used his Independence Day national address to praise the Jakarta trials, and met personally with General Wiranto (by then a candidate in the 2004 presidential elections) to perform an act of reconciliation that received strong condemnation from victims' groups and civil society organizations. On December 14, 2004, Gusmao and newly elected Indonesian president Susilo Bambang Yudhoyono reached an agreement in Bali to create a joint East Timor–Indonesia Commission for Truth and Friendship (CTF) to look at gross human rights violations in 1999. The CTF had a one-year mandate, which was renewed for a second year to review all materials documented by the aforementioned Indonesian National Commission of Inquiry, the Indonesian *ad hoc* court, the Special Panels hybrid court, and the CAVR truth and reconciliation commission. After expressing that it would be unfair to continually ask each Indonesian president to apologize, President Gusmao targeted the human rights groups calling for an international tribunal: "For us it is (closed). If you want to open it, do it yourself."[5]

Going it Alone

Despite the grand theater of Indonesia's obstruction, East Timor's ambivalence and the UN's acquiescence, the SCU had continued to conduct its trials since its early formulation of priority cases. By 2005 the SCU trials remained the only opportunity to achieve legal accountability. Aside from the primary inhibitor to justice, that is, the inability to extradite perpetrators, the hybrid court faced challenges related to inadequate resources, competency, and turnover among staff, cultural and linguistic issues, and divergent priorities between national and international actors by the nature of the mixed model.

The UN did not endow the hybrid court with the resources and support to effectively prosecute cases. The UNMISET forensic lab itself was rather rudimentary, reflecting that the criminal process was an afterthought and not sufficiently funded. Transportation was difficult in this mountainous terrain that had poor infrastructure and impassable roads, and UNMISET had only a few vehicles at its disposal. Shockingly, sometimes witnesses, victims, and suspects would travel to the tribunal together from the countryside in a single UN vehicle due to logistical constraints. Witnesses missed valuable time during the planting and harvest seasons and once in the capital, they could either stay with family or reside in the temporary accommodations at the SCU compound on the edge of town. Witnesses were occasionally not picked up to return from the court to their temporary residence, were not properly counseled, and were not told in advance that the accused would be in the courtroom. Only one person was available to staff the Witness Management Unit that was responsible for such duties. As a result, the majority of rural Timorese considered the trial process to be only for the elites and few local citizens ever attended the proceedings.

Short-term contracts and high staff turnover repeatedly obstructed the court's operation; only one judicial panel operated for most of the first three years until a second and a third started functioning after mid-2003 at which time it was instructed to prepare for its closure, issuing its final four indictments in December 2004. Trials were frequently postponed, sometimes for months at a time, or delayed for a host of reasons: no vehicle or driver was available to pick up witnesses, a judge could not attend, staff members were on vacation, the departure of a judge could force a new trial, lawyers regularly sought adjournments and continuances to prepare cases, or personnel simply did not appear. Though the interpreters were diligent, they were unfamiliar with the courtroom's technical legal terms. Participants could not be informed or did not have information when trials were postponed because of the absence of modern communication infrastructure and thus they arrived at the court with no place to stay and no trial to attend. The Court of Appeal was unable to function for more than a year due to a shortage of international judges related to the Timorese government's preference for Portuguese-speaking judges; thus, thirty-four serious crimes cases were pending when it reopened in July 2003. Although its performance improved by the summer of 2004, appeals were difficult since early trials had no transcript.

Limited resources also created systemic bias that resulted in a poor defense for the accused. The prosecutor's office enjoyed far more resources than did the defense, possessing more than 100 staff while the public defenders had only several assistants. At its peak in 2002, the SCU had 106 staff: Thirty-one international, sixteen UN volunteers, twenty UN police, twenty-nine national staff, and ten national trainees working as prosecutors, investigators, forensic experts, and translators before it began to be downsized in 2003. By contrast, the defense was perennially underfunded and performance suffered as a result. No witnesses were called in the first fourteen trials that took place before the Special Panels as nine inexperienced Timorese public defenders had to defend individual clients accused of serious crimes against professional international prosecutors. After the court's underwhelming debut, its conduct improved over time, as it began following a work schedule, improving the quality of translation and hiring better judges and staff. In September 2002, UNMISET created a Defense Lawyers Unit consisting of only one lawyer, which expanded to seven international defense lawyers, three legal researchers, and a director by the time the court closed in May 2005. After the arrival of the international staff, defense improved marginally but training of local defenders was largely ignored as a result.

Establishing a common *lingua franca* in the courtroom was exceedingly difficult with the polyglot of available languages. A majority of Timorese speak the indigenous Tetum language, around half understand Bahasa Indonesian, and less than 5 percent are fluent in either Portuguese or English. The SCU's choice to place English in the central role in the courtroom essentially skewed the hybrid balance toward internationals over the local population; legal mentors rarely learned Tetum, transcriptions were done in English, and then translated and indictments often were read to a defendant in a language that the accused did not understand. In April 2004, a simultaneous interpretation system was introduced that alleviated some of these short-term dilemmas, yet capacity-building was still hindered by linguistic and cultural gaps. According to a 2003 UN report, the reluctance of international advisers to learn local languages contributed to the poor rate of skill transfer from internationals to nationals.[6] In a January 2005 international review of East Timor's domestic jurists participating in both the Special Panels and the ordinary courts, all twenty-two failed the qualifying exams, perhaps due to difficulties in learning Portuguese, and were replaced by four international judges (later increased to six), exemplifying the underlying strain between international expectations and local capabilities.

The complexity of distinct authorities in the hybrid model also creates extraordinary challenges when national and international prerogatives diverge as highlighted in the *Armando dos Santos* case. In an environment where domestic politics impacted the developing jurisprudence of the court, a simmering tension between the lower-level Special Panels (two international judges and one Timorese) and the higher-level Court of Appeal (two Timorese judges and one international) reached a crescendo when in July 2003 the Court of Appeal applied the Portuguese penal code as a subsidiary law to convict Armando dos Santos for genocide (*jenosidiu* in Portuguese) on an appeal, though he had never been charged with genocide but rather crimes against humanity. At issue was which subsidiary law to use, Indonesian or Portuguese. Sergio Vieira de Mello, the UN transitional administrator, had recognized Indonesian law as the proper subsidiary law, thus the applicable laws for the SCU were UNTAET regulations, Indonesian law not in conflict with UNTAET legislation, UN Security Council Resolution 1272, and internationally recognized human rights standards. After independence in May 2002, the applicable laws became international law, Timorese domestic law, UNTAET regulations, and Indonesian law. The Special Panels continued to use UNTAET regulations and Indonesian law while the Appeals Court argued that Portuguese law was technically the appropriate code since Portugal was the officially recognized sovereign of the territory prior to UN administration. Good relations with Portugal, Timor's rare supporter at the UN during the Indonesian occupation, was a chief priority of the new government and the Court of Appeal, also the highest domestic court, promoted the government's relationship with Portugal and its desire to see Portuguese, the language of resistance to Indonesia, as an official language. In fact, Timorese judges were sent to Portugal for training and several prominent judicial officials have returned from the Community of Portuguese-Speaking Countries, but nevertheless 80 percent of domestic court actors have essentially no Portuguese-speaking ability.

The impact of the *dos Santos* case was very evident during subsequent trials as the judges of the Special Panels increasingly issued judgments that ran counter to the law established by the Court of Appeals and reflected growing animosity between the two benches. At length, the lower court Special Panels explained the miscarriage of the Court of Appeal decision and refused to follow it, arguing that Indonesian law was still subsidiary law, that the Court of Appeal cannot promulgate law, and that the Court of Appeal violated the constitution, the rights of the accused, and international human rights standards. The Special Panels contended that the Court of Appeal convicted the accused of a crime for which he had not been charged and an offense not in the regulations. The national parliament finally clarified that Indonesian law continued to apply as the default subsidiary law in October 2003, but the *dos Santos* conviction for a crime under Portuguese law was not overturned as some suspect the Timorese government wanted to demonstrate its commitment to its Portuguese-language policy and there was a growing desire to discontinue the trials.

At the conclusion of the trials process on May 20, 2005, ninety-five separate indictments had been issued encompassing 391 accused persons for a total of 684 murders, resulting in 285 arrest warrants, including for thirty-seven Indonesian military officers from the army, four Indonesian police chiefs, sixty Timorese army officers and soldiers, the former civilian governor of East Timor, and five former district administrators. A total of fifty-five cases were heard and eighty-seven defendants were tried; of these, eighty-four were convicted and three acquitted, twenty-four of the accused pleaded guilty. A further thirteen defendants had their cases withdrawn by the SCU or dismissed by the Special Panels; one defendant was ruled mentally unfit to stand trial. Moreover, 186 outstanding murder cases were investigated without issuing indictments, and 469 additional murder cases could not be investigated due to the closure of the courts; the investigative arm closed six months prior to the close of cases. As a result of the lack of cooperation by Indonesian authorities, the court's convictions all related to relatively low-level perpetrators: Timorese militia members and junior army officers, aside from one former resistance fighter. Of those indicted, 339 remained at large outside the court's jurisdiction.

Closing Down the Court

With the closure of the hybrid court, which was touted for its ability to build capacity in the judicial sector, the responsibility to prosecute serious crimes was handed over to Timor's newly formed judiciary. Yet judges, prosecutors, and public defenders in the domestic courts lacked training and professionalism; none had worked as a judge, only one had been a prosecutor, and few had law degrees (Open Society Institute and Coalition for International Justice 2004). One international mentor for the local courts said that "judges don't know the law; they haven't even read the constitution. They make arbitrary decisions not based in law and are unqualified."[7] Meanwhile the courts still faced a backlog of 5,000 defendants awaiting trial.

In April 2005, UN Security Council Resolution 1599 called on the UN Secretariat to preserve a copy of all SCU records. The SCU did collect, analyze, and store evidence, leaving the potential for future prosecutions; however, government offices holding these records were ransacked during violence in May 2006 and looters stole 138 computers containing registry files and forensic evidence against Indonesian soldiers and others. Further demonstrating the fits and starts of the transitional justice process, in 2007, UNMIT sought to assist the Office of the Prosecutor General in resuming the investigative functions of the former SCU in order to complete investigations into the serious human rights violations of 1999. Although the serious crimes investigations were reopened under UNMIT authority in February 2008, the UN recognized the infeasibility of restarting the prosecutorial component and the new investigating team did not have the power to initiate prosecutions. Thus, the serious crimes process was essentially restarted after a three-year hiatus, though only to support investigations by the disinterested Timorese government.

Eruptions of political violence, including an attempt to kidnap President Jose Ramos-Horta, continued to mar progress toward peace and justice while an acceptance of a pattern of impunity took hold. In 2008, President Ramos-Horta pardoned nine former militia members convicted of crimes against humanity, including Joni Marques who had been sentenced to thirty-three years by the Special Panels in 2001. Acts of clemency either represented the inability to inculcate the value of accountability or the continued emphasis on stability among Timorese political leaders. The choices certainly reflect the divergence between international human rights norms and the sovereign prerogatives of national authorities.

Conclusions

Indonesia's resistance to any sort of accountability process for the crimes against humanity that transpired in 1999 stymied hopes to extradite prominent Indonesian suspects. Lacking the international political will to pursue the goals of justice and accountability, the UN let Indonesia off the hook in the effort to assign individual criminal responsibility for human rights violations. Lukewarm support for the hybrid court among the Timorese political leadership and the broader public further undermined the SCU's investigations, which operated in a political vacuum. Nevertheless, by carrying on with the trials, the Special Panels established a rather thorough documentation of crimes committed in the conduct immediately before and after the 1999 referendum. An evidentiary record of abuse was submitted by the five-year process and some degree of respect for human rights was enshrined in the oral rendition of atrocities by militia members.

Moreover, prominent perpetrators were formally indicted, including some of the major decision-makers such as the Indonesian politicians and generals in charge of the invasion, occupation, and withdrawal policies. Still residing in Indonesia, none spent a day in prison, though Generals Zacky Anwar Makarim, Adam Damiri, and Wiranto, Colonel Suhartono Suratman, and Regional Police Chief Timbul Silaen were indicted by the SCU for authority over the 1999 violence. Other notorious militia leaders were tried and sentenced and faced significant punishments of ten to fifteen year jail terms. Overall, the legacy of the UNTAET can be seen as guiding a national self-determination process to the successful achievement of full independence but not as attaining accountability for the human rights violations that occurred along that pathway.

Notes

1. See, Michael Richardson. 2000. "Jakarta Setting Stage for Army Prosecutions." *International Herald Tribune*. January 22.

2. Combating terrorism also made Indonesia, the world's largest predominantly Muslim nation and partner in the "war on terror," an essential ally of the West. Several large-scale bombings in the 2000s against Western targets in Bali and Java demonstrated the real and growing security threats faced by Indonesia from religious organizations like *Jemaah Islamiyah*.
3. Later, a second truth and reconciliation commission would be formed jointly by East Timor and Indonesia to look at the gross human rights violations of 1999. The multiplicity of mechanisms operating in the transitional justice sphere was not necessarily an asset and was occasionally disruptive of the process that continued the longest, the Serious Crimes Unit.
4. Although these cases were retained by the Office of the General Prosecutor, none were tried since the court process was about to conclude.
5. See, Olivia Rondonuwu. 2008. "East Timor PM Satisfied with Indonesia's Regret." Reuters, July 16.
6. See, UNMISET. 2003. "Strategic Plan for East Timor Justice Sector: Post UNMISET Continuing Requirements and Suggested Mechanisms." September 24.
7. Fernando Lathore, IFES mentor for Ordinary Crimes, interview with author, August 13, 2003, Tutuala.

References

Cohen, David. 2003. *Intended to Fail: The Trials Before the Ad Hoc Human Rights Court in Jakarta*. New York: International Center for Transitional Justice.

Dunn, James. 2001. *Crimes Against Humanity in East Timor, January to October 1999: Their Nature and Causes*. New York: United Nations.

East Timor-Indonesia. 2008. *Per Memoriam Ad Spem: Final Report of the Commission of Truth and Friendship (CTF)*.

Judicial System Monitoring Program. 2007. *Digest of the Jurisprudence of the Special Panels for Serious Crimes*. Dili, East Timor: JSMP.

Kingsbury, Damien, and Michael Leach. 2007. *East Timor: Beyond Independence*. Clayton, Australia: Monash University Press.

Open Society Institute and Coalition for International Justice. 2004. *Unfulfilled Promises: Achieving Justice for Crimes against Humanity in East Timor*. New York: OSI.

Pigou, Piers. 2003. *Crying Without Tears: In Pursuit of Justice and Reconciliation in Timor-Leste: Community Perspectives and Expectations*. New York: International Center for Transitional Justice.

Rae, James. 2009. *Peacebuilding and Transitional Justice in East Timor: Commitment, Competence, and Cultural Accommodation*. Boulder, CO: First Forum Press.

Reiger, Caitlin, and Marieke Wierda. 2006. *The Serious Crimes Process in Timor-Leste: In Retrospect*. New York, NY: International Center for Transitional Justice.

Robinson, Geoffrey. 2003. *East Timor 1999 Crimes Against Humanity*. New York: UN Office of the High Commissioner for Human Rights.

United Nations. 2006. Report of the Secretary-General on Justice and Reconciliation for Timor-Leste. New York, NY: United Nations. S/2006/580.

United Nations. 2000. Report of the Security Council Mission to East Timor and Indonesia. New York, NY: United Nations. S/2000/1105.

CHAPTER 13

Unfinished Business: The Commission for Reception, Truth, and Reconciliation in East Timor

WENDY LAMBOURNE

Introduction

East Timor has emerged as one of the world's newest nations after a turbulent history comprising 450 years of Portuguese rule followed by civil war, invasion, and twenty-five years of Indonesian occupation characterized by human rights abuses, massacres, and violence. The United Nations (UN) and international non-government organisations (NGOs) have supported significant peace-building efforts, including attention to both justice and reconciliation strategies to promote healing and rebuilding of relationships within communities divided by violence, as well as the establishment of political, economic, and security structures and institutions. The animosities between the different Timorese political factions stemming from the violence in 1974 have continued to affect relationships in the newly independent East Timor. The relationship between East Timor and Indonesia is critical, as the relationship has not only defined the competing ideologies of the different political parties, which emerged following the departure of the Portuguese in 1974, but has continued to divide the Timorese, especially following the post-referendum militia violence in 1999, which was driven by the desire of some groups seeking to maintain ties with Indonesia, albeit in a new system of government that would allow East Timor a measure of regional autonomy. As discussed in Chapter 11, an estimated 2,000 East Timorese were killed while 500,000 civilians were displaced (including 200,000 to 250,000 to West Timor), and hundreds of women were raped. Approximately, 60,000 houses were burnt, and 70 percent of the infrastructure was destroyed. In Suai, in the South not far from the West Timor border, people were massacred as they took shelter in the cathedral. The militia and their families, as well as other pro-autonomy supporters and victims, fled to West Timor.

The population of East Timor has thus remained divided politically since 1974 between the supporters of incorporation or autonomy within Indonesia and the supporters of independence. In the aftermath of the militia violence of 1999, a division existed between those who led the militia, those who followed the militia, their families, and those who were targets of the militia violence (Nishikawa 2002). Within the East Timorese population, families may be divided, with some supporting autonomy, others actively supporting independence, some coopting with the militia, and others changing their minds over the years. The conflict that erupted in 1999 was thus not about age-old enmities but rather political divisions dating from 1974 exacerbated by the experience of violence and mass human rights violations, which has significance for the promotion of justice and reconciliation for the East Timorese.

Reconciliation is needed between different sectors of the East Timorese population, many of whom live in the same communities, as well as between East and West Timorese, East Timorese and Indonesians more generally, and between East Timorese and those members of the international community such as Australia, which supported the Indonesian invasion and annexation of East Timor in the 1970s and failed to prevent the subsequent violence and human rights abuses. Justice and reconciliation have frequently been seen as competing objectives in transitional societies in which mass abuse of human rights has occurred either by a former repressive regime or during a civil war or genocide.

However, the UN International Commission of Inquiry on East Timor (UNICIET), established in response to the post-referendum violence, recommended in its report in January 2000 the establishment of both an international tribunal and a truth commission to promote both justice and reconciliation for the East Timorese. Despite the extreme violence and losses suffered by East Timorese at the time of the 1999 referendum, their new government chose to support the recommendation of a truth and reconciliation commission to deal with the minor crimes perpetrated at this time.

The perceived tension between justice and reconciliation, and the coordination challenges of having both legal trials and a truth commission operating simultaneously, has been difficult for East Timor. Most significant for community perceptions about the success of the truth commission was the expectation that it was intended as complementary rather than a substitute for prosecutions. The international, Indonesian, and Timorese failure to effectively implement prosecutions of serious crimes, as detailed in Chapter 12 of this volume, thus had a detrimental effect on Timorese experiences of the truth commission and its ability to promote reconciliation in relation to the less serious crimes under its jurisdiction.

Creating the Commission for Reception, Truth, and Reconciliation

Following the recommendation of the UNICIET, the UN High Commissioner for Human Rights (UNHCHR) together with the UN Transitional Administration in East Timor (UNTAET) held workshops in Dili to consult with East Timorese groups and international truth commission experts on the possibility of a truth commission in East Timor. A workshop of East Timorese civil society to consider transitional justice mechanisms was held in June 2000 and recommended that the first national congress of the National Council of Timorese Resistance (CNRT) consider a proposal to establish an independent truth and reconciliation commission. The CNRT proposed at its congress in August 2000 that such a truth commission be set up and emphasized the significance of truth in its vision of reconciliation:

> Reconciliation is a process, which acknowledges past mistakes including regret and forgiveness as a product of a path inherent in the process of achieving justice; it is also a process which must involve the People of Timor-Leste so that the cycle of accusation, denial and counter-accusation can be broken. This process must not be seen only as a conflict resolution or mere political tool which aims at pacification and reintegration of individuals or groups in the context of their acceptance of independence and sovereignty of Timor-Leste but, above all, must be seen as a process where truth must be the outcome (Commission for Truth, Reconciliation, and Reception Final Report 2005, 18).

A steering committee was established comprising representatives of the CNRT, East Timorese non-government organisations, UNTAET, the UNHCHR, and two advisers from the International Center for Transitional Justice (ICTJ). The committee consulted widely throughout East Timor as well as in the refugee camps of West Timor and concluded that the mechanism set up would need to provide a concrete program to heal relationships, reduce the possibility of violence, and avoid impunity (Schlicher 2005, 15). It would need to have a firm legal basis as well as being grounded socially and culturally in the community.

The East Timorese Transitional Administration subsequently agreed on December 13, 2000 to the proposal to establish a Commission for Reception, Truth, and Reconciliation (known by its Portuguese acronym, CAVR) focusing its activities in three areas: Facilitating the reintegration of East Timorese refugees (reception), establishing a historical record about human rights abuse (truth), and recommending legal and institutional safeguards to protect human rights in the future (reconciliation) (Gorjao 2001, 151). The CAVR was established by UNTAET in July 2001 as an independent statutory authority under Regulation 2001/10. The commission had three main purposes: To investigate human rights violations during the period between April 25, 1974 until October 25, 1999 (truth seeking), to assist in the reception and reintegration of those who committed lesser crimes (community reconciliation), and to report its findings and make policy recommendations to the East Timorese government for further action on reconciliation and the promotion of human rights.

Extensive community consultations were held regarding the structure, functions, and selection of national and regional commissioners of the CAVR. Seven national commissioners were chosen from almost 300 candidates, and their official inauguration ceremony was held on January 21, 2002. Following a public nomination process in each district, twenty-nine regional commissioners, including ten women, were sworn in on May 12, 2002. The CAVR was included in the new East Timorese constitution at independence on May 20, 2002.

The CAVR national commissioners were: Jacinto das Neves Raimundo Alves (coordinator of the Association of former Political Prisoners), Maria Olandina Isabel Caeiro Alves (chair of Women Against Violence), Isabel Amarel Guterres (member of Jesuit Refugee Service), Father Jovito Rego de Jesus Araujo (Catholic priest and former member of the Students National Resistance Organization), Jose Estevao Soares (founding member of pro-autonomy political organization, Forum for Peace, Democracy, and Justice), Reverend Agustinho de Vasconselos (Minister of the Protestant Church of East Timor), and Chairperson Aniceto Longuinhos Guterres Lopes (lawyer and founding member of prominent human rights organization, Yayasan Hak). The CAVR was initially established with a two-year mandate of operations from April 2002, but this was first extended by six months to October 2004 and again extended twice more to enable completion of the final report by October 31, 2005. Its headquarters were set up in the renovated Portuguese colonial prison at Comarca in the Balide district of Dili, with a view to the prison being maintained as a memorial after the conclusion of the CAVR's work.

The Work of the CAVR

The CAVR's thirteen district teams engaged in statement-taking, reconciliation, and support for victims, covering sixty-five sub-districts throughout East Timor. Almost 8,000 statements were collected from survivors and families of victims regarding human rights violations between 1974 and 1999, including ninety-one statements from East Timorese living in West Timor. A total of 216 community reconciliation events were facilitated for 1,403 deponents throughout East Timor, and six national healing workshops were conducted. Urgent reparations were provided for 690 of the most seriously affected victims.

Eight national public hearings were held: Victims' Hearing (November 2002), Political Imprisonment (February 2003), Women and the Conflict (April 2003), Forced Displacement and Famine (July 2003), Massacres (November 2003), the Internal Political Conflict of 1974–1976 (December 2003), Self-determination and the International Community (March 2004), and Children and Conflict (March 2004). These public hearings were broadcast throughout East Timor via live television and radio. Their goal was to maximize the public availability of information, to stimulate discussion, and provide a basis for healing. In addition, 6,500 people attended fifty-two sub-district Victims' Hearings throughout the country.

Particularly significant was the public hearing on the internal political conflict held in December 2003, which focused on the 1974–1976 civil war. Portuguese leaders participated by telephone and President Xanana Gusmao and other former leaders of the Armed Forces for the National Liberation of East Timor, as well as leaders of the other factions, participated in person in Dili. By all accounts, the event was very emotional and healing for the leaders involved, as well as for the Timorese in the general population. As described by Burgess, "the hearing ended in a gathering of these former allies and enemies, arm in arm, many crying, covered live on national radio and television" (2006, 199).

The particular vulnerability of women during the conflict was recognized by the CAVR as demonstrated by the national public hearing on "Women and the Conflict" held on April 28–29, 2003. Thirteen women gave testimony at the hearing covering human rights violations perpetrated in eleven districts over the twenty-five years of Indonesian occupation. Again the hearing was emotional and was intended to promote understanding and healing, as well as respect for women and their experiences (Commission for Reception, Truth and Reconciliation Final Report 2005). Of the 7,669 statements documented by the CAVR, 1,642 (21 percent) were from women and of all the violations reported, 853 counts of sexual violence were recorded. Women's participation in the CAVR was described as "moderate" but without the intensive efforts to ensure a gender balance and to reach out to women in rural communities, the participation would have most likely been considerably less (Wandita et al. 2006). The reception component of the CAVR's mandate included providing information and monitoring the reception of refugees returning from West Timor. The final report identifies some of the challenges faced by returnees in finding accommodation, work, and acceptance in the community. An outreach program was conducted in West Timor in collaboration with Indonesian NGOs involving direct discussions with refugees and dissemination of information through the media and videos of community reconciliation meetings.

Community Reconciliation Process

The community reconciliation process (CRP) was a particularly significant component of the CAVR both for the Timorese and as a potential model for other truth commissions. The CRP was used for lesser crimes such as looting, burning, minor assault, theft, killing of livestock, and the destruction of crops. Each CRP was set up at the request of a deponent (perpetrator) and the community was then invited to participate (rather than individual victims). The deponent's participation and agreement was registered with the Office of the General Prosecutor, resulting in amnesty from future prosecution so long as no more serious crime was identified during the course of the CRP.

The CRP incorporated the grassroots Timorese reconciliation process of *nahe biti*, which refers to the symbolic rolling out of a mat as a venue to discuss and settle an issue among interested parties through consensus (Babo-Soares 2005; Ximenes 2004). The process involved voluntary acceptance of culpability and agreement on reconciliation acts such as reparation, community service, or public apology, and was usually finalized with a symbolic ceremony exchanging "betel nut" to show sincerity and commitment. The significance of the mat is that it cannot be rolled up again until the conflict has been resolved. As an indication of the community's commitment to the process, many CRPs that commenced in the morning continued into the late night or even early morning of the following day (Burgess 2006). Reconciliation in this manner is traditionally seen as a bridge to achieve much greater harmony and peace in society.

The CRP resonated with traditional values in its emphasis on the community rather than the individual, and the opportunity for the perpetrator to engage with the community in an exchange, which was both ceremonial and practical. The sanctions or compensation requested by the victims more often than not involved a heartfelt confession and public apology, along with symbolic payments, in recognition of the inability of deponents to pay more and "the desire of communities to settle matters, to delve into the issues deeply, but then leave them behind and not leave hanging threads into the future" (Burgess 2006, 194). It was also commonly accepted that the East Timorese perpetrators were led and manipulated by the Indonesian military, which was seen as ultimately responsible.

The CRP was thus seen as culturally and socially appropriate and embedded, producing a local community ownership unprecedented among truth commissions around the world. The existence of district commissioners and holding of victims' hearings as well as CRPs in subdistricts created an extent of coverage also not previously seen in other truth commissions. An interim review conducted by the CAVR in 2003 found that both victims and perpetrators reported significant positive effects on their relationships and daily lives, and that they expected the effects to be sustained over time (Burgess 2006).

The CAVR Final Report

The CAVR final report took more than a year to finalize, at least in part because of the complications of having to produce three different language versions (Indonesian official version and translations in Portuguese and English), which all needed to be cross-checked against each other and updated each time in case of any amendments.[1] The 2,000-page report *Chega!* (Portuguese for "no more, stop, enough!") was completed and delivered to President Gusmao on October 31, 2005. In his address at the presentation, CAVR chair Aniceto Guterres Lopes said that the dissemination of the report and implementation of its recommendations remained "an item of unfinished business that is essential to the healing process, the deepening of a culture of human rights and rule of law, and the learning of lessons both nationally and internationally."[2] He recommended the establishment of a successor organization to the CAVR for this purpose and to ensure the security, management, and development of the CAVR archives.

President Gusmao subsequently presented the report to the parliament on November 28, 2005 and inaugurated the post-CAVR Technical Secretariat on December 20, 2005. However, Gusmao was criticized by organizations such as Amnesty International for delays in making the report public, as required under the law that established the CAVR. On January 20, 2006, Gusmao presented the report to the UN Secretary-General Kofi Annan, and *Chega!* was finally made public. A ICTJ Press Release (2006) described the CAVR report as "scientifically rigorous and morally brave" because of its thorough accounting of the human rights violations perpetrated in East Timor between 1974 and 1999, and its call to end impunity for the perpetrators." Unfortunately, the public dissemination and impact of the report, and its reception nationally and internationally, were weakened by the fact that very soon after its release there were new outbreaks of violence in East Timor—this time triggered by accusations of discrimination within the military.

The CAVR report provided the most scientifically accurate estimate of the number of Timorese who were killed or died as a result of hunger and illness between 1974 and 1999 and directly as a result of the Indonesian occupation. The figure of 102,800 was based on the CAVR database, a retrospective mortality survey and a census of public graveyards. The report also found that 85 percent of the human rights violations reported to the CAVR were committed by Indonesian security forces, while approximately 10 percent were committed by pro-independence forces led by the Revolutionary Front for an Independent East Timor.[3] Significantly, the latter admitted responsibility and cooperated with the CAVR, unlike the Indonesian forces. As a result, the report recommended that the Indonesian government should declassify information that could contribute to justice and educate the public about the crimes committed in East Timor, while the international community should pursue criminal accountability for the Indonesian perpetrators. The report also recommended the establishment of a reparations program for the victims of human rights violations, to be jointly financed by the Timorese government, the permanent members of the UN Security Council, the Indonesian government, and other governments and businesses, which profited from the war and related activities in East Timor. However, Indonesia's state secretary dismissed the CAVR report, claiming that "Western countries also colonized Asia and Africa in an even worse manner" (ICTJ Press Release 2006).

Other recommendations of the report included specific strategies and goals for the promotion and protection of human rights in the future; the establishment of a community-focused mechanism for conflict prevention and resolution based on the lessons learned from the CRP; further initiatives to promote reconciliation in the Timorese political community; a continuation of contacts and goodwill with East Timorese living in Indonesia, and a national memorialization program (Commission for Reception, Truth and Reconciliation Final Report 2005).

Evaluation of CAVR

The strengths of the CAVR included its participatory approach at the village level and the interactive community reconciliation process based on traditional justice *nahe biti*. These features helped to ensure a sense of local ownership and inclusion, which was quite unprecedented for a truth and reconciliation commission. The public acknowledgment of suffering seemed to be an important benefit of the community reconciliation process, as well as the public hearings and the "truth-telling" collection of testimony. The historical account of human rights violations covering the whole period from 1974 until 1999 provided in the final report was also a significant contribution to justice and reconciliation for the Timorese.

The CAVR also helped alleviate pressure on the formal justice system by dealing with less serious crimes out of the court system. This provided both a sense of closure for the deponents and reduced the desire and incidence of revenge when the former militia returned to their villages. The CAVR was able to contribute to encouraging refugee repatriation, even though there was dissatisfaction that not more had returned, as will be discussed further in the following section. One of the weaknesses of the CAVR was the inadequate participation of women in the CRPs, despite women being employed locally by the CAVR, and the lack of attention given to the needs and rights of victims in terms of preparation and protection, compared with the focus on deponents. The CAVR was also accused of creating a justice gap and experience of accidental immunity because of its role in raising expectations regarding prosecutions for serious crimes, which were not forthcoming. This sense of "unfinished business" to some extent undermined the reconciliation experienced in the communities through the CRPs dealing with less serious crimes. These and other aspects of perceived unfinished business resulting from the work of the CAVR will be discussed in more detail in the following section, drawing on the results of field research conducted in East Timor in July 2004.

Unfinished Business

Despite the relative success of the CAVR, East Timorese have reported a strong desire for justice for the militia who raped and killed during the violence of 1999.[4] The CAVR conducted reconciliation processes for those who committed minor crimes such as burning houses and verbal abuse. But in relation to serious crimes, all it could do was record people's stories with the assumption that acknowledgement and truth-telling would contribute to their healing. The expectations of the victims of serious crimes were therefore not fulfilled. They told the CAVR interviewers their stories and expected the perpetrators of the crimes against them would be arrested and punished, but in many cases this did not occur. Not only were the Serious Crimes Unit (SCU) in Dili and the court in Jakarta seen as failing to deliver justice (see Chapter 12 for a complete discussion), but because the truth-telling process was seen as linked to the implementation of justice, the CAVR was also perceived as having failed at least in the area of dealing with serious crimes.

It was not in the CAVR's mandate to provide justice or reconciliation for serious crimes. The CAVR's focus was twofold: Reconciliation in relation to minor crimes and truth-telling for serious crimes. The community-based, participatory reconciliation process that was implemented in every region of East Timor focused on the reintegration of the perpetrators of minor crimes back into the community. As such, it was extremely successful, setting a world first example of a nationally constituted and financed truth commission, which operated at a grassroots level incorporating traditional reconciliation processes. The perception was that the East Timorese truly owned this process even though they relied on CAVR officials for its implementation.

However, the victims and perpetrators who did not get a chance to go through the process before the CAVR official mandate ended have been left feeling dissatisfied. The victims were unable to instigate a CRP, so if the perpetrator/s who committed crimes against them did not come forward, then they were unable to participate in the CRP. There was also a backlog of deponents who had requested a CRP, which could not be conducted before the CAVR's mandate ended. According to Burgess (2006), it was estimated that more than 3,000 perpetrators would have been prepared to participate in the CRP hearings if the program had been extended. Furthermore, it was confusing for victims who were often victims of both serious and non-serious crimes, not to mention the deponents who were also often victims. As a result, it seemed rather arbitrary to many East Timorese which crimes were dealt with under the CRP, leaving them with a sense of unfinished business relating to those crimes and perpetrators not dealt with.

This view was reflected by two victims of serious crimes in Suai who expressed their frustration at not being invited to participate in a CRP. Two deponents who were also victims of non-serious crimes, both living in Suai, similarly expressed their dissatisfaction with the CRP because the crimes perpetrated against them were not dealt with even though they had gone through a CRP for the crimes they had committed against others. Victims of serious crimes in Suai and Liquica expressed their dissatisfaction and anger at being interviewed many times by the CAVR and SCU but there was "no result." However, victims of non-serious crimes and deponents who had participated in a CRP agreed that it was helpful.

The feeling of unfinished business was also felt by East Timorese who, after the CAVR, still did not know the "truth" about who killed family members or the location of their remains. The CRPs also raised new issues and crimes, which in many cases remained unresolved because the CAVR ran out of time to investigate and hold further CRPs. Indeed, one of the missing ingredients for the CAVR's contribution to reconciliation was the failure to empower local communities to continue the traditional reconciliation processes on an ongoing basis, without relying on the official imprimatur of the CAVR. Unfortunately the CAVR appears to have unwittingly created a dependency of the people on an official organization to provide the space for conducting their own traditional reconciliation. The mistake appears to have been to conceive of the reconciliation process as something which only the commission could provide and, as a result, that it would have an endpoint, which would coincide with the end of the CAVR's mandate. Of course, individuals do not think and feel that way. Their need for reconciliation does not suddenly stop on a particular date, nor does it stop at those who committed less serious crimes.

The CAVR thus focussed only on the truth-telling aspect and was not empowered to conduct reconciliation in relation to serious crimes. This was unsatisfactory for both the perpetrators/deponents who could not participate in a CRP for serious crimes, and for the victims who participated in the truth-telling process. The victims have been left with unfulfilled expectations that something would be done with their "evidence" and that the stories they told to the CAVR interviewers as part of the "truth-telling" process (as distinct from the CRP) would be passed on and lead to the arrest and punishment of the perpetrators. Emotional wounds were opened by "telling the truth" but without any apparent follow-up or result in relation to justice or reconciliation process. The deponents were also dissatisfied because they, the so-called "small people," were expected to go through a CRP while the "big people" or "big fish" (leaders of the militia and others who directed the violence) were still living freely and comfortably in Jakarta or West Timor, or sometimes even in East Timor.

The CAVR was only the latest in a series of attempts to promote return and reintegration of refugees from West Timor. Before independence, Gusmao was heavily involved and because of the general trust and respect he could personally command, was able to convince many of the pro-autonomy supporters and other militia to return. UNTAET also managed a "come and see" program for refugees to check out their homes and villages before deciding to bring their families back to East Timor. Most East Timorese wanted the militia and their families still in West Timor to be able to return to East Timor, but many stayed in West Timor because they had jobs and better economic security than if they returned, as well as because they feared retribution or arrest if they returned. Victims living in East Timor wanted the militia who had committed serious crimes to return and to face justice. These victims also said they would reconcile with the militia who had committed serious crimes, but only if they received justice. This was consistent with their attitude toward the crimes of Indonesian General Wiranto: Reconciliation and justice were both possible and both necessary.

Kent (2004) also reports that many East Timorese saw both reconciliation and justice as necessary for real peace. However, some Timorese thought reconciliation was possible as long as the perpetrators were then held accountable, while others said they could only reconcile after justice had been served. The latter perspective is reflected by Guterres (2003) who says that the perpetrators could be forgiven once they had received justice or gone through a court procedure. Another significant aspect of unfinished business among East Timorese was the perception of a lack of socioeconomic justice. This was indicated by Timorese who identified the need for a job, health care, safe water, help with school fees and assistance to start a small business. The CAVR might have provided some reconciliation in the communities, but without a more complete experience of justice including socioeconomic as well as legal justice, East Timorese peace and security is less likely to be sustainable. This prediction was in fact borne out with the outbreak of violence in 2006. It is therefore suggested that a greater focus was needed on socioeconomic justice either through the CAVR and reparations, or a separate government program.

Conclusions

The CAVR was noteworthy for its emphasis on grassroots, public participation, and its holistic, integrated, and culturally appropriate approach to justice and reconciliation. According to Burgess, the CAVR "conducted significantly more grass-roots programs, and of a more varied approach, than any previous truth and reconciliation commission" (2006, 197). The public hearings were focused on healing and reconciliation and the victims were prioritized and treated with dignity, including the provision of reparations when it was revealed that these were urgently needed. Despite its groundbreaking achievements, however, the CAVR raised expectations, which were not fulfilled regarding the implementation of criminal prosecutions for perpetrators of serious crimes, and the ability to satisfy demand for community reconciliation processes.

The built-in assumption of complementarity rather than amnesty for serious crimes, and the promotion of CRPs for all perpetrators of less serious crimes, contributed to these unfulfilled expectations. Truth-telling in the CAVR mandate was associated with legal justice and the promise of subsequent prosecutions for serious crimes, rather than being seen as an end in itself, which could contribute to reconciliation. It is possible to conclude from the CAVR experience that reconciliation without legal justice may be possible for non-serious crimes, but the same is not necessarily true for serious crimes. Truth-telling on its own may be insufficient for victims of serious crimes to feel a sense of justice and reconciliation, especially if the perpetrators are not present and/or if they perceived the process of reconciliation instituted for the perpetrators of non-serious crimes to be more thorough and complete.

The lessons to be learnt from the East Timorese experience include the importance of seeing reconciliation as a long-term process so that any institutions that are established with a short-term mandate need to focus on setting up sustainable processes, which can continue after the institution is disbanded. The breakout of violence in 2006 and ensuing political instability undermined the Timorese government's focus on the release and follow-up to the recommendations of the CAVR report. Instead, the government focused its attention on the Commission on Truth and Friendship with Indonesia.

As outlined above, care should be taken not to leave victims with a false sense of expectations about legal follow-up to their statements to a truth commission when there is no amnesty provision and there are legal trials operating simultaneously. The critical role of coordination between transitional justice bodies is extremely important, as it has also been more recently in Sierra Leone. On a more positive note, the experience of the CAVR illustrates how the incorporation of traditional justice and reconciliation processes into the mechanisms of a truth commission is possible and desirable in terms of increasing its acceptance, ownership, and effectiveness. The CAVR also demonstrates the value of including both victims/survivors and perpetrators facing each other and having the opportunity to communicate and restore their relationship as a means of promoting community reconciliation. Finally, the East Timorese experience shows us the importance of socioeconomic justice for sustainable reconciliation, and the need to focus on political justice if violence is to be avoided in future.

There is a need for both reconciliation and justice in East Timor in order to promote social and political transformation, meet the needs of victims and perpetrators for closure and healing, and satisfy international law requirements regarding prevention and prosecution of crimes against humanity. The East Timorese suffered for many years and are understandably angry that the main perpetrators have not faced justice. This poses an obstacle to reconciliation in East Timor and a continuing threat to future peace and security within the region. Truth commissions and legal trials need to work together in combating a culture of impunity and building a human rights culture as a basis for sustainable peace. The East Timorese could show us the way to incorporate both reconciliation and justice into a successful peace-building strategy if the political will could be found to prosecute those most responsible for the militia violence and human rights violations.

Notes

1. Only parts of the report were translated into Tetum by the CAVR, and it was hoped that the full report would subsequently be translated.
2. Address by Aniceto Guterres Lopes, chair of CAVR, at the presentation of the Commission for Reception, Truth, and Reconciliation Timor-Leste Final Report to the president on October 31, 2005. An English translation is available at: www.etan.org/et2005/october/31/31anicet.htm.
3. Human rights violations identified and documented in the report included unlawful killings and enforced disappearances, forced displacement and famine, detention, torture and ill treatment, violations of the laws of war, sexual violence, violations of the rights of the child, and violations of economic and social rights (Commission for Reception, Truth and Reconciliation Timor-Leste Final Report 2005).
4. These observations are based on field research interviews that I conducted in East Timor in July 2004 with victims of serious and non-serious crimes and perpetrators of non-serious crimes living in Dili, Suai, and Liquica. Further data was derived from the reports of external reviewers of the CRP, Lia Kent, and Piers Pigou, who also conducted interviews in East Timor in 2004.

References

Amaral-Guterres, Isabel. 2002. "East Timor–Reconciliation and Justice." *Eureka Street.* May.

Babo-Soares, Dionisio. 2005. "*Nahe Biti*: Grassroots Reconciliation in East Timor." In *Roads to Reconciliation*, ed. Elin Skaar, Siri Gloppen, and Astri Suhrke. Lanham, MD: Lexington Books.

Burgess, Patrick. 2006. "A New Approach to Restorative Justice–East Timor's Community Reconciliation Process." In *Transitional Justice in the Twenty-First Century: Beyond Truth versus Justice*, eds. Naomi Roht-Arriaza and Javier Mariezcurrena Cambridge: Cambridge University Press.

Burgess, Patrick. 2004. "Justice and Reconciliation in East Timor: The Relationship between the Commission for Reception, Truth and Reconciliation and the Courts." *Criminal Law Forum* 15:135–158.

Coakley, Victoria. 2001. "Towards Justice and Reconciliation in East Timor." *Alternative Law Journal* 26:229–241.

Commission for Reception, Truth and Reconciliation Timor-Leste Final Report. 2005.

Gorjao, Paulo. 2001. "The East Timorese Commission for Reception, Truth and Reconciliation: Chronicle of a Foretold Failure?" *Civil Wars* 4:142–162.

Guterres, Francisco da Costa. 2003. "Reconciliation in East Timor: Building Peace and Stability." Paper prepared for Swedish International Development Agency. Stockholm, Sweden.

ICTJ Press Release. 2006. "Timorese Truth Commission Report Reveals Shocking Brutality, Calls for End to Impunity." January 20. Available at: www.ictj.org/en/news/press/release/773.html.

Kent, Lia. 2005. "Community Views of Justice and Reconciliation in Timor-Leste." *Development Bulletin* 68:62–65.

Kent, Lia. 2004. "Unfulfilled Expectations: Community Views on CAVR's Community Reconciliation Process." Dili: Judicial System Monitoring Program.

Nishikawa, Yukiko. 2002. "East Timor: Unfinished Business." *Peace Conflict and Development* 2:1–11.

Schlicher, Monika. 2005. *East Timor Faces up to its Past: The Work of the Commission for Reception, Truth and Reconciliation*. Aachen: Missio.

Wandita, Galuh, Karen Campbell-Nelson, and Manuela Leong Pereira. 2006. "Learning to Engender Reparations in Timor-Leste: Reaching Out to Female Victims." In *What Happened to the Women? Gender and Reparations for Human Rights Violations*, ed. Ruth Rubio-Marin. New York: Social Science Research Council.

Ximenes, Fausto B. 2004. "The Unique Contribution of the Community-Based Reconciliation Process in East Timor." Paper developed for the International Center for Transitional Justice and the Institute for Justice and Reconciliation, May.

PART VI

Conclusion

CHAPTER 14

The Quest for Justice: Lessons Learned

STEVEN D. ROPER AND LILIAN A. BARRIA

Introduction

Over the past three decades, considerable debate has taken place regarding the strengths and the weaknesses of the various transitional justice mechanisms that have been adopted after a transition to democracy. The mechanisms chosen by states during the cold war period were generally domestic, including trials, amnesties, and truth and reconciliation commissions (TRCs). However, the 1990s witnessed several important innovations including the establishment of international and later hybrid criminal tribunals, culminating in the creation of the International Criminal Court (ICC). The contributors to this volume discuss diverse transitional justice mechanisms implemented following severe human rights violations (often perpetrated by a government). How should we assess these methods of transitional justice? Given the nature of the conflict and the human rights abuses, is any mechanism superior?

These questions are difficult to answer because of the different motivations involved in the adoption of transitional justice mechanisms. For those who advocate trials, retributive justice not only provides closure for the victim but also serves a larger social role by deterring future atrocities (Morris 1997). Those who advocate TRCs note the healing and reconciliation properties involved in testifying and forgiving (Drumbl 2000). Finally, transitional justice mechanisms are often chosen based on the hope that they can ultimately lead to political stability, peace, and security (Shinoda 2002). Given the different goals of the various forms of transitional justice, it is not surprising that the four country cases in this volume adopted multiple methods of accountability, often at the same time. The question remains, however, whether these diverse mechanisms can work in tandem and whether the simultaneous use of different mechanisms leads to a more complete process of accountability or actually diminishes the individual effectiveness of each of the mechanisms. In this chapter, we draw upon the conclusions of the contributors to this volume to provide some comparative lessons from the four country cases. Given the regional, cultural, and historical diversity of the cases in this volume, the lessons learned here can be applied to various situations in which democratizing states are dealing with human rights abuses and attempting to balance justice, peace, and reconciliation.

Transitional Justice Mechanisms

Domestic Trials and Amnesties

In Chapter 1, we noted that in established democracies, domestic trials are the preferred mode for addressing human rights violations. How successful is this mechanism of transitional justice in democratizing countries seeking to establish the rule of law? The cases of Argentina and Bosnia-Herzegonvina (BiH) show mixed results in the implementation of domestic trials. Di Paolantonio discusses the legacy of the 1985 "Trial of the Military" in Argentina. His initial conclusion is that the domestic trial was not a good option for Argentina to pursue after its transition back to democracy because of the unresolved conflicts in the society. While President Raul Alfonsin attempted to limit the trial to the top nine military leaders, the public demanded further prosecutions. With a military challenge to the new democratic regime, Alfonsin issued a series of amnesties to forestall the prosecution of junior officers. The subsequent Menem government issued further amnesties that covered the military leaders who were convicted in 1985. The Argentinean approach favored political stability and peace rather than justice for victims. Therefore, Di Paolantonio ultimately concludes that the justice denied in the 1980s brought about further demands in the 1990s and the 2000s that led to the overturn of the earlier amnesties and a renewal of trials. He argues that civil society was critical in providing justice to victims. The state was hesitant to expand criminal prosecutions in the 1980s due to the concern for democratic consolidation, but as democracy became further entrenched in the 1990s, civil society was able to force the state to try those who were responsible for the Dirty War.

Lowry and McMahon describe the transfer of cases back to BiH from the ICTY and the significant difficulties facing BiH domestic courts in prosecuting these complex human rights cases in a politically and ethnically charged environment. In the case of BiH, it is also important to consider the complex government and legal structure created after independence was declared in 1992. Within the state of BiH, there is the Federation of Bosnia and Herzegovina (FBiH) and the *Republika Srpska* (RS). The FBiH and the RS have a strong degree of autonomy from the national (state) level, each with their own ministries of justice and interior. As Lowry and McMahon point out, judicial capacity-building is difficult to achieve at the same time as nation-building. While creating (or re-creating) an impartial, professional, and effective legal system is an essential component of democratic consolidation, the rule of law and transitional justice, Lowry and McMahon argue that this "is neither a simple nor a quick fix" (19). As they note, building legal norms and institutions in newly independent states must be embedded within a larger nation-building project, which makes domestic trials even more difficult to implement.

Truth and Reconciliation Commissions

Like many countries over the last thirty years, Argentina, Sierra Leone, and East Timor adopted a TRC to address previous human rights violations. In the chapter on Argentina, Crenzel discusses after the transition to democracy in 1983, the issues involved with implementation of the TRC when both victims and perpetuators were unwilling to cooperate with the process. In its initial stages, civil society demanded trials; however, as the TRC gained legitimacy, human rights groups became full participants in gathering testimony and uncovering the truth. The military, however, refused to cooperate with the inquiry, partly due to the fear that the evidence gathered by the National Commission on the Disappearance of Persons (CONADEP) would be used in the subsequent military trials. CONADEP's final report, thus, was not an exercise in reconciliation but the prelude to domestic trials. Crenzel credits the commission with strong civil society participation; however, the report focused on identifying perpetuators within the military, ignoring the role that civil society played in the violence that transpired during the military regime. He observes that the CONADEP report is an apolitical and ahistorical document that does not accurately portray the reality of the Dirty War.

When discussing the Sierra Leone case, Dugal argues that outreach, education, and local community engagement is absolutely vital to the success of a TRC. The Sierra Leone TRC began its work late and as a consequence, personnel in charge of gathering testimony were often also in charge of outreach, which hampered both activities. Dugal explains that the recommendations of the TRC's final report were often ignored and that Sierra Leonean nationals were not allowed to consult the TRC's archives for a period of twenty-five years. In essence, the very people who need to know the "truth" in order for reconciliation to occur are forbidden from reading the files. Dugal also notes that TRC outreach was vital because the commission operated at the same time as the hybrid Special Court for Sierra Leone (SCSL). While the TRC and the SCSL worked effectively to dedifferentiate their mandates, the concomitant use of a TRC and trials requires careful consideration as both rely on testimony to fulfill their goals.

Lambourne notes that civil society was extensively consulted in the creation of the East Timorese Commission for Reception, Truth, and Reconciliation (CAVR). Public hearings involving victims and perpetuators were structured based on the local culture and thus were highly successful. Many perpetuators were willing to participate in the process, and those who committed minor crimes were able to be reintegrated into their communities. However, some of the victims thought that the TRC was supposed to assist in criminal prosecutions (as in the case of Argentina). This was particularly true when testimonies uncovered serious crimes that were supposed to be sent to the East Timor hybrid court. Many of these cases were not prosecuted, leaving the victims unsatisfied with too little accountability. Other victims did not have the opportunity to find out the "truth." For many, the TRC process ended too soon, and more victims and perpetuators would have participated had the CAVR operated for a longer period of time. Lambourne concludes that a formal institution like the CAVR was not needed to continue with the process of reconciliation and that there was a failure to empower the community to continue the healing process after the end of the TRC in 2005.

International Criminal Tribunals

As the International Criminal Tribunal for the former Yugoslavia's (ICTY) mandate nears it end (officially 2013) and cases are devolved back to BiH, it is an opportune time to reflect on the relative successes and failures of the tribunal. As Clark points out, there are many methods by which we can evaluate the ICTY, and she examines the outreach of the ICTY in order to assess its record in communicating its mission, goals, and legitimacy to the populations in BiH as well as Croatia and Serbia. Clark concludes that the failure to significantly engage in outreach activities has hampered the ICTY's ability to provide justice, reconciliation, and peace. The jurisprudential effect of the ICTY on the ground can only be as successful as the tribunal's communication and engagement with the local population. Therefore, one lesson that is learnt from the analysis of the ICTY is that the international community, at the beginning, must design outreach programs that involve and educate locals. If not, then the purpose and activities of the institution can actually be counterproductive to reconciliation and ultimately peace maintenance. Given the current cases before the ICC, this lesson seems as important today as it was in 1993 when the ICTY was created.

Hybrid Criminal Tribunals

Stensrud notes the many liabilities that the SCSL has faced including a limited budget (based on voluntary contributions) and a restricted mandate. A lack of commitment by the international community has stymied the process of providing justice, and she argues that a hybrid criminal court will only be effective if properly implemented and funded so that it is part of a larger reform of the domestic judicial system. The problems faced by the SCSL are not necessarily an indictment against the logic of a hybrid model. Stensrud is not critical of the model itself but rather of its implementation. Rae also highlights the budgetary and political problems associated with the Serious Crimes Unit (SCU) in East Timor. Limited staff and resources did not allow for the full participation of the victims or the effective defense of the accused. Capacity-building of the local judiciary, one of the main benefits touted with regards to the hybrid model, was not accomplished. East Timorese were unclear as to what the process would achieve, particularly as many of the high-ranking perpetuators were in Indonesia, which refused to extradite them. The international community did not force Indonesia to cooperate due to political considerations, and the new East Timorese government undermined the process as it began to value its economic relationship with Indonesia more than its quest for accountability and justice.

Conclusions: Lessons Learned

One of the first issues to consider with human rights violations is whether there is political will to address them, either domestically or internationally. In transitioning societies and in newly independent states, leaders have to weigh the benefits of holding past perpetuators accountable against potential political instability. Criminal prosecutions, either through the national judiciary or an international or a hybrid criminal court, can have the unintended consequence of increasing hostility and reinforcing divisions in transitioning societies attempting to deal with past atrocities. In the case of Argentina, the Alfonsin government resisted calls by civil society for widespread accountability of the military by issuing amnesties in an effort to stop military unrest. In East Timor, President Xanana Gusmao opposed continuing efforts to hold Indonesian leaders accountable hoping for better economic relations with Indonesia. Political will depends on the existence of institutions and a legal culture, which supports the rule of law. In the case of East Timor, the problems of the SCU reflect the pains of nation- and state-building for a newly independent country. In the case of Sierra Leone, the SCSL has been constrained by a fragile peace after a decade-long conflict. In both countries, legal institutions were under-institutionalized before the outbreak of the conflict.

In addition to political will, financial commitment is required to implement different accountability mechanisms. Whether it is travel by TRC commissioners or establishing a hybrid court, any effort will fall short if financing is not forthcoming by the stakeholders. For example, one of the chief reasons why the international community moved away from a purely international criminal tribunal model such as the ICTY to a hybrid model such as the SCSL and the SCU was due to financial considerations. As the ICTY was established through United Nations Chapter VII authority, it was guaranteed funding while the SCSL and the SCU were funded through voluntary contributions. As Stensrud notes, the lack of strong commitment by the international community has constrained the work of the SCSL. However, others argue that in post-conflict environments, money should not be spent on these trials, which can be very costly, but instead should be devoted to rebuilding the domestic judiciary or even providing compensation to victims (Kritz 1996).

How civil society is involved in the process can also have a strong impact on the perceived success of accountability mechanisms. As Crenzel and Di Paolantonio discuss, civil society groups in Argentina were very active in both the TRC and trial process. In the case of the ICTY, individuals in Bosnia, Serbia, and Croatia have felt detached from the tribunal, particularly as it was located in the Netherlands rather than in the localities where the crimes took place, and the personnel were purely international and did not have links with the communities affected. In Sierra Leone, Dugal points to the problems of outreach and educating the community about the work of the TRC. In the case of BiH, the ICTY was a purely international effort without a strong regional component, which, according to Clark, hurt the legitimacy of the tribunal in the eyes of the local population.

While mechanisms are put in place to address past violations, it is also important to focus on how these violations can be avoided in the future. Domestic judicial capacity-building is vital in preventing future violence and part of the calculation in selecting a transitional justice mechanism should be how to best promote the rule of law. Rae points out that the training of the domestic judiciary that was envisioned by the SCU was not very effective, partly due to issues of language and personnel turnover. Stensrud argues that the SCSL was more of an international court than domestic and that the international judges and prosecutors were much more important to the process than local judicial officials.

On the broader issue of reconciliation and the establishment of a historical record of abuses, the ICTY has failed to serve as a vehicle for reconciliation among ethnic groups in the former Yugoslavia, and indeed some might argue that it has perpetuated ethnic resentment. While Lambourne points out that reconciliation for minor crimes seems to have been achieved in East Timor through the TRC, Gusmao accused the SCU of undermining the process of reconciliation between East Timor and Indonesia. In the case of Argentina, one might question how much reconciliation has taken place given that the demand for trials continues decades after the Dirty War.

When authoritarian regimes and civil wars come to an end, both perpetrators and victims of human rights violations must find ways to address the past in order to move forward. Impunity for perpetrators can increase the risk of retaliation and further atrocities leading to new cycles of violence that can undermine the new democratic regime. Victims may feel resentful if no one is held accountable for their suffering. If impunity is allowed, the political system that is being re-built may be democratic in form but lack the essential component of accountability. If human rights violations are not addressed, it makes it difficult for present and future generations to have faith in democracy and the rule of law.

New democratic governments turn to transitional justice mechanisms to promote peace, justice, truth, and reconciliation. However, in post-conflict societies, these goals can sometimes compete with each other. There will be questions as to what type of transitional justice mechanism to implement, which goals to prioritize, and the appropriate time frame in which to initiate the transitional justice process. The main concern for newly formed democratic regimes is how the diverse transitional justice mechanisms can provide justice, assist in the reconciliation of divided societies, and ultimately promote lasting peace (Gibson 2005).

The pursuit of justice by the newly formed democratic regime can focus on retribution (*i.e.*, punishment for wrongdoings by the state) or on restoration (*i.e.*, emphasizing personal responsibility and forgiveness between perpetrator and victim). Retributive justice focuses on the role of the state in punishing perpetuators for human rights violations. Advocates of retributive justice believe that criminal punishment, whether through domestic or international courts, is the best way to break from the past, to ensure that there are no future crimes, and to build the rule of law by combating impunity. Atrocities are made public, condemned, and punished. In this view, TRCs and amnesties undermine the rule of law because the law requires consequences for violations.

Yet in a post-conflict environment in which a state is transitioning to democracy, retributive justice can have a number of limitations. The most notable are the impracticality of trying everyone who might be deemed responsible for violations, the long duration and costs of trials, and the lack of unbiased judges and judicial infrastructure needed for free and fair trials. If there are thousands of perpetrators, it will be impossible to bring all of them to trial. Moreover in post-conflict societies, domestic court systems often lack independence and sufficient resources (especially qualified judges, as in BiH and East Timor). In addition, as the case of child soldiers in Sierra Leone demonstrates, there can be instances when it is difficult to clearly distinguish between perpetuators and victims. Finally, there is the question whether punishment by the state results in healing for victims and their relatives. As Mamdani argues "to punish perpetrators is not the same thing as to benefit victims" (1997, 24).

Rather than focusing on laws, judges, and the state, restorative justice is centered on the victims, the perpetuators, and the communities where the violations took place in order to repair and re-build relationships. Advocates of restorative justice see great value in the work of TRCs because they are created to reconcile individuals and communities rather than to punish the perpetrators. Members of society are asked to testify in order to create a narrative about the violence that took place, which serves a larger social good. At the same time, TRCs are victim-centered and focus on restoring the individual dignity of the victim by having perpetrators admit to their crime, apologize, and ask for forgiveness. These actions foster a dialog between the victim and the perpetrator that can contribute to the process of healing. However, it is important to ask whether restorative justice truly leads to reconciliation. Bell argues that "expecting victims to give up retributive desires in favour of reconciling narratives may not contribute to their 'healing' at all" (2003, 1095).

Reconciliation has increasingly become the focus of transitional justice mechanisms. Indeed, one of the greatest challenges in seeking to promote reconciliation is the lack of a clear definition of what this means. Bloomfield defines reconciliation as "a process through which a society moves from a divided past to a shared future" (2003, 12). However, the question remains how a society reconciles to create a "shared future"? Daly argues that "while the word itself is seen on every transitional government's 'to do' list, its precise meaning is unclear" (2003, 73). Achieving reconciliation requires a minimal level of tolerance between victims and perpetuators that will lead to a re-building trust in the political process. For this to happen, there must be willingness on the part of all concerned to treat others fairly and live with them in harmony and peace. As has been discussed in this volume, the types of mechanisms that can be used to promote reconciliation are as complex and varied as the definition of the word itself.

What is clear is that reconciliation cannot be imported into post-conflict societies. Reconciliation processes need to be based on local structures, experiences, needs, and values. Local culture and traditions can provide important resources for reconciliation. Sustainable reconciliation also requires the involvement of civil society, which can play a crucial role in strengthening the reconciliation processes through advocacy, public education, and community empowerment. The ownership of initiatives that aspire to promote reconciliation should be in the hands of locals. Huyse argues that "lasting reconciliation must be home-grown because in the end it is the survivors who assign meaning to term and the process" (2003, 23).

The ultimate goal of justice and reconciliation is to promote a lasting peace in a society that has experienced violence. While "negative peace" refers to the absence of violence, "positive peace" involves the restoration of relationships, the creation of social systems that serve the needs of the whole population, and the constructive resolution of past conflict (Galtung 1996). Societies have several options when reckoning with past atrocities, and as the chapters in this volume illustrate, there is ample room for experimentation. In Argentina, Sierra Leone, and East Timor, retributive and restorative justice were combined through the use of trials and a TRC. Depending on the crimes, the needs of victims and the society, various transnational justice mechanisms can be used at the same time. Therefore, the problem of achieving justice is not a function of the choice between retribution (trials) and restoration (truth-seeking process), but rather how these mechanisms are designed, combined, and communicated. As the cases we have reviewed demonstrate, the problems associated with transitional justice have less to do with adopting one specific model than with the steadfast involvement of governments and civil society in the quest for to end impunity and foster reconciliation. When this determination is present, and the mechanisms adopted are designed locally to fit the circumstances of the particular case, then and only then can there be a realistic hope of promoting peace, justice, truth, and reconciliation.

References

Bell, Christine. 2003. "Dealing with the past in Northern Ireland." *Fordham International Law Journal* 26:1095–1147.

Bloomfield, David. 2003. "Reconciliation: An Introduction." In *Reconciliation After Violent Conflict: A Handbook*, ed. David Bloomfield, Teresa Barnes, and Luc Huyse. Stockholm: IDEA Publications.

Daly, Erin. 2002. "Transformative Justice: Charting a Path to Reconciliation." *International Legal Perspective* 12:73–183.

Drumbl, Mark A. 2000. "Punishment, Postgenocide: From Guilt to Shame to Civis in Rwanda." *New York University Law Review* 75:1221–1326.

Galtung, Johan. 1996. *Peace by Peaceful Means: Peace and Conflict Development and Civilization*. London: SAGE Publications.

Gibson, James L. 2005. "The Truth about Truth and Reconciliation in South Africa." *International Political Science Review* 26:341–361.

Huyse, Luc. 2003. "The Process of Reconciliation." In *Reconciliation After Violent Conflict: A Handbook*, ed. David Bloomfield, Teresa Barnes, and Luc Huyse. Stockholm: IDEA Publications.

Kritz, Neil J. 1996. "Coming to Terms with Atrocities: A Review of Accountability Mechanisms for Mass Violations of Human Rights." *Law & Contemporary Problems* 59:27–131.

Mamdani, Mahmood. 1997. "From Justice to Reconciliation: Making Sense of the African Experience." In *Crisis and Reconstruction: African Perspectives*, ed. Mahmood Mamdani, and Colin Leys. Uppsala, Sweden: Nordiska Afrikainstitutet.

McGregor, Lorna. 2006. "Reconciliation: I Know It When I see it." *Contemporary Justice Review* 9:155–174.

Morris, Madeline H. 1997. "The Trials of Concurrent Jurisdiction: The Case of Rwanda." *Duke Journal of Comparative & International Law* 7:349–374.

Shinoda, Hideaki. 2002. "Peace-Building by the Rule of Law: An Examination of Intervention in the Form of International Tribunals." *International Journal of Peace Studies* 7:41–58.

INDEX